Robert Burton

Philosophaster

MEDIEVAL & RENAISSANCE
TEXTS & STUDIES

VOLUME 103

The Renaissance Society of America
Renaissance Texts Series

VOLUME 15

Robert Burton

Philosophaster

Edited and Translated by

◆

CONNIE McQUILLEN

Medieval & Renaissance texts & studies
Binghamton, New York
1993

Library of Congress Cataloging-in-Publication Data

Burton, Robert, 1577–1640.
    [Philosophaster. English & Latin]
    Philosophaster / Robert Burton ; edited and translated by Connie McQuillen.
        p. cm. — (Medieval & Renaissance texts & studies ; v. 103)
(Renaissance texts series ; v. 15.)
    Includes bibliographical references.
    ISBN 0–86698–123–3 (clothbound)
    1. College and school drama, Latin (Medieval and modern)—England—Oxford—
Translations into English.   2. College and school drama, Latin (Medieval and
modern)—England—Oxford. I. McQuillen, Connie, 1945– . II. Title. III. Title:
Philosophaster. IV. Series.
PA8485.B8P513 1992
872'.04—dc20   92–16389
                                                           CIP

∞

This book is made to last.
It is set in Baskerville, smythe-sewn
and printed on acid-free paper
to library specifications

Printed in the United States of America

For Will and Kathleen

Table of Contents

Acknowledgments

I thank the curators of the libraries holding the Burton manuscripts: Jeanne T. Newlin, Harvard Theatre Collection, Harvard College Library, Cambridge, Massachusetts, and Laetitia Yeandle, The Folger Shakespeare Library, Washington, DC. Both were most gracious in allowing me to work with the manuscripts and in assisting this research. I also thank the librarians of the Robert Burton Collection, Honnold Library, Claremont, California for providing me with copies and information about the letters of Edward Bensly to Paul Jordan-Smith. I appreciate permission granted by the libraries to use and quote from the manuscripts.

I thank the many friends and colleagues who have helped with this edition, the editors and readers at MRTS, the English faculty at Washington State University, the Classics faculty at the University of Idaho, especially Nicolas Kiessling who first introduced me to Burton and his philosophasters and Cecelia Luschnig who has, for many years now, helped me tend this unruly bunch. I thank my dearest friends, Teoman Sipahigil and Kathleen Quinn, for their help, and my children, Will and Kathleen, for their patience.

Abbreviations

The following abbreviations are used for works frequently cited in the commentary.

AM	Robert Burton, *The Anatomy of Melancholy*, ed. Holbrook Jackson (New York: Vintage Books, 1977).
Bensly	Letters of Edward Bensly to Paul Jordan-Smith. December 1929 to March 1930. Robert Burton Collection, The Honnold Library, Claremont, CA.
Shakespeare	References to Shakespeare's plays are from *The Complete Works of Shakespeare*, ed. David Bevington, 3rd ed. (Glenview: Univ. of Chicago Press, 1980).
Cooper	Thomas Cooper, *Thesaurus Linguae Romanae et Brittanicae* (London, 1565; rpt. Menston: The Scolar Press, 1969).
D-JS	"Index and Biographical and Bibliographical Dictionary" in Floyd Dell and Paul Jordan-Smith, eds. *The Anatomy of Melancholy* (New York: Tudor Publishing, 1927).
Deferrari	Roy J. Deferrari *A Latin-English Dictionary of St. Thomas Aquinas based on the "Summa Theologica" and selected passages of his other works* (Boston: Daughters of St. Paul, 1960).
Erasmus, *Ad.*	*Adagiorum Chilias Prima, Secunda, Tertia*, eds. Felix Heinimann and Emanuel Kienzle, vol. 2 of *Opera Omnia* (Amsterdam: North-Holland Publishing, 1981).
——, *Alc.*	"Alcumistica," *Colloquia*, ed. L. E. Halkin, F. Bierlaire, R. Hoven, vol. 1 of *Opera Omnia* (Amsterdam: North-Holland Publishing, 1972).
——, *Mor.*	*Moriae Encomium*, ed. Clarence H. Miller, vol. 4 of *Opera Omnia* (Amsterdam: North-Holland Publishing, 1979).
JS	"Notes" in *Robert Burton's Philosophaster*, ed. Paul Jordan-Smith (Palo Alto: Stanford Univ. Press, 1931).

Kiessling	N. K. Kiessling, *The Library of Robert Burton* (Oxford Bibliographical Society, 1987).
Loeb	The Loeb Classical Library Series (London: William Heinemann; Cambridge: Harvard Univ. Press).
LS	Charlton T. Lewis and Charles Short, *A Latin Dictionary* (1879; rpt. Oxford: Clarendon Press, 1975).
OCD	*Oxford Classical Dictionary*, 2nd ed. (1970).
OED	*Oxford English Dictionary* (1971).
Pontano, *Ant.*	"Antonius Dialogus," *I Dialoghi*, ed. Carmelo Previtera (Florence: Sansoni, 1943).
——, *Ch.*	"Charon Dialogus," *I Dialoghi*, ed. Carmelo Previtera (Florence: Sansoni, 1943).
Rulandus	Martinus Rulandus, *A Lexicon of Alchemy*. trans. A. E. Waite (Frankfurt, 1612; rpt. London: John M. Watkins, 1964).
Thomas	Thomas Thomas, *Dictionarium Linguae Latinae et Anglicanae* (Cambridge, 1587; rpt. Menston: The Scolar Press, 1972).

Unless otherwise noted, citations from classical authors are from the Oxford Classical Texts (OCT). Abbreviations used for reference to the works of the classical authors are:

Cicero	*Att.*	Epistulae ad Atticum
	Fam.	Epistulae ad Familiares
Ovid	*Met.*	Metamorphoses
Horace	*C.*	Carmina, or Odae
	Sat.	Sermones, or Satirae
	Epist.	Epistulae
Juvenal	*Sat.*	Saturae
Plautus	*Am.*	Amphitruo
	As.	Asinaria
	Bacch.	Bacchides
	Capt.	Captivi
	Cas.	Casina
	Cist.	Cistellaria
	Merc.	Mercator
	Mil.	Miles Gloriosus
	Most.	Mostellaria
	Pers.	Persia
	Poen.	Poenulus
	Ps.	Pseudolus
	Trin.	Trinummus
	Truc.	Truculentus
Terence	*Ad.*	Adelphi
	And.	Andria

	Eun.	Eunuchus
	Heaut.	Heautontimorumenos
	Hec.	Hecyra
	Phorm.	Phormio
Vergil	*Aen.*	Aeneid
	Ecl.	Eclogae

Introduction

In *The Anatomy of Melancholy* Robert Burton defines philosophasters as "[qui] licentiantur in artibus, artem qui non habent, eosque sapientes esse jubent, qui nulla praediti sunt sapientia, et nihil ad gradum praeterquam velle adferunt" [those licensed in the arts who have no art, those judged to be wise who have no wisdom and have no qualifications for a degree except desire].[1] In a marginal note he adds, "Hos non ita pridem perstrinxi, in Philosophastro, Comoedia Latina, in Aede Christi Oxon. publice habita, anno 1617, Feb. 16" [Not long ago I satirized them in Philosophaster, a Latin comedy publicly performed in the Hall of Christ Church, Oxford, on February 16, 1617/18]. A holograph copy of the play is extant: MS. Thr. 10, Harvard Theatre Collection, Harvard College Library. On the title page of this manuscript, Burton notes that, although the play was presented "a studiosis aedis Cristi Oxoniensis alumnis" in 1617/18, it had in fact been written in 1606 and revised in 1615. His original statement is "Comoedia noua / Inchoata Anno domini 1606 / Alterata, renouata, perfecta / Anno domini 1615." He later changed "Inchoata" [begun] to "Scripta" [written], and the somewhat ambiguous "renouata" to "reuisa."[2] In both the prologue and epilogue, he also mentions that he wrote his play eleven years earlier, asking the audience's patience should anything seem "well-known" or "commonplace" or "too well-worn." In the prologue he adds, "Emendicatum e nupera scena ne quis putet" [no one should think that this story has been borrowed from a recent play]. Because Burton originally wrote "e vulgari scena" [from a public play], many have noted similarities, or lack of similarity, between *Philosophaster* and Ben Jonson's *Alchemist*.[3] What is more obvious, however, is the considerable resemblance, both

---

[1] *The Anatomy of Melancholy*, pt. 1, sec. 2, mem. 3, subs. 15.

[2] On photocopies of Harvard MS. Thr. 10, one can see that "perfecta" has also been canceled and that "interpolata" added in the margin of the manuscript. These emendations are not Burton's but those of William Buckley who edited the manuscript in the mid-nineteenth century. See pages 11-13.

[3] See William E. Buckley, *Philosophaster Comoedia, Nunc primum in lucem producta* (Hert-

in content and conventions, *Philosophaster* bears to several "recent plays," most of them presented on the academic rather than the public stage.

Philosophaster is topical satire on seventeenth-century education. It follows in the tradition of *The Parnassus Trilogy, Club Law, Pedantius*—those university plays F. S. Boas describes as "academic in a more special and intimate sense; [they] deal with the studies and the experiences of scholars young and old, with the notable figures of contemporary university life, with the immemorial feud of town and gown."[4] In *Philosophaster*, Burton has all these "well-worn" elements: he deals with the distinction between true scholars and false; he has not one but several pedants, including the pedant in love; a student who abandons his studies; townsmen abused by university men. As in other academic plays such as Tomkins's *Albumazar*, Burton deals with deceit and theft. *Philosophaster* has an alchemist who cheats a nobleman of his gold; the physician who mistreats his patients; a greedy bawd with her "meretricious daughters." And as in the Cambridge play *Ignoramus*, Burton mixes in a little religious satire. The leader of the philosophasters is the Jesuit Polupragmaticus with his appropriately named servant Aequivocus who is not only better at equivocating but also more clever and devious than his very clever and devious master.

Like many of his contemporary playwrights for the university stage, Burton uses the conventions of classical comedy. Entrances are announced by creaking doors or by "ecce," meetings are far too "opportunè," and characters occasionally burst into song. There is the love story typical of New Comedy from Menander to Terence: the young man falls in love with a young girl he cannot have because she is of questionable virtue and station. But, "ecce," by the final scene she is discovered to be both virtuous and of noble birth, somehow misplaced as a youth, and now free to marry her lover. Another typical figure of Roman comedy is the clever slave. Burton has not one but two, now transformed into clever servants. One is Aequivocus, the Jesuit's servant; the other is Dromo, the nobleman's servant who sees through the deceptions of the philosophasters more quickly and completely than any other character.

Burton's characters are stock figures whose names define their types. His seven philosophasters are Polupragmaticus (The Busybody); the mathemati-

---

ford, 1862), xi-xii; Paul Jordan-Smith, *Robert Burton's "Philosophaster"* (Palo Alto: Stanford Univ. Press, 1931), xii-xiv; G. E. Bentley, *The Jacobean and Caroline Stage* (Oxford: Oxford Univ. Press, 1956) 3:100; Nicholas Dewey, "Robert Burton and the Drama," (Ph.D. diss, Princeton Univ., 1968), 136–37; Marvin Spevack, ed., *Robert Burton. Philosophaster* Renaissance Latin Drama in England, 1st ser., no. 8, ed. Marvin Spevack and J. W. Binns (Hildesheim: George Olms Verlag, 1984), 7; Michael O'Connell, *Robert Burton* (Boston: Twayne Publishers, 1986), 93–94.

[4] F. S. Boas, "University Plays," *The Cambridge History of English Literature*, pt. 2, ed. A. W. Ward and A. R. Waller (New York: G. P. Putnam's Sons; Cambridge: Univ. Press, 1910), 6:344. On academic drama see also Frederick Boas, *University Drama in the Tutor Age* (Oxford, 1914; rpt. New York: Benjamin Blom, 1966) and Leicester Bradner, "Latin Drama of the Renaissance," *Studies in the Renaissance* 4 (1957): 31–70.

cian Pantometer (All Measure); the alchemist and physician Pantomagus (All Magic); the sophist Simon Acutus (The Sharp); the theologaster Theanus; the pedantic grammarian Pedanus; and the poetaster Amphimacer, whose name is that of the Greek poetic meter scanned as long, short, long.

These philosophasters ensconce themselves in a university recently established by the local duke who is aided by his advisors Eubulus (Good Counsel) and Cratinus (The Strong). The local townsmen, who at first fear the establishment of the university, are Sordidus (The Pinch-penny), Cornutus (The Horned) and Rubicundus (The Red). They are appropriately and respectively robbed, cuckolded and beaten by the university men. Also abused and twice deceived is the nobleman Polupistos (Great Faith or Trust).

The deceptions and impostures of the philosophasters are at length detected by two wandering scholars, Polumathes (All Learning) and Philobiblos (Lover of Books). By the final scene the duke learns of the numerous abuses brought on by the philosophasters and the university men. The duke is distraught and prepared to close the school, but changes his mind at the urging of Polumathes and Philobiblos. The philosophasters are rounded up and severely punished; the university is re-established with stronger statutes and a new administration.

The story is rather simple and the plot episodic and it may well be argued that there is little in *Philosophaster* that is new, even beyond its generic similarity to academic satire and classical comedy. What distinguishes the play—and what no doubt appealed to its seventeenth-century audience—is Burton's wit and "virtuosity" and the extent of his borrowings.

Burton's Borrowings

Philosophaster is a patchwork of borrowings, some long and some short: scenes, episodes, characters, quotations, commonplaces, and allusions from contemporary as well as classical texts are all woven together into something of a continuous whole.

Burton's philosophasters, especially his primary pretender, the Jesuit Polupragmaticus, seem inspired by Desiderius Erasmus. In his *Moriae Encomium*, Erasmus has Folly set forth the foolishness of those "qui sapientiae speciem inter mortales tenet"[5] [who hold the appearance of wisdom among mortals]. Among the groups she satirizes are the philosophers, "barba pallioque verendi; qui se solos sapere praedicant. . . . Ii cum nihil omnino sciant, tamen omnia se scire profitentur"[6] [venerable with their beards and gowns, who assert that they alone are wise. . . . Although they know nothing at all, they profess to know everything]. They show their scorn for the

[5] Desiderius Erasmus, *Moriae encomium*, ed. Clarence H. Miller, vol. 4 of *Opera Omnia* (Amsterdam: North-Holland Publishing, 1979), 138.
[6] Erasmus, 144.

common folk, says Erasmus's Folly, when they confuse the uneducated with academic jargon: with triangles, tetragons, and circles, and mathematical figures of this sort, imposing one on another to produce what looks like a labyrinth, and then lining up series of letters as if in battle lines, and repeating them first in one order and then in another[7]—which is just what Polupragmaticus tells his fellow philosophasters to do in Act I, scene 1. In Act IV, scene 2 of *Philosophaster*, Simon Acutus asks Polupragmaticus how to become famous. Part of the Jesuit's advice is to publish. He elaborates, using Folly's description of "qui libris edendis famam immortalem aucupantur" [those who strive to win eternal fame by publishing books], who write without thought whatever pops into the head, care not if the work is contemptible, publish another's work as their own, praise one another.[8]

Burton's alchemist also owes much to Erasmus. In his "Alcumistica," Erasmus has a certain Lalus relate the story of a gentleman who was cheated by an alchemist. Burton borrows heavily from this colloquy for Act IV, scene 1, and Act IV, scene 4, expanding Erasmus's prose into dialogue between the alchemist Pantomagus and his victim Polupistos.

But the author to whom Burton is most indebted is the Italian humanist Giovanni Pontano.[9] The characters Theanus and Pedanus are interlocutors in Pontano's "Charon Dialogus," where both are shades of pedantic grammarians. Burton's Pedanus remains a "grammatista," but his Theanus becomes a rhetorician turned "theologaster." In the "Charon Dialogus," the shade Pedanus reports to the god Mercury a conversation he has had with the shade of Vergil concerning how many wine jars Acestes had given to Aeneas and with which foot Aeneas first touched the Italian shore. He also reports that the shade of Juvenal admonished him to beat young boys with a "ferula," not a "virga." Meanwhile the shade of Theanus approaches and the two grammarians argue about the proper use of "oportebat" and "oportuit," "debueras" and "debuisti." Burton takes the conversation between Pontano's Theanus and Pedanus, condenses it, and gives it to his own Theanus and Pedanus in Act II, scene 2 and Act III, scene 5.

In Pontano's "Antonius Dialogus," a number of interlocutors stop by the Porticus in search of a certain Antonius. One such interlocutor is Suppatius who has returned from seeking a wise man, discouraged that he has found none. He relates his adventures and tells of the conversations he has had with several foolish people, including some who pretend to be wise. In *Philosophaster*, Suppatius becomes Polumathes and Philobiblos, the two wandering scholars and true philosophers. Pontano's several foolish people become one or another of Burton's philosophasters.

---

[7] Erasmus, 144.

[8] Erasmus, 140–42.

[9] It was Edward Bensly who noted Burton's indebtedness to Pontano. See the end of this introduction.

Burton does not conceal his indebtedness to Pontano, for in Act I, scene 5, when Polumathes and Philobiblos are introduced, Polumathes says that he, like "Supputius in Pontano" has been in search of a wise man.[10] He tells Philobiblos of his own adventures in almost the same words Suppatius uses to tell of his adventures in Italy.

Relating other adventures, Pontano's Suppatius tells of his conversations with a certain "literator" who objected to his use of the verb "marcescere," a grammarian who objected to the phrase "iniuriam patior," and another grammarian who insisted upon using the noun "fricatio" instead of the proper "frictio." In Burton's play (Act III, scene 5), Philobiblos appropriates the role of Suppatius and Pedanus, the roles of the three pedants. In Act IV, scene 7, of *Philosophaster*, two speeches of Lodovicus Pantometer and one of Simon Acutus also borrow closely from the adventures of Suppatius.

From other interlocutors in the "Antonius Dialogus," Burton takes the description of a mad wife (Act III, scene 2), and predictions of impending disaster from seven-year-old cocks (Act IV, scene 5).

Burton's indebtedness to other authors is of a different sort. He frequently has his characters quote, or misquote, the classics: in the first two scenes alone the philosophaster Polupragmaticus quotes and misquotes Juvenal; Lodovicus quotes Plautus and Terence; Theanus, Cicero; Amphimacer, Ovid; Aequivocus, Plautus; the duke, Cicero; his counselor, Seneca. In all, Burton uses more than 60 quotations from classical authors and more than 30 Latin maxims and proverbs which were collected by Erasmus in his *Adagia*.

In the epilogue to *Philosophaster*, Burton notes that his play is neither stuffed with jokes nor salted with wit. This seems a fair assessment, if by "jokes" one understands the slap-stick humor of Roman comedy, and by "wit" a biting satire, for Burton does little more than repeat contemporary commonplaces, such as characterizing the Jesuit as equivocator. What is funny in *Philosophaster* is its element of self-parody: it is a play about pedants which is rather pedantically stuffed with quotations, borrowings and allusions. The humor depends upon the audience's recognition of the source and Burton's use or misuse of that source. An exaggerated Plautine convention, a misquotation from Vergil, a frequent proverb from Erasmus, an episode from Pontano moved from Italy to Oxford—all are jokes between the academic playwright and his academic audience.

---

[10] In both *Philosophaster* and *The Anatomy of Melancholy*, Burton refers to Pontano's character as "Supputius," not "Suppatius." Burton owned a copy of Pontano's dialogues: Joannes Jovianus Pontanus, *Librorum omnium, quos soluta oratione composuit, tomus secundus, cui insunt, de aspiratione, lib. II. Item, dialogi, festivissimi, diversorum argumentorum, nempe Charon. Antonius. Actius. Aegidius. Asinus. De sermone, lib. VI. Belli, quod Ferdinandus . . . gessit, libri totidem* (Basle, 1538). See N. K. Kiessling, *The Library of Robert Burton* (Oxford Bibliographical Society, 1987), no. 1263.

The Three Manuscripts

FOLGER MS. V.a. 315; HARVARD MS. Thr. 10; HARVARD MS. Thr. 10.1

The complete text of Burton's *Philosophaster* is extant in two manuscript copies; part of the text has been preserved in a third contemporary source.

Folger MS. V.a. 315, The Folger Shakespeare Library, Washington, DC (hereafter called the Folger) is a manuscript book in quarto on 43 leaves of paper, 18 by 14 cm., bound in calf. The title page reads in part: "Philosophaster. Comoedia noua. . . . Auctore Roberto Burton . . . 1617." On the flyleaf is the inscription: "Liber Wm[i] Burton Lindliaci Leicestrensis de Falde Com: Staff: 1618: ex dono fratris mei Robt[i] Burton Authoris."

The text is written in Elizabethan secretary script mixed with italic characters. Some blank spaces have been left in the text, occasionally with an "x" in the margin. The text contains several corrections and additions made by a different hand, with different pen and ink.[11] Corrections are made by cancellation; additions have been inserted into the text with a caret or added in blank spaces left in the text. Some accent marks and palaeographic *notae* have also been added.

The manuscript formerly belonged to Lord Mostyn of Gloddaeth. It was sold to Quaritch in July, 1920, and acquired by the Folger Shakespeare Library, most likely in 1928.[12] The Folger Library also holds a letter written by William Buckley to Lord Mostyn on April 17, 1890, listing words and lines which Mr. Buckley had determined were missing from the Mostyn manuscript after he compared it with his own copy of *Philosophaster*.

Harvard MS. Thr. 10, Harvard Theatre Collection, Harvard College Library, Cambridge, MA (hereafter called the Harvard) is a manuscript book on 45 leaves of paper in quarto, 15 x 19 cm, bound in tooled calf. The title page reads in part: "Philosophaster. Comoedia noua. . . . Auctore Roberto Burton . . . 1617."

The text is written in Elizabethan secretary script, in a formal or set hand. Corrections, by the same hand, are generally made by cancellation with the emended word written directly above the one canceled. Following the epi-

---

[11] The hand of the corrections is also Elizabethan secretary. Pen strokes in the corrections are wider than those of the text; brown ink was used for the corrections, black for the text. See Appendix I for a complete list of these additions and corrections to the Folger MS.

[12] The original catalogue number for this manuscript was Folger MS. 1828.2. Ms. Laetitia Yeandle, Curator of Manuscripts, Folger Shakespeare Library, writes: "Other books and catalogues with [Mr. Folger's] code number '1828' were acquired in 1928. Unfortunately, I could find no card for the manuscript in Mr. or Mrs. Folger's card catalogue (which is most unusual) and so cannot tell you from whom he acquired it, probably about 1928." Letter received from Ms. Laetitia Yeandle, October 15, 1986.

logue, in the same hand, are the names of the actors from the 1617/18 performance. Following that, in an unidentified seventeenth-century hand, are
"Collections out of Dr. Sherlocks vindication of the doctrine of the Trinity"
(1690). The text is preceded and followed by notes in the hand of W. E. Buckley. Buckley also made approximately 250 penciled notes in the text or in the
margin of the text itself.[13] A rough draft of Buckley's letter to Lord Mostyn
is kept with the manuscript. It is written on the back of an envelope addressed
to Buckley and postmarked "Exeter Ap 14 90" and "Banbury Ap 15 90."

Buckley purchased the manuscript in 1846 from W. Pickering, Bookseller.
In the preface to his edition of *Philosophaster*, he states that Pickering had purchased the manuscript

> in April, 1843, at the sale by Messrs. Sotheby and Wilkinson, of the
> Library of Jeremiah Milles, D.D., formerly Dean of Exeter, and Presi-
> dent of the Society of Antiquaries, whose bookplate is pasted inside
> the cover. Dean Milles died in 1784, and it is conjectured that the
> MS. had belonged to Thomas Milles, D.D., Bishop of Waterford and
> Lismore, previously Canon of Christ Church, and Regius Professor of
> Greek at Oxford in 1706-7. . . . He, most probably, became possessed
> of this MS. at Oxford; for though Burton bequeathed his printed
> books mainly to the Bodleian Library, yet he left his MSS. to his
> executors; and within half a century after his death they would, in the
> common course of things, have passed into other hands.[14]

After Buckley's death, the manuscript was sold in 1894 to W. A. White of
New York. His son, Harold T. White, and daughter, Mrs. Hugh D. Marshall, do-
nated the manuscript to the Harvard College Library in December, 1941.[15]

Harvard MS. Thr. 10.1 (hereafter called the Goffe playbook) is a manuscript
book with "Parts in plays . . . att CtCh/acted . . . copyd" barely legible on the
spine of the volume. It contains 72 leaves of paper, 14.8 x 10 cm, bound in
vellum. Although it contains a few miscellaneous writings, the manuscript is
primarily a collection of four actors' parts in plays written by students at Christ
Church, Oxford.[16] On folios 8v-19v is the part of Antonius in an unidentified
Latin play; on 21-46v, the part of Poore in an unidentified English Comedy; on

---

[13] See pages 11-13.

[14] William E. Buckley, *Philosophaster Comoedia, Nunc primum in lucem producta* (Hertford,
1862), x-xi.

[15] Harvard College Library bookplate: "This volume is from the collection of early
English books, chiefly of the Elizabethan period, formed by William Augustus White of
the class of 1863, of Brooklyn, New York. It is part of a gift made by his son Harold T.
White, '97, and his daughter Mrs. Hugh D. Marshall, December 26, 1941."

[16] On fols. 3-7 is a summary in Latin of Porphyrius' "Isagoge," and on fols. 71v-72v,
"A songe upon ye losse of an actors voyce."

57–71, that of Amurath from Thomas Goffe's *The Courageous Turk*; on folios 48–54 is the part of Polupragmaticus in Burton's *Philosophaster*. Folios 48–54 are in the hand of Thomas Goffe, who played Polupragmaticus in the 1618 performance of the play.[17] In this manuscript book, Goffe records just his character's speaking parts and cues—the last two or three words of the previous character's speech.

Goffe uses an Italic script. Some words are corrected, generally by cancellation with the emended word written above. Some lines and cues are added interlinearly. For the corrections and additions, Goffe uses a different pen with wider stroke and darker ink.

The Harvard Theatre Collection acquired MS. Thr. 10.1 in 1960.

Holograph Status of the Manuscripts

The Harvard and Folger manuscripts are clearly written by different hands, yet both have been reported to be Burton holographs. However, in a study of Burton's hand, (*Manuscripta* 29, 1985), I determine that only Harvard MS. Thr. 10 is a Burton holograph.[18] Numerous samples of Robert Burton's handwriting are available. For that study I use a fragment of a letter written in 1605 to his brother William, a letter written in 1635 to John Smyth of Nibley, and annotations in several books which belonged to Burton.[19] Burton's hand remains quite consistent over the thirty-year period in which these materials were written, and while the hand is fairly typical of Elizabethan secretary script, some features of his writing are distinctive, especially the letters "g," "h," "u/v," and the letter combinations "ha," "ho." All these peculiar forms are found in the text and in the corrections or additions to the Harvard manuscript. None are evident in the text of the Folger. Similarly, a comparison of other characters supports these same conclusions: the text of the Harvard manuscript, the two letters, and the annotations in Burton's books were all written by the same hand; the text of the Folger manuscript was written by a different hand.[20] Both manuscripts have been corrected. The corrections in the Harvard are more complete and are holograph. The

---

[17] See David Carnegie, "The Identification of the Hand of Thomas Goffe, Academic Dramatist and Actor," *The Library* 26 (1971): 161–65.

[18] Connie McQuillen, "Robert Burton's *Philosophaster*: Holograph Status of the Manuscripts," *Manuscripta* 29 (1985): 148–153.

[19] On the 1605 letter, see Richard L. Nochimson, "Robert Burton's Authorship of Alba: A Lost Letter Recovered," *Review of English Studies* 21 (1970): 325–31. For the 1635 letter, see T. C. Skeat, "A Letter by Robert Burton," *British Museum Quarterly* 22 (1960): 12–16. Many of Burton's books are well annotated. See N. K. Kiessling, *The Library of Robert Burton* (Oxford Bibliographical Society, 1987).

[20] The hand was compared with samples of William Burton's writing. While it is clear that William wrote the inscription of the flyleaf ("Liber Wm^i Burton . . ."), he did not copy the text of the play.

corrections in the Folger manuscript are not extensive and do not provide a wide variety of characters for comparison with Burton's autograph, but the evidence at least suggests that those corrections may have been made by Robert Burton.

Relationship of the manuscripts

Harvard MS. Thr. 10 and *Folger MS. V.a. 315* are very closely related. They contain enough errors[21] peculiar to both to suggest that one was copied from the other or that both were closely copied from another manuscript now lost. The differences between the two manuscripts are relatively insignificant. The scribe of the Folger uses different abbreviations to introduce speakers; he uses many more Latin *notae* and abbreviations; his spelling, punctuation and capitalization are not consistent with that of the Harvard, but are very close. The text of the Folger manuscript has only five words and one stage direction (the introduction of "Theanus" as the speaker at line 545) not found in the Harvard. The text of the Harvard manuscript, on the other hand, has approximately 35 words and phrases, eight stage directions, two half-lines and nine whole lines not found in the Folger. All but one interlinear addition or correction in the Harvard is included as text in the Folger, that of "renouata" instead of "reuisa" on the title page.

Many of the differences between the two manuscripts can be attributued to scribal error. The scribe of the Folger was careless or at least working rather quickly. He not only omitted words and lines, but frequently dropped letters from words. He wrote over letters he had previously written, erased, inserted words and lines interlinearly. Burton, on the other hand, seems to have copied the Harvard manuscript very carefully. He occasionally dropped letters from words and added words interlinearly, but such mistakes and corrections are relatively few.

Because of the peculiar errors the manuscripts share, and because the Harvard contains words and lines missing in the Folger, one obvious conclusion to the relationship of the manuscripts would be that the Folger was copied from the Harvard. Yet the blank spaces in the Folger manuscript complicate this conclusion. Many of those gaps, whether filled in or left blank, occur where the Harvard is quite legible. The Folger manuscript was corrected by a second hand, yet on several folios where the blank spaces occur, even though other words were corrected on that folio, the blank spaces were left blank.

It is possible, of course, that Burton copied his manuscript from the Folger, emending his own play as he copied it, or that both manuscripts were

---

[21] In line (139), both manuscripts have "Philoblo" for "Philobiblo." At lines 1269-70, the character Polupragmaticus is given two consecutive speeches; at lines 1302-6, he has three consecutive speeches; at lines 1051-54, Philobiblos has three consecutive speeches; at line 1363, "ET" speaks. There is no "ET" in the play.

copied from another source or sources. Yet were this the case, one would expect less similarity between Harvard and Folger.

In the editor's preface to the Roxburghe edition, William Buckley suggests that some mistakes in the Harvard manuscript "look like those of one copying from dictation."[22] Buckley's evidence would seem to depend upon such words as "similat" in line 312 (which he emends to "simil ac") or "huiusque" in line 1453 (which Buckley emends to "huiusce"). Such words are evidence of phonetic spelling but not necessarily of copying from dictation, especially since the readings are preserved in both manuscripts. The evidence from corrections and errors, strong in the Folger though slight in the Harvard, suggests that both manuscripts were copied from a written source.[23] But whether Folger was copied from the Harvard, or Harvard from the Folger, or both from a lost manuscript cannot now be determined.

Harvard MS. Thr. 10.1, on the other hand, is not so closely related to the other extant manuscripts. While the Goffe playbook records only approximately 250 of the more than 2230 lines of the complete *Philosophaster*, the variant readings are numerous.

Many variants are synonyms, such as Goffe's "quid" for "cur" (lines 105 and 1656) or "pseudophilosophi" for the "philosophastri" (line 120) found in the Folger and Harvard manuscripts.[24] Some sentences express similar ideas in different words. Line 140, for example, in the Goffe playbook reads "Vel si verbo dictum vultis, sum Iesuita." The same line in both Harvard and Folger is "Vel si mauis Iesuita, vt dicam semel." In some instances, the word order is different, as for example at line 1314 where Goffe has "Terram mouere, incoli lunam, et stellas et huiusmodi" but Burton has "Moueri terram, stellas et lunam incoli et huiusmodi." In other instances, sentences are shortened. At line 810, Goffe's "Dicam quod fuit, et quod futurum sit ad vnguem praedicere" is "Quod fuit et quod futurum, ad vnguem praedicere," in both Harvard and Folger. At line 1276, Goffe's "Ne quid vltra de hoc roges" is but "ne roges" in the other manuscripts.

Other discrepancies between the playbook and the other manuscripts are more substantial. In Act IV, scene 2, the Harvard and Folger manuscripts record for the character Polupragmaticus 21 lines that are not in the playbook; the epilogue in the playbook omits seven lines but includes an additional line not found in the other manuscripts. The last scene of Act IV is scene 7 ac-

---

[22] Buckley, x.

[23] Most of the visual errors in the Folger manuscript are those of homoeatarcta. I.e., the scribe's eye is attracted to similar beginnings of words or sentences and therefore omits a line or several lines of text. For the scribe of the Folger manuscript, the similar beginning was often the introduction of the character speaking. The most obvious evidence of visual error in the Harvard manuscript occurs in the final scene (line 1985) where Burton's eye was apparently attracted to a previous line (1983).

[24] Line numbers given here are those of this text.

cording to Burton, scene 8 according to Goffe. The early lines in that scene are the same in all three manuscripts, but assigned to different characters in the playbook. Moreover, Goffe records Polupragmaticus' final lines in the scene as "Quando ita vis, placet" cued by "Haec condo" spoken by "Ta" (presumably the character Tarentilla). These lines appear nowhere in the other manuscripts, nor is Tarentilla on stage in the final scene of Act IV.

If one can assume that Polupragmaticus's cues and speeches recorded in Harvard MS. Thr. 10.1 are Goffe's prompt copy for the actual performance of *Philosophaster*, and that Harvard MS. Thr. 10 and Folger MS. V.a. 315 were copied sometime after that performance (since both manuscripts refer to the time and date of performance and note that the audience "plauserunt"), then it would seem that Burton not only revised but also augmented his play sometime after its production.

Early Editions

William E. Buckley, *Philosophaster Comoedia, Nunc primum in lucem producta.* Hertford, 1862.

The first edition of *Philosophaster* was limited to 65 copies prepared for the Roxburghe Club. The edition has a brief preface, biographical information about the actors in the 1618 performance of the play, a list of plays acted at Christ Church from 1547 to 1617, "errata" and "corrigenda et variae lectiones," and the text of eighteen of Burton's poems.

Buckley edited the Latin text of *Philosophaster* from Harvard MS. Thr. 10. A comparison of the edition with the manuscript indicates that Buckley used only this manuscript for the printed text, but standardized Burton's capitalization, punctuation, orthography and syntax.[25]

Buckley's Editing of Harvard MS. Thr. 10

Buckley pencilled over 250 notations in the text of Harvard MS. Thr. 10, whether mere underlining of words, marginal notes, addition or deletion of letters, words or punctuation. The majority of these notations, over 200, involve the standardization of Burton's spelling and grammar to classical forms and correspond to almost half of the changes in the printed *Philosophaster*. To anyone reading the manuscript itself, Buckley's pencilled notations are obviously later additions. But on photocopies of the manuscript, Buckley's emendations are difficult to distinguish from Burton's original text.

---

[25] Buckley was aware of a second manuscript copy but perhaps not until several years after the publication of *Philosophaster Comoedia*. On April 17, 1890, Buckley wrote to Lord Mostyn, then the owner of Folger MS. V.a. 315, thanking him for the use of the "William Burton copy" of the play and listing words and lines omitted in that copy.

One type of notation Buckley frequently used was to underline a word in the text and write another word or letters in the margin. For example, in line 133, he underlined Burton's "Aristotilis" and wrote an "e" in the margin. In his printed text, he spelled the word "Aristotelis." Likewise in line 149, he underlined Burton's "Empericus," wrote "pir" in the margin, and spelled the word "Empiricus." In line 785, he underlined "hic" and entered "huic" in the margin and in the edition.

Buckley also made notes and marks in the text itself. He lined out some words, such as "repit" in line 1355 or "modo" in line 1397; he added others, such as "mihi" in line 1397 and "cum" in line 1803. But most of the marks in the text delete or add single letters. For example, Buckley crossed out the "u" in "emplaustris" (line 326), "h" in "Iathro" (line 95) and the second "r" in "proprius" (line 990); he added "u" to change "ascultans" to "auscultans" in line 991, and "asculto" to "ausculto" in line 993, and an "h" to change "cacexiae" to "cachexiae" in line 1482. In several places he canceled one letter, usually a vowel, and wrote another letter above the line ("conspicuum" to "conspicuam," line 407; "tantam" to "tantum," line 761; "fingas" to "finges," line 1313). In still other places he wrote over Burton's letters. Most frequently he changed a Burton "i" to "y," as in "olimpo" to "olympo" (line 501), "pithagorico" to "pythagorico" (line 1165), "metaphisicaliter" to "metaphysicaliter" (line 1184). Several times he changed "e" to "i," as in "demidium" to "dimidium" (line 772), "duodecem" to "duodecim" (line 1212), "latefundiis" to "latifundiis" (line [32]).

Twenty-five of Buckley's notations suggest emendations that he evidently rejected. On three occasions where Burton used the word "illico," Buckley wrote "ilico" in the margin but used "illico" in his printed text. In line 937, he underlined "Paternosters" and wrote "-ros" in the margin; in line 949, where Burton has "suos," Buckley wrote "eius" in the margin; in line 995, he crossed out "autem, si" and wrote "si autem" in the margin. Nevertheless in his edition he preserves the readings "Paternosters," "suos" and "autem, si."[26]

Buckley includes with his edition a list of 56 "corrigenda et variae lectiones." He indicates that he altered the manuscript reading 43 times, once changing word order, once changing punctuation, three times giving emendations: "educae" to "aeruca," "jocis nec" to "jocisve" and "non" to "nec." On three other occasions, he indicates that he was unsure of the manuscript reading. For example, on page 47, line 10 of his text (line 874) he gives the reading "ustae" but questions "vestae? cestae? costae?" and offers the variant reading "vesti?" All other "corrigenda" are in orthography and syntax.

These "corrigenda et variae lectiones" are quite misleading, however, be-

---

[26] Buckley also underlined approximately twenty other words and occasionally wrote an "x" in the margin, but made no change in the printed text. These marks usually indicate proper names, difficult readings, or words Buckley listed in his "corrigenda et variae lectiones."

cause they are far from complete. Of more than four hundred changes in orthography, Buckley lists only 20. While he gives "chromatium" as a variant reading for the manuscript "cromatium," he does not mention that in the line before he changes "rithmica" to "rhythmica," and just five lines later "peripate" to "parhypate," and "hepaton" to "hypaton." He lists only one change in punctuation, from the manuscript "a quo," to "a quo"; but in fact he modernizes the punctuation throughout. He notes the correction of Burton's "cessurum academiam" to "cessuram academiam," but not the other instances in which he makes nouns and adjectives agree. He gives "perduint" for "perduant," "designabit" for "designet," and "subridebis" for "subrides," but there are more than 30 other instances in which Buckley put Burton's verbs back into their "classically proper" conjugation, mood, tense or voice.

Paul Jordan-Smith. *Robert Burton's "Philosophaster."* Palo Alto: Stanford University Press, 1931.

This edition of *Philosophaster* includes the first English translation of Burton's play. Jordan-Smith states in the introduction to the edition that his aim was "interpretation, rather than a literal rendering." He translates Burton's Latin into seventeenth-century prose, using where fitting "those expressions that are familiar to the readers of *The Anatomy of Melancholy*." But in so doing, as he himself admits, Jordan-Smith takes considerable liberties with the Latin.[27]

With the translation are eight pages of notes and annotations. Many of the notes are helpful, but several are incomplete where, for example, Jordan-Smith cites a source as simply "From Ovid," or "From Terence" without identification of the text or line number. This edition also contains a brief preface, a reprint of the eighteen *Poemata* from the 1862 edition, a poem from *Riders Dictionarie*, Burton's Latin preface to *Riders Dictionarie*, his will, Anthony à Wood's account of his life from *Athenae Oxonienses*, 1721, and a chronological table of Burton's life and contemporary events.

The Latin text reprinted in this second edition is that prepared by William Buckley for his 1862 edition of the play. Jordan-Smith acknowledges that Buckley prepared the text from a single manuscript and that a second manuscript is extant:

William Burton's copy, which was formerly in Lord Mostyn's Library. Since both of these manuscripts are in Robert Burton's autograph they should, properly, have been compared;

Nevertheless, he merely reprints the Buckley text, arguing that "the Roxburghe text, apart from a misspelling here and a comma there, is the best

---

[27] Jordan-Smith, xx.

text now in existence, for Robert Burton's manuscript contained his own latest corrections."[28] Unfortunately, that text contains more Buckley emendations than Burton corrections.

Marvin Spevack, Ed., *Robert Burton. Philosophaster*. RENAISSANCE LATIN DRAMA IN ENGLAND. 1st ser., No. 8. Ed. Marvin Spevack and J. W. Binns. Hildesheim: Georg Olms Verlag, 1984.

This third edition of *Philosophaster* is a facsimile of the Latin text of Harvard MS. Thr. 10. With the facsimile is a brief discussion of Renaissance Latin drama, *Philosophaster*'s place in that tradition, and a brief bibliography of academic drama. The introduction to *Philosophaster* includes information on Burton's life, works, the *Philosophaster* manuscripts, and a ten-page summary of the play, followed by a bibliography for *Philosophaster*.

Burton's hand is quite legible and this facsimile useful. However, since it is a photocopy of Harvard MS. Thr. 10, Buckley's pencilled notations—particularly those made in the text rather than in the margins of the manuscript—are visible but not always distinguishable in the facsimile.

Burton's Latin

If *Philosophaster* had been printed in the early seventeenth century, Burton's Latin text might have appeared much as it does in William Buckley's 1862 edition: that is, with all the errors and inconsistencies removed, for as W. Speed Hill notes, "when an author submitted a manuscript to a printer, he did so with the expectation that it would be 'styled' by the printer."[29] That "styling" included standardization of orthography, punctuation and capitalization. But Burton did not publish his play, nor is there any indication that he intended to. He prepared his copy of *Philosophaster* with great care, and in it we have an example of a finished yet unstyled Neo-Latin literary text written by a leading scholar of the early seventeenth century.

Burton makes some errors in syntax, but they are not numerous and at times difficult to distinguish from scribal error. One such mistake is nonagreement in gender. For example, in lines 227–28 and 233, he gives "academiam cessurum" for "academiam cessuram." In line 406, he has "frontem elatum" for "frontem elatam," and in line 2113 "frontes nouos" for "frontes

---

[28] Jordan-Smith, xix.

[29] "The Calculus of Error, Confessions of a General Editor," *Modern Philology* 75 (Feb. 1978): 254. Hill quotes Philip Gaskell, *A New Introduction to Bibliography* (Oxford: Oxford Univ. Press, 1972), 339: "Most authors, in fact, expect their spelling, capitalization, and punctuation to be corrected or supplied by the printer, relying on the process to dress the text suitably for publication, implicitly endorsing it (with or without further amendment) when correcting proofs."

nouas." Errors of non-agreement also include verbs and relative pronouns. In lines 1166–67, Burton has "concentum . . . quae" for "concentum qui"; in line 968 he has the "Ancilla" say "experti fuimus" instead of "expertae fuimus"; in lines 1153–55, he has "mulierum versutiam qui . . . edocti" instead of "quae . . . edoctae." And he occasionally uses the reflexive possessive adjective "suus, sua, suum" where the pronouns "eius/eorum" are more appropriate.

Despite these errors or idiosyncracies of usage, Burton's grammar and syntax generally follow the rules of grammar set forth in contemporary school texts. His orthography, however, does not always agree with that given in the major dictionaries of the period: Thomas Cooper, *Thesaurus Linguae Romanae et Britannicae* (1565), Thomas Thomas, *Dictionarium Linguae Latinae et Anglicanae* (1587), and *Riders Dictionarie* (1612). For example, Burton consistently uses "Aristotiles," "inditium," "spetie," "rithmis," and "ascultabo." The dictionaries give the spellings "Aristoteles," "indicium," "specie," "rhythmis," and "auscultabo." Burton also consistently uses "inprimis" and "faelix." Here the authorities are divided. Cooper gives "in primis," Thomas lists "inprimis" but prefers "imprimis," *Riders* "inprimis"; Cooper gives "felix," *Riders* "foelix," Thomas both "foelix" and "felix" but prefers the latter.

Burton's spelling is far from consistent. He interchanges the letters "i" and "y," as in line 763 where he uses "Anticeras," but just two lines later, "Antyceras," and in line 500, "olympum" but "olimpo" in line 501. The "ae" dipthong is also a problem. In line 223, he has both "pratorem" and "praetor." Nor is he consistent with the letter "h." On the title page he has "Cristi" two times, "Christi" once. In line 52 he uses both "rhombum" and "romboidem." At times he exchanges "e" and "i" (as in "peregrinantes" and "perigrinationis," "peripateticum" and "perepateticus") and "c" and "t" ("exercitium" and "exertitium," "precio" and "pretio," "meretriciam" and "meretritiam," for example). The dictionaries give the spellings "Anticyras," "Olympus," "praetor," "rhombus," "rhomboidem," "peregrinantes," "peripaticus," "exercitum," "pretio," and "meretriciam."

The spelling in the Folger manuscript is no more consistent nor does it always agree with that of the Harvard. For example, where the Harvard manuscript reads "exercitium," the Folger has "exertitium," and where Harvard has "exertitium," Folger has "exercitium." Likewise the two times Burton uses "peregrinantes," the scribe of the Folger manuscript uses "perigrinantes," but where Burton uses "perigrationis," the scribe has "peregrationis." In almost every instance of a familiar word, Thomas Goffe gives the preferred Renaissance spelling. But with unfamiliar words, all three manuscripts are likely to give different readings. For example in line 144, Burton has "chyrosophia," the scribe of the Folger "chirosophia," and Goffe, "cheirosophia." In line 54, Burton has "Icosaeadron," Folger "Icosaradron," and Goffe "Icoseodron." In line 51, for Burton's "paralapippidum," Folger has "par lappidum" and Goffe "paralelapippedum." None of these words appears in the dictionaries.

Capitalization and Punctuation

Although he occasionally nods, Burton tends to follow the basic rules of capitalization set forth in the school books of the sixteenth and seventeenth centuries: "Great letters are written in the beginning of" sentences, proper names, "the more eminent words in a sentence," and "everie vers in a Poem."[30] Burton uses two types of "great letters." One is considerably larger than other letters and almost ornamental; these he most often uses to indicate acts and scenes and lists of characters in a scene. His other capital is only slightly larger than his normal script and is prevalent with the letters "m," "n," "v," "p," and "o."

On punctuation, the grammars state that "a point or paus is a note of distinction, signifying the space of breathing, or how long one may staie his breath."[31] Burton tends to omit "a full prick after a perfect sentence" at the end of sentences which coincides with the end of a line of verse. He frequently ends what are clearly interrogative sentences with periods and what seem to be declarative sentences with question marks. He uses a virgule after a period for clear breaks in the dialogue, such as at the end of a scene. He seldom uses colons "which suspend a sentence somwhat long, by dividing it in the midst" or semicolons "staying a sentence longer then a Comma, and not so long as a Colon." But he is quite fond of the comma "which staieth a sentence a little by distinguishing its shorter parts" to indicate pauses in the dialogue.[32] He also uses a dash to indicate longer pauses.

Burton has no accent marks on the few words of Greek in *Philosophaster*. In Latin he uses an accent "for difference sake"[33]: the circumflex on ablatives of the first declension to distinguish them from nominatives or vocatives and on adverbs such as hîc and quî to distinguish them from the pronouns. He also uses the circumflex on syncopated verbs such as "nostîn," and on the vocative of second declension nouns ending in "ius." He uses the acute accent on the final vowels of adverbs.

Prosody

Opposite the title page of both the Harvard and Folger manuscripts is a note in which Burton cites Matthew Gwinne and Rudolph Gualter on Latin

---

[30] Charles Hoole, *Latin Grammar fitted for the use of schools. Wherein the words of "Lilie's Grammar" are (as much as might bee) reteined; many errors thereof amended; many needless things left out: many necessaries, that were wanting, supplied; and all things ordered in a Method more agreeable to Children's Capacitie.* (London, 1651; rpt. Menston: The Scolar Press, 1969), 6. See also Iohn Bird, *Grounds of Grammar* (Oxford, 1639; rpt. Menston: The Scolar Press, 1971), 3, and Ben Jonson, *The English Grammar* (1640; rpt. Menston: The Scolar Press, 1972), 35.

[31] Hoole, 10. See also Bird, 10 and Jonson, 83–84.

[32] Hoole, 10.

[33] Hoole, 274.

prosody and announces that he has "done the same" in his own play. That is, for the dialogue of *Philosophaster*, Burton uses iambic meter in six, seven or eight feet.

In its pure form, the iambic senarius is simply six iambic feet scanned

$$\smile\,\acute{-}\,\smile\,- \quad \smile\,\acute{-}\,\smile\,- \quad \smile\,\acute{-}\,\smile\,-$$

The septenarius is seven complete feet and a half foot:

$$\smile\,\acute{-}\,\smile\,- \quad \smile\,\acute{-}\,\smile\,- \quad \smile\,\acute{-}\,\smile\,- \quad \smile\,\acute{-}\,\smile\,\asymp$$

The octonarius is eight full iambic feet:

$$\smile\,\acute{-}\,\smile\,- \quad \smile\,\acute{-}\,\smile\,- \quad \smile\,\acute{-}\,\smile\,- \quad \smile\,\acute{-}\,\smile\,-$$

However, all three meters allow substitutes in any foot except the last which must be a pure iambus ($\smile\,\acute{-}$) or a tribrach ($\smile\,\acute{\smile}\,\smile$). Any one of the following could be substituted for the iambus in the other feet: spondee ($-\,\acute{-}$), anapest ($\smile\,\smile\,\acute{-}$), dactyl ($-\,\smile\,\acute{\smile}$), or proceleusmatic ($\smile\,\smile\,\acute{\smile}\,\smile$). In the iambic meters of Plautus and Terence, the ictus (or beat, marked above $'$) tends to coincide with the normal accent of the Latin word.[34] This is true in Burton's dialogue as well:

> Compónite, compónite, compónite, ínquam ócyus
>
> Túnicas, tógas, bárbas, véstes, hábitus.
>
> Sed éstne cértus híc admíssiónis díe? (lines 38-40)

In his songs, Burton uses a trochaic meter ($\acute{-}\,\smile$), most often in four feet and with end rhyme:

> Pérsonátus égo
>
> Síc meípsum tégo (lines 1189-90)

Váleté Acádemíci

Ét combíbonés optími

Ósunénsesqué relíqui

Et núnc et ín perpétuum (lines 1485-89)

> Phaébus dúm perérrat órbem
>
> Lústrans quóque práeter spém
>
> Mártem vídet ét Venérem
>
> Síne thálamó cubántem (lines 1679-82)

---

[34] For a more complete discussion of Latin comic meter, see *OCD*, "Meter, Latin," or George E. Duckworth, *The Nature of Roman Comedy* (Princeton: Princeton Univ. Press, 1971), 361ff.

This Edition

Text

I have used Harvard MS. Thr. 10, Burton's holograph, as the copy text for this edition. I edited the manuscript with two (sometimes contradictory) goals: to reproduce the text as Burton wrote it and to produce a text intelligible to modern readers of Latin. Certain compromises have been made.

Since *Philosophaster* is readily available in facsimile, a diplomatic transcription is not necessary. Therefore, I silently expand all abbreviations, separate ligatures and modernize long "s." However, Burton wrote a Renaissance, not a classical Latin text, and so I usually keep the peculiarities of his spelling. I silently emend scribal errors. These are sometimes difficult to distinguish from Burton's idiosyncratic spelling, but as a rule, I silently emend only those words where Burton omits single letters and the result is neither a Latin word nor a variant spelling. I have listed in Appendix II phonetic variations in spelling found in all three manuscripts. Emendations to the copy text are marked with an asterisk *.

With syntax, it is often more difficult to distinguish scribal mistake and author idiosyncracy. If I have erred, it may be in keeping some mistakes, or at least listing too many of them in the textual notes. I emend non-agreement of adjectives and nouns and of relative pronouns and antecedents. Burton and the scribe of the Folger do occasionally repeat these "errors" (e.g., twice modifying "frontes" with the masculine form of the adjective). Nevertheless, Burton usually makes his nouns and adjectives agree and uses the "proper" gender and inflections of nouns. Relative pronouns are more problematic. On three occasions Burton uses the masculine form to refer to female characters. Since the female characters were played by males, I first considered these "errors" one of Burton's jokes. But any intentional misuse of relatives is neither consistently nor usually done, so I emend the syntax but list all emendations in the textual notes.

I silently emend capitalization of the first letter in proper names, in the first word of a sentence, and a line of verse. I keep capitalization of what Burton seems to have considered important words in a sentence, particularly those words that are regularly capitalized in all three manuscripts ("Academia," "Dux," "Idiotae," for example). I keep Burton's accents in Latin and add accents in Greek. I silently emend, standardize and modernize punctuation throughout.

I have numbered the lines of the text to match those given by Marvin Spevack in his facsimile edition of *Philosophaster*. Because Spevack began his numbering with the prologue, I give line numbers for the introductory prose sections of the manuscript in parentheses. Burton usually wrote stage directions in the margin of the manuscript. I transcribe these directions into the body of the text in square-bracketed italics. To keep the line numbering consistent with the Spevack facsimile, I count stage directions as part of the following line of text.

Textual Notes

I list in the textual notes my emendations of the Harvard text and variant readings found in the Folger and Goffe manuscripts. I exclude accidental errors of transcription; variant spellings are given in Appendix II. Additions or corrections made to the three manuscripts are noted, but only those additions and corrections which help to determine the relationship of the manuscripts. My notations are as follows: "Erasure" means that a word has been rubbed out. "Cancellation" means that the word has been crossed out with one or more strokes. If the word erased or canceled can be deciphered, it is given in the notes. A correction written "above" an erasure or cancellation is not on the line of text, but slightly above it. A word or letter written "over" another word or letter indicates that the original has been corrected on the line of text, not erased or canceled. An "interlinear" word has been inserted above the text, usually with a caret and without erasure or cancellation.

Additions and corrections to the Folger manuscript not made by the principal scribe are said to be in Hand b. Only major additions and corrections by Hand b are listed in the textual notes. A complete list of additions and corrections by this second hand (including ornamental serifs, single letters, *notae*, etc.) are given in Appendix I.

In the textual notes, the first reading, followed by a bracket], is that of this text. The abbreviations for the three sources are:
F: Folger MS. V. a. 315
F¹: Folger MS. V. a. 315, Hand b
G: Harvard MS. Thr. 10. 1, the Goffe playbook
H: Harvard MS. Thr. 10.

Om. indicates that words are omitted; *add.*, that they have been added at the end of a line. Emendations to copy text are marked with an asterisk *.

Translation

I have translated Burton's verse dialogue into modern English prose, following the Latin text as closely as possible. If all the characters seem to speak with one voice in translation, it is because they do so in Latin. Burton makes no distinctions in grammar or vocabulary for philosophasters, courtiers, or townspeople, and for the most part, neither do I. Pedants are only slightly more pompous and pedantic than rustics.

I have been a little freer in translation of Burton's songs and poems. Here I have attempted to catch something of the meter, although not of rhyme.

My primary sources for general terms and phrases are Thomas Cooper, *Thesaurus Linguae Romanae et Brittanicae* (London, 1565) and Thomas Thomas, *Dictionarium Linguae Latinae et Anglicanae* (Cambridge, 1582). For technical, specialized or less familiar terms, I use Charles Estienne, *Dictionarium*

Historicum, Geographicum, Poeticum (Paris, 1596); Martinus Rulandus, *A Lex-icon of Alchemy* (Frankfurt, 1612), trans. A. E. Waite; Roy J. Deferrari, *A Lat-in-English Dictionary of St. Thomas Aquinas* (Boston: Daughters of St. Paul, 1960).

Commentary

Terms, people and places that may not be familiar to the reader are explained or identified in the commentary. My first sources for such people, places and things are Renaissance texts (such as Cooper, Estienne, Rulandus); where those are silent or inadequate I turn to modern dictionaries or texts. I note, insofar as I have been able to unearth them, quotations or paraphrases of classical or contemporary authors. If the quotation is exact, I do not give the Latin. If it is not exact, I include the Latin with translation in brackets. Unless otherwise noted, all citations from classical authors are from the Oxford Classical Texts and all translations are my own.

Except for rather general information, I indicate at the beginning of the notation my source for the commentary. Where I have been led to a source by others, I acknowledge them. I include many annotations from Paul Jordan-Smith's 1931 edition of *Philosophaster*. If I use the exact or complete notation, I enclose it in quotation marks. Where I expand the commentary, I list "JS" at the beginning of the notation.

I have also used several comments from personal letters written to Jordan-Smith by Edward Bensly. Seventeen of these letters, dated from December 1929 to March 1930, are held in the Robert Burton Collection of the Honnold Library, Claremont, CA. Most of these letters begin with a brief personal greeting followed by notes suggesting revision of translation or reference to classical or contemporary sources. Jordan-Smith used many of Bensly's references in the 1931 *Philosophaster*, others he did not use. The most important of these is Bensly's identification of Pontano as one of Burton's major sources. I indicate Bensly as my source for those references Jordan-Smith did not use and cite Bensly rather than Jordan-Smith when the references in his letters are more complete than the annotations in the 1931 edition.

I refer to *The Anatomy of Melancholy* where Burton repeats or expands on either a relevant idea or obscure allusion in *Philosophaster* or where he more fully identifies a person or place. References are given by partition, section, member, etc. with page numbers from the Holbrook Jackson edition in parenthesis. I make no attempt to identify all shared phrases or quotations or to comment on other similarities between *The Anatomy of Melancholy* and *Philosophaster*.

Philosophaster

Versus per totum sunt Comici Iambici, Senarii, Septenarii, Octonarii, vel Iambi mixti, qui singulis in locis pedes habent indifferentes, excepto vltimo vbi semper Iambus. Nostrates enìm veteres, exteri, neoterici, quos vidi, audiui, legi comici id vnum agunt et plerunque sunt aucupati, vt in Iambum versus continuò desineret. (5)

Matthias Gwinne, praefatio ad suum Vertumnum.

Comici enim quia populi plausum venantur, communem magis loquendi consuetudinem, quam Carminum anxiae rationes et pedum constitutionem obseruant quarè omnibus promiscuè utuntur.

Rodolphus Gualter Tigurinus, De [syllabarum et] carminum ratione, liber secundus. (10)

Idem ego feci per totam hanc Comoediam.

The verses throughout are comic iambics in six, seven, or eight feet, or mixed iambics which have indifferent scansion in various positions except the last which is always an iamb. Our own, the ancient, foreign, and neoteric writers of comedy whom I have seen, heard, and read do the same, and they are especially careful that the verse end in an iamb.

Matthew Gwinne in the preface to *Vertumnus*[1]

Writers of comedy, because they strive for the applause of the people, observe the common custom of speech more than the strict rules of verse and laws of meter. Therefore, they use all meter indiscriminately.

Rudolph Gualter of Tigure, *De syllabarum et carminum ratione*, bk. 2.

I have done the same throughout this Comedy.

---

[1] See Jordan-Smith, 12, for the complete quotation.

Philosophaster

COMOEDIA NOVA

Scripta Anno domini 1606.
Alterata, reuisa, perfecta
Anno domini 1615. Acta demum
Et publicè exhibita Academicis   (20)
In aulâ Aedis Cristi, et a
Studiosis Aedis Cristi Oxoniensis
Alumnis, Anno 1617 Februarii
Decimo sexto, die lunae
Ad horam sextam pomeridianam.   (25)

Auctore Roberto Burton
Sacrae Theologiae Baccalaureo
Atque Aedis Christi Oxoniensis Alumno.
1617

Osuna scena, oppidum Andalusiae   (30)
In Hispaniâ Baeticâ.

Philosophaster

A NEW COMEDY

Written in 1606.
Altered, revised, completed
In 1615. Finally acted
And publicly presented to the University
In the Hall of Christ Church
By the student members of Christ Church, Oxford
On Monday, February 16, 1617
At five o'clock in the afternoon.

Written by Robert Burton, SD
And alumnus of Christ Church, Oxford
1617

Scene: Osuna, a town in Andalusia,
The Province Baetica, Spain

Argumentum

Desiderius Osunae Dux, Osunam Andalusiae vrbeculam de nouo insti-
tuit Academiam, latefundiis et priuilegiis abundè locupletatam: pro-   (35)
mulgatione factâ per omnem Europam, vt si qui studiosi nouam hanc
Academiam studendi causâ visitarent, eos se donaturum, non tam
priuilegiis, sed et salario se digno, caeterisque necessariis. Ad quam
promulgationem vndiquaque philosophorum fit concursus, tum et   (40)
philosophastrorum, lenarum et meretricum. Huc etiam appulerûnt
duo peregrinantes philosophi Polumathes et Philobiblos vt sapientem
consulerent, qui post moram aliquot mensium in Osunâ mores omni-   (45)
um pseudophilosophorum propalant et sugillant, ob quam causam
tandem ab ipso duce corruptam Academiam repurgaturo, multis modis honorantur. Oppidani interìm consultatione habitâ de nouâ hâc
erectâ Academiâ, concludunt futuram in rem suam et suis suffragiis
approbant. Ad praescriptum itaque diem omnes omnium ordinum
philosophi et studiosi post conuiuium, quod in Lapitharum desinit, li-   (50)
berè admittuntur. De bonis hic non agitur. Philosophastri prae caete-
ris egregii, et qui totam ferè fabulam agunt, hi sunt: (55)

POLUPRAGMATICUS Iesuita cum AEQUIVOCO seruo suo qui
varias formas induit, politicum, aulicum, theologum, magum, quo habitu indutus, Polupistum quendam e rure nobilem mirâ verborum
grandiloquentiâ deludit. Stephanioni vero alteri nobili, cuius filium
Antonium erudiendum susceperat, iisdem artibus imponit.   (60)

LODOVICUS PANTOMETER prae se ferens Mathematicum,
veteratorem agit suis praestigiis, rude vulgus circumueniens.   (65)

PANTOMAGUS Alcumista, Medicus, rudi etiam vulgo miserimè

Argument

Desiderius, the duke of Osuna, recently established the little town in Andalusia as a university, well endowed with money and lands. Throughout all of Europe it is made known that anyone who comes to this new university to study will be given not just benefits, but also an appropriate stipend and other necessities. In response to this announcement, philosophers stream in from all over, and right behind them, philosophasters, pimps and whores. But two wandering scholars in search of a wise man, Polumathes and Philobiblos, also arrive here. After a few months in Osuna they expose and bring to public ridicule the true character of all the pseudophilosophers; for this they receive many honors from the duke who will clean up his corrupt university. In the meantime, the townspeople, after meeting to discuss this newly built university, conclude that it will profit them and vote their approval of it. And so, on the appointed day, after a banquet which ends in a Lapithean Feast,[1] philosophers and students of every sort are freely admitted. This play is not about true scholars. These are the notable philosophasters who make up almost the entire cast:

POLUPRAGMATICUS, a Jesuit, with AEQUIVOCUS his servant, takes on various guises: a politician, courtier, theologian and magician. As a magician, with a wonderful grandiloquence of words, he deceives Polupistos, a certain nobleman from the country. In truth, with these same skills, he also tricks Stephanio, another nobleman whose son, Antonius, he has undertaken to educate.

LODOVICUS PANTOMETER, pretending to be a mathematician, is a crafty fellow, fooling the common people with his deceptions.

PANTOMAGUS, an alchemist, physician, and outstanding fabricator of

---

[1] JS: "The Lapithae were a people of Thessaly, celebrated in mythology as having had a contest with the Centaurs. Pirithous, one of the Lapithae, was married to Hippodame. The Centaurs were invited to the wedding feast, where one of them got drunk and carried off the bride. The banquet ended in a brawl." See Ovid, *Met.* 12.210–530.

abutitur suis pharmacis ridiculis, nugarum artifex egregius, tum et Polupistum nobilem, Chimistam se similans, variis technis bis circumscri-
bit aurum se posse dicens conficere, cuius verbis ille inescatus aureos
sibi montes pollicetur, multaque regali quâdam magnificentiâ perfici-   (70)
enda proponit, sed pro auro (quod aiunt) carbones inuenit, post rem
familiarem decoctam, secundo iam delusus abiit.   (75)

SIMON ACUTUS sophistam agit verbis factisque, post varias eas-
que absurdas confabulationes hoc demùm in votis habet, vt a Iesuita
edoctus sicut ille charus singulis et celebris euadat, et ob haec, noua
quaedam dogmata et paradoxa liberiùs effingit.   (80)

AMPHIMACER poetaster rithmos quosdam in amicae gratiam ri-
diculè componit, quosuis obuios eodem tenore salutans.

THEANUS Theologaster, postquam Rhetorem egisset, ordines init
et fit Collegii sui subpraefectus, vbi per annos aliquot tanquam fucus
consenescens, suasu tandem Pedani, pauperis olìm alumni sui, rus   (85)
abit, quouismodo sacerdotium captaturus.

PEDANUS grammatista, quum per annum vnum et alterum pauper alumnus in Academiâ vixisset, pueris edocendis ruri operam elo-
cat, politicis criticisque se demum stolidè immiscens, duo Simoniacè   (90)
init sacerdotia, et ad Academiam decoro habitu reuersus, barbâque
reuerendâ conspicuus Irenarchae dignitatem apud suos, et inter Academicos Doctoratus gradum ambit, Sacellanum Ducis prae se ferens.   (95)

ANTONIUS, tyro, Stephanionis filius (ab Aequiuoco Iesuitae seruo
corruptus, mendatiorum fabro peritissimo, singulis imponente, et herum et medicum circumueniente) pictis chartis, aleae compotationi ve-
nerique totum se deuouet, hoc solum in votis habens quo artificio pe- (100)
cuniam emungat a patre, et vt amicae placeat, quam cantilenis, Musicâ
et donis ambiens; paulo post grauidam fecit, lenae vetulae consiliis
adiutus et illecebris inescatus, quae lotricem se fingens et sutricem, (105)
plures egregiâ formâ puellas tanquam filias enacta, poetam, medicum,
Antonium, caeterosque illectans, suburbanis hortis lupanar exercuit.

Deîn post varios errores, propter frequentes imposturas, et multi-   (110)
plices abusus, multae eaeque variae ad ducem semèl et simul deferun
tur queremoniae in philosophastros hosce sibi inuicèm ob laetiorem for-

trifles, miserably abuses the ignorant folk with his ridiculous medicine. Also, pretending to be an alchemist and saying that he can make gold by various techniques, he twice tricks the nobleman Polupistos who, taken in by these words, expects mountains of gold[2] for himself and proposes to do many great things with a certain royal magnificence. But instead of gold (as they say), he finds charcoal.[3] After he has wasted the family fortune, he departs, deceived for a second time.

SIMON ACUTUS, playing the sophist in word and deed, after various absurd conversations, at length makes this his goal: to learn from the Jesuit how to become dear to people and well-known. To this end he more freely fashions certain new and paradoxical doctrines.

AMPHIMACER, a poetaster, composes ridiculous verses to please his girlfriend, greeting whomever he meets in the same fashion.

THEANUS the theologaster, after he had played at being a rhetorician, enters orders and becomes subprefect of his college. Growing old there for many years just like a drone bee, he is at length persuaded by Pedanus, once another poor scholar, to go to the country to find a benefice of some kind.

PEDANUS, a grammarian, who for many years had lived at the university as a poor scholar, finds work in the country teaching young boys. Then, after foolishly meddling in politics and criticism, he obtains two benefices by simony. Having returned to the university in elegant costume, notable with his distinguished beard,[4] he canvasses for the office of Justice of the Peace among his own kind, and within the academic community goes after a doctoral degree while passing himself off as the duke's chaplain.

ANTONIUS, a freshman, the son of Stephanio, (having been corrupted by Aequivocus, the Jesuit's servant who is most skilled at lying and deceiving everyone, including his master and the physician,) devotes himself completely to cards, dice, drinking, and love. He has only one thing in mind: how to squeeze money from his father so he can please the girl he is courting with little songs, music and gifts. A little later, encouraged by the advice and lured by the deceit of an old bawd, he gets the girl pregnant. This bawd runs a brothel in a suburban garden, pretending to be a seamstress and laundress, keeping several lovely young girls as if they were her daughters, deceiving the poet, the doctor, Antonius, and others.

At length, after various complications brought on by the many impostures and numerous abuses, various and sundry complaints and written appeals from country and town all together and at one time are delivered to the duke against the philosophasters, who meanwhile are congratulating

---

[2] Terence, *Phorm.* 68: "montis auri pollicens." [Promising mountains of gold] Erasmus, *Ad.* 1.9.15: "Aureos montes polliceri." [To be promised a mountain of gold.]

[3] Erasmus, *Ad.* 1.9.25: "Thesaurus carbones erat." [The treasure was charcoal.]

[4] See Erasmus, *Ad.*, 1.2.95: "Barba tenus sapientes." [Bearded, therefore wise.]

tunam intereà congratulantes, multique supplices libelli e rure et vrbe.
Stephanio queritur ob filium deperditum, quem Iesuitae fidei com-
mendarât. Polupistos se bis delusum a mago et medico. Oppidani ob   (115)
ciues verberatos, res suffuratas, etc. Antonius querelam defert de Aequiuoco. Ab alias res querantur alii.

Hisce tam diuersis diuersorum querimoniis incensus et irretitus
Dux, exilium Studiosorum et Academiae subuersionem minitatur. Et   (120)
sane subuertisset illicò, si Polumathes et Philobiblos iam tum opportunè non interuenissent, quorum suasu sententia reuocata est, et
eorum consilium sequutus, philosophastros et delatores ad Tribunal   (125)
suum sistit. Philosophastri et lena vnà cum meretricibus filiis diuersorum criminum accusantur, idque coram ab iis quos priùs eluserant, a
Polumathe deteguntur omnes, et pro varietate criminum variè mulc-
tantur. Polupistos aurum suum restitutum habet, sed et inter sutrices   (130)
Camaenam, vnicam filiam suam, inuenit et agnoscit, quam iamdiu
crediderat demortuam, sed a lenâ olìm ereptam et ab Antonio grauidam factam, Antonio eidem vnico Stephanionis filio, laeto parentum
consensu, nuptam dat. Atque hunc in modum poenis persolutis,
consopitis querelis, rebusque demùm compositis, restauratâ nimirum   (135)
Academiâ, nouis decretis sancitis, Polumathe et Philobiblo procura-
toribus a Duce constitutis–pacatus Dux, reconciliata plebs, placati   (140)
delinitique omnes in gratiam redeunt, et hymnum canentes in laudem
Philosophiae, aequis animis discedunt.

themselves on their good fortune. Stephanio complains that his son, whom he had entrusted to the care of the Jesuit, has been led astray. Polupistos that he has twice been cheated by the magician and the doctor; the townspeople that they have been beaten and their things stolen, etc. Antonius brings a complaint against Aequivocus. Others complain about other matters. The duke, incensed and infuriated by these diverse complaints of diverse people, threatens the banishment of the students and the destruction of the university. And certainly he would have destroyed it then and there had not Polumathes and Philobiblos so opportunely intervened. At their persuasion, the duke changes his mind and, following their advice, calls the philosophasters and their accusers to his tribunal. The philosophasters and the bawd with her whorish daughters are accused of various crimes, and in the presence of those whom they had previously deceived all are exposed by Polumathes. For the variety of their crimes they are variously punished. Polupistos has his gold restored, but also among the seamstresses discovers Camaena, his only daughter whom he had long believed dead, but who had once been stolen by the bawd and now is pregnant by Antonius. With the happy consent of the parents, he gives her hand in marriage to this same Antonius, only son of Stephanio. And so in this manner with punishment given, complaints are quieted, matters settled, the university truly restored, sanctioned by new decrees with Polumathes and Philobiblos established as procurators by the duke. The happy duke, the reconciled people, and all the others now pacified and soothed, give thanks and, singing a hymn in praise of Philosophy, quietly depart.

Drammatis Personae

Desiderius	Osunae Dux	(145)

Eubulus Cratinus	} Ducis Consiliarii	

Polumathes Philobiblos	} Duo Peregrinantes Philosophi	(150)

Sordidus Cornutus Rubicundus	} Oppidani et Ciues Osunenses	

Polupragmaticus: Iesuita, Magus. etc.   (155)
Aequiuocus: Iesuitae Seruus
Lodouicus Pantometer: Mathematicus
Pantomagus: Medicus, Chimista
Simon Acutus: Sophista   Philosophastri
Theanus: Theologaster
Pedanus: Grammatista   (160)
Amphimacer: Poetaster
Antonius: Tyro, Stephanionis Filiis

Stephanio:	Nobilis e rure	
Polupistos:	Nobilis e rure	(165)
Dromo:	Polupisti Seruus	
Staphila:	Anus et Lena	

Camaena Tarentilla	} Lenae Filiae et Sutrices Habitae	
		(170)

Dramatis Personae

Desiderius	The Duke of Osuna
Eubulus Cratinus	The Duke's Counselors
Polumathes Philobiblos	Two Wandering Scholars
Sordidus Cornutus Rubicundus	The Townsmen and Citizens of Osuna

Polupragmaticus: A Jesuit, Magician, etc.
Aequivocus: The Jesuit's Servant
Lodovicus Pantometer: A Mathematician
Pantomagus: A Physician and Chemist
Simon Acutus: A Sophist   Philosophasters
Theanus: A Theologaster
Pedanus: A Grammarian
Amphimacer: A Poetaster
Antonius: A Freshman, Son of Stephanio

Stephanio	A Nobleman from the Country
Polupistos	A Nobleman from the Country
Dromo	Polupistos' Servant
Staphila	An Old Woman and a Bawd
Camaena Tarentilla	The Bawd's Daughters, Pretending to be Seamstresses

Lictor.	Promus.	Seruus.
Patientes.	Tibicines.	
Ancilla.	Puer.	Etc.

Sergeant at Arms.   Drawer.   Servant.
Patients.   Lute Players
A Maid.   A Boy.   Others.

Prologus

Quod est poetis nunc, quod antiquis fuit
Solenne, et vsu sempèr in ludis erit,
Orare, adesse vt mente benignâ velint,
Pro more solenni nos petituri sumus.   5
Si quid peruulgatum hâc fabulâ fuerit
Absoletum si quid, quod minùs arriserit,
Emendicatum e nuperâ scenâ aut quis putet,
Sciat quod vndecem abhinc annis scripta fuit,
Inter blattas et tineas in hunc diem delituit,   10
Ab authore in aeternas damnata tenebras,
Aliorum importunitate nunc in scenam venit.
Et hoc inpraesentiàrum scire vos aequum fuit.
Comoediae summam eloqui non est opus,
Nomen vel ipsum quae sit abundè docet.   15
Scenaque prima, ne quis ignoret tamen,
Haec terra quae vos tenet est Andalusia.
Hoc oppidum Osuna, a duce huiusce loci
Iam de nupero erecta Academia.
Viros vndequaque accersiuit doctissimos.   20
Mox aderunt, vnà omnes admittendi illicò.
Hic non agetur de bonis; pseudophilosophi
Quid perpetrarînt, fabulae finis docet.
Nec plura dicam; cuncta se sponte explicant.
Vos vnum hoc obitèr admonitos volo: 25
Philosophastros, si qui tales saltem sient
Quamprimùm vt eant, pleni rimarum sumus.

Prologue

As is the custom of comic playwrights now—
Established by the ancients and one that will endure:
To ask those present for an open mind—
We will now seek solemnity.
  If anything in this story should seem well known,
If anything is commonplace or, what would be less pleasing,
If anyone should think this adapted from a recent play,
Let him know it was written eleven years ago
But hidden among the roaches and moths until this day,
Condemned by its author to eternal darkness.
Now, at the urging of others, it comes onto the stage.
You should know this much of the circumstance.
  There is no need to tell what the comedy is about;
The name itself well teaches what that may be.
The foremost scene, lest anyone not know,
This land which holds you is Andalusia,
The town Osuna, the university
Quite recently erected by the local duke.
He has summoned from far and wide most learned men.
Soon they will have come to be admitted one and all.
This play is not about true scholars;
The end of the tale teaches what pseudophilosophers do.
I shall say no more. All unfolds of its own accord.
  By the way, I want to warn you:
Philosophasters, if any such be here,
Leave at once for we are full of chinks.[1]

---

[1] Terence, *Eun.* 105: "plenus rimarum sum" [I am full of chinks.] Cooper: *full of chinkes*: "that can kepe no counsayle, but blabbe out all that he heareth." See also Plautus, *Curc.* 510.

Sed salua res est, nullus exurgit loco.
Nemo reus, digni omnes Academici.
Opere magno rogatos vos omnes volo–   30
Attentionem nostrae vt praestetis re gregi,
Saltem Theatro quanta vulgari datur.

ACTUS PRIMUS
Scena Prima
Polupragmaticus. Lodouicus Pantometer.
Pantomagus. Simon Acutus.   35
Aequiuocus [*cum togis et reliquo apparatu.*]

[*Dum alii loquuntur reliqui se parant.*]
POLUPRAGMATICUS: Componite, componite, componite inquam
    ocyùs Tunicas, togas, barbas, vestes, habitus.
LODOUICUS PANTOMETER: Sed estne certus hic admissionis dies?   40
POLUPRAGMATICUS: Certo certius, hodie ad horam decimam
    Dux aderit, vnàque admittendi Academici.
    Tu libros hos tuque instrumenta haec cape,
    Tu prae te feres mathesin, tu philosophiam,
    Tu medicinam, ego qualemcunque scientiam.   45
LODOUICUS PANTOMETER: Sed vnde scientiam?
POLUPRAGMATICUS: Stipes, librum hunc cape.
    Edisce hinc verba quaedam sesquipedalia.
LODOUICUS PANTOMETER: Sed qui verbis aut arte hâc vti potero?
POLUPRAGMATICUS: Qui? Sic. Si fueris ad mensam, vel in colloquio,
    Cape quadram aut librum; si sit altera parte longior   50
    Dic esse paralologrammum rectangulum,
    Dic Rhombum vel Romboidem; si multilaterum
    Ac regulare Poligonum; secus, Trapesium.
LODOUICUS PANTOMETER: Egone haec?
POLUPRAGMATICUS: Panem scinde in formam Icosaeadron.
    Dic conum, cylindrum, prisma, paralapippidum.   55
    Habensque sempèr in promptu hunc circinum,
    Describes figuras quasdam geometricas.
    Docebis in dato cubo pyramidem efficere,
    Ex dato pyramide octeadron, ex octeadro
    Docaedron, tetrahedron aut exaedron.   60
LODOUICUS PANTOMETER: Ego nunquam recordabor horum nominum.
POLUPRAGMATICUS: Loqueris inde de Algorismo et Algebrâ,
    De numeris contractis, surdis, sursolidis,
    De radice zanzenique, zinzizanzizeqique et huiusmodi.

But all is well, no one rises from his place.
No one is guilty, all are worthy scholars.
    Now I ask you all earnestly:
Give attention to our company,
At least as much attention as you grant the public stage.

ACT I
Scene one
Polupragmaticus. Lodovicus Pantometer.
Pantomagus. Simon Acutus.
Aequivocus, [*with togas and other stuff*]

[*While some are talking the others get ready.*]

POLUPRAGMATICUS: Come, get ready, quickly I say. Bring the tunics, togas, beards, clothes and habits.

LODOVICUS PANTOMETER: Are you sure that this is the day of admission?

POLUPRAGMATICUS: More than sure. Today at the tenth hour the duke will be here and also the students to be admitted to the university. You take these books, you these instruments. You will pretend to mathematics, you philosophy, you medicine, and I just knowledge in general.

LODOVICUS PANTOMETER: But where do we get this knowledge?

POLUPRAGMATICUS: Stupid. Just take this book. Learn from it certain sesquipedalian words.

LODOVICUS PANTOMETER: But how will I be able to use these words or this art?

POLUPRAGMATICUS: How? Like this. If you are at table or in conversation, take a square or a book. If one side is longer, say that it is a rectangular parallelogram, say a rhombus or a rhomboid. If it is multilateral and regular, call it a polygon. Otherwise, a trapezoid.

LODOVICUS PANTOMETER: I'm to say that?

POLUPRAGMATICUS: Cut a slice of bread in the form of an icosahedron; say it is a cone, a cylinder, a prism, or a parallelepiped. Having this compass always close by, you will describe some geometric figures. You will show how to make a pyramid in a given cube, an octahedron from the given pyramid, and from the octahedron a decahedron, tetrahedron, or hexahedron.

LODOVICUS PANTOMETER: I'll never remember the names of those things.

POLUPRAGMATICUS: After that, you will talk about algorisms and algebra, or about contracted numbers, surds, subsolids, about the zenzic root, the zenzizenzic root—and things of this sort.[1]

---

[1] OED: *Surd*: Of a number or quantity (esp. a root): That cannot be expressed in finite terms or ordinary numbers or quantities. *Zenzic*: a. of a number or root; b. a square

LODOUICUS PANTOMETER: Zinzizan: quid hoc?
POLUPRAGMATICUS: Vel de Musicâ: 65
   Vocali, Harmonicâ, Rithmicâ, Organicâ.
   Vt Cromatium iuuetur hemitonio,
   De b fa b mi, elamire et elami,
   Inducendis aptè in cheli et in organo,
   De diapente, diapason, et diateseron   70
   Vt sonent meson proslambomenos,
   Hypate, hepaton, peripate, meson, hepaton,
   Lichanos, nete, trite, paranete, et nete diazeugmenos.
LODOUICUS PANTOMETER: Ludis operam, numquam haec imitari potero.
POLUPRAGMATICUS: Nihil est.
LODOUICUS PANTOMETER: At haec si quis demonstrari velit?   75
POLUPRAGMATICUS: Tum dic ab a et c, et ab a ad d, et l per e alterum
   Duc rectam per n et o et ipsum d diagonalitèr
   Et per sextum primi scindet medium f aequale c altero.
LODOUICUS PANTOMETER: Hoc tam obscurum vt nemo possit intelligere.
POLUPRAGMATICUS: Eo melius. Sic demonstratur quod demonstran-
   dum erat.   80
   Tuum est disputare de Infinito, Ente, Vacuo,
   Naturâ Naturante et Exietate Scoti,
   De causalitate causae et quidditatiuâ materiâ,
   De Gabrielitate Gabrielis, et spiritali animâ.
SIMON ACUTUS: Vellem quod iubes si possem.
POLUPRAGMATICUS: Potes fingere,   85
   Iactare et mentiri et hoc satis.

LODOVICUS PANTOMETER: Zenzizan: what's that?

POLUPRAGMATICUS: Or you can talk about music: vocal, harmonic, rhythmic, instrumental. Say that the chromatic scale is useful to harmony; talk of "b fa," "b mi," "e la mi re," and "e la mi,"[2] and the proper manner of playing the lyre and lute. Speak of fifths, octaves, double octaves, or the sound of the meson proslambanomenos, the hypate, hypaton, parhypate, meson, hypaton lichanos, the nete, trite, paranete, and nete diazeugmenos.[3]

LODOVICUS PANTOMETER: You are doing all of this for nothing. I'll never be able to imitate that.

POLUPRAGMATICUS: It's nothing.

LODOVICUS PANTOMETER: But what if someone wants a demonstration?

POLUPRAGMATICUS: Then say from 'a' and 'c' and from 'a' to 'd,' and 'l' through another 'e,' draw a straight line through 'n' and 'o,' and 'd' will cut the middle of 'f' diagonally through a sixth of the first, equal to another 'c.'[4]

LODOVICUS PANTOMETER: But this is so obscure no one could understand it.

POLUPRAGMATICUS: So much the better. Thus is demonstrated what must be demonstrated. Now your job is to discuss infinity, being, vacuity, 'natura naturans,'[5] and the haecceity of Scotus.[6] Talk of the causality of cause and the materiality of matter, the Gabriality of Gabriel, and the spirituality of spirit.

SIMON ACUTUS: I would what you order, if I were able.

POLUPRAGMATICUS: You are able to make things up, to throw them around and to lie, and this is enough.

---

number. So various compounds denoting higher powers or roots, as zenzicube (the square of the cube, the sixth power) . . . Zenzizenzic . . . Zenzizenzizenic, etc.

[2] JS: " 'elami': The note E, sung to the syllable 'la' or 'mi,' according as it occurred in the hexacord." See also Shakespeare, *The Taming of the Shrew*, 3.1.77.

[3] These are the strings of the lyre or notes from the scales of ancient Greek music. See *Music*, OCD.

[4] Compare Erasmus, *Mor.* 144. Folly, describing philosophers, says, "Tum vero praecipue prophanum vulgus aspernantur, quoties triquetris, et tetragonis, circulis, atque huiusmodi picturis mathematicis, aliis super alias inductis et in labyrinthi speciem confusis, praeterea literis velut in acie dispositis ac subinde alio atque alio repetitis ordine, tenebras offundunt imperitioribus." [In truth their scorn of the common folk is evident when they confuse the uneducated with triangles, tetragons, and circles, and mathematical figures of this sort, imposing one on another to produce what looks like a labyrinth, and then lining up series of letters as if in battle lines, and repeating them first in one order and then in another.]

[5] Deferrari: "the nature that serves as the cause of everything that happens according to nature, by which is meant God."

[6] In scholastic philosophy, a term especially associated with Duns Scotus. OED: *haecceity*: The quality implied in the use of *this*, as *this* man; 'thisness'; 'hereness and nowness'; that quality or mode of being in virtue of which a thing is or becomes a definite individual; individuality.

SIMON ACUTUS: Dabo operam.

POLUPRAGMATICUS: Ne dubites. Vnica virtus erit impudentia.

    Heus Medice, tu prae te feres Spagiricum,

    Disputabis de parimiro, lili, tartaro, mummia,

    Elixir extrahendo, caementis, gradationibus,   90

    Quopacto sit sublimandus Mercurius,

    Saturnus calcinandus, florificanda Venus,

    Ferrum crocificandum, reuerberandus Iuppiter.

    Audîn quae dico?

PANTOMAGUS: Dictum sapienti satìs.

POLUPRAGMATICUS: Aut si te mauis Iathromathematicum,   95

    Tum sit sermo de crisi et morbis cronicis,

    De Ioue directo aut stationario, Marte retrogrado,

    De tetragono radio, partili et platico.

    Tenesne?

PANTOMAGUS: Teneo.

POLUPRAGMATICUS: Suum quisque curet officium,

    Ego meum; bilinguis, ambodexter, omniscius,   100

    Iactabo quiduis, proùt dabitur occasio,

    Callere me omnes linguas, artes, scientias,

    Nescire aut haesitare stolidum existimo.

    Sed verbo dicam, Iesuitam prae me feram.

SIMON ACUTUS: I'll give it a try.

POLUPRAGMATICUS: Don't worry. The one and only virtue will be impudence.[7] You there, physician, you will pretend to be a spagyrist. You will discuss paramirum, lilium, tartarus, mummia, the drawing out of elixir, cementum and gradations.[8] You will tell how Mercury ought to rise, Saturn to calcine, Venus to flower, iron to saffronate and Jupiter to reverberate.[9] Do you hear what I'm saying?

LODOVICUS PANTOMETER: A word to the wise is sufficient.[10]

POLUPRAGMATICUS: Or, if you prefer, be an Iathromathematician.[11] Then there might be talk about crisis or chronic diseases, about Jupiter moving from west to east or standing stationary, about Mars moving backwards, or about a tetragonal radius in particular or in general. Do you understand?

LODOVICUS PANTOMETER: Perfectly.

POLUPRAGMATICUS: Let each one of you take care of his own duties, I'll take care of mine. As bilingual, ambidexterous, and omniscient, I'll boast of whatever I wish, just as the occasion is given.[12] I know every language, art, science, and consider it stupid either not to know or to hesitate. In a word, I'll pretend to be a Jesuit.

---

[7] Compare Juvenal, *Sat.* 8.20: "nobilitas sola est atque unica virtus" [Nobility is the one and only virtue.]

[8] JS: " 'Paramirum' is a term used by Paracelsus in two of his medical works—*Paramirum de quinque entibus omnium morborum* and *Opus paramirum secundum*, issued at Cologne in his collected works (1589–1590); it seems to have been an unguent or elixir taken from dead for living bodies." " 'Mumia' was bitumen or pitch, taken from mummies, in the belief that it would prolong life. It was freely used in sixteen- and seventeenth-century medicine." Rulandus: *Lilium*: "Mercury and its Flowers. Also Tincture of the Philosophers, Quintessence of Sulphur, Fixed Flowers, Fixed Sulphur." *Tartarus*: "Calculus of Wine, called Wine-stone by similitude, the stone, or deposit, which cleaves to the sides of vessels. Paracelsus uses it for stone in the bladder or kidneys, or the albuminous deposit in the other members which causes gout." *Cementum*: "a sharp and penetrating Mineral Substance by which the metallic layers to be cemented or welded, are, chemically speaking, reverberated upon." *Gradatio* "is the gradual Exaltation of Metallic Qualities by which their weight, colour and fixity are excellently increased. It accomplishes the transmutation of matter into its essential substance, provided it is performed gradually. It also manifests concealed potency without changing the original species."

[9] JS: "These metallurgical terms were employed by alchemists and referred to the processes used in refining or changing the metals. 'Saturn' = lead; 'Venus' = copper; 'Jupiter' = tin. 'Iron saffronated' = 'crocus of iron' or 'iron sulphate.' 'Reverberated' refers to heating in what was called a reverberating furnace."

[10] Plautus, *Pers.* 729; Terence, *Phorm.* 541: "Dictum sapienti sat est."

[11] OED: Those who practice medicine in conjunction with astrology. See also *AM* pt. 2, sec. 1, mem. 4, subs. 2 (16): "Paracelsus goes farther, and will have his physician predestinated to this man's cure, this malady, and time of cure, the scheme of each geniture inspected, gathering of herbs, of administering, astrologically observed; in which Thurnesserus and some iatromathematical professors are too superstitious in my judgment."

[12] For Burton on the hypocrisy of Jesuits, see *AM* Democritus (55).

SIMON ACUTUS: Cur Iesuitam?

POLUPRAGMATICUS: Quid non audet hoc genus hominum? 105
    In regum aulas, gynesia, quo non ruit?
    Quod intentatum reliquit scelus?
    Hos agam Ruffinos, et ad vnguem exprimam.
    Sed heus Aequiuoce, nostîn officium tuum?

AEQUIUOCUS: Here, ne dubites de sedulitate meâ. 110
    Lacti lac, ouum ouo non magis est simile
    Quam ego tibi; quod dico, dissimulo.
    Aequiuocare iamdudùm ab vtroque parente didici.
    Amphibologia enim mater meretrix et lena fuit;
    Pater Agyrta, magus et impostor vnicus. 115
    Ego vero qualis quantusque sum, totus sum tuus.

POLUPRAGMATICUS: Benè se res habet, suas quisque partes agat.

Scena Secunda
Desiderius. Eubulus. Cratinus.
Lictor. Philosophastri. Etc. 120

DESIDERIUS: Eubule, quis nouae iam status Academiae?

EUBULUS: Bellus et magnificus, parata sunt omnia,
    Bibliothecae, scholae, reditus, salaria.

DESIDERIUS: Sed vbi sunt interim scholares, vbi Academici?

EUBULUS: Prastò sunt.

CRATINUS: Ingredi iube.

DESIDERIUS: Paretur conuiuium. 125
                [Intrant philosophastri.]

DESIDERIUS: Aspectus haud ingratus ita me deus amet.

SIMON ACUTUS: Why a Jesuit?

POLUPRAGMATICUS: What will this sort of man not dare? Do they not hasten to royal halls or to a woman's chambers? What crimes remain untried? I'll play the ruffin, and I'll play it to the hilt.[13] But, Aequivocus, do you know your job?

AEQUIVOCUS: Don't worry, sir, about my sedulity. Milk to milk, egg to egg is not more similar than I to you.[14] When I speak, I dissemble. I learned to equivocate long ago from both parents.[15] My mother Amphibologia was both a whore and a bawd, my father Agyrta, a magician and unparalleled imposter.[16] I am all yours, as much as I am and what sort I am.

POLUPRAGMATICUS: Then all is well. Let each one play his own part.[17]

Scene two
Desiderius. Eubulus. Cratinus.
Sergeant at Arms. The Philosophasters.
Others.

DESIDERIUS: Eubulus, what now is the status of our new university?

EUBULUS: It is beautiful and stately. Everything is ready: the libraries, the colleges, the revenue, the stipends.

DESIDERIUS: But where are the scholars, the academics?

EUBULUS: They are here.

CRATINUS: Tell them to come in.

DESIDERIUS: Let a banquet be prepared.
                    [*The Philosophasters enter.*]

DESIDERIUS: Not an unpleasant sight, thank heaven. Welcome to you all,

---

[13] OED: *Ruffin*: the name of a fiend; the devil. LS: "Ad vnguem" is literally "to the finger nail." The expression is "borrowed from sculptors, who, in modelling, give the finishing touch with the nail; or joiners, who test the accuracy of joints in wood by the nail." Erasmus, *Ad.* 2.5.91.

[14] Plautus, *Am.* 601: Sosia describing Mercury who is disguised as Sosia: "neque lact' lactis magis est simile quam ille ego similest mei." [Nor is milk more similar to milk than that "I" is to me.] Plautus, *Bacch.* 6: "sicut lacte lactis similest" [as much alike as two drops of milk.] Erasmus, *Ad.* 1.5.10: "Non tam ovum ovo simile." [Egg is not so similar to egg.] *Ad.* 1.5.11: "Non tam lac lacte simile." [Milk is not so similar to milk.]

[15] For the Jesuits and equivocation, see Bevington on the "equivocator" in *Macbeth* 2.3.8ff., as a possible reference to "the trial of the Jesuit Henry Garnet for treason in the spring of 1606, and to the doctrine of equivocation said to have been presented in his defense; according to this doctrine a lie was not a lie if the utterer had in his mind a different meaning in which the utterance was true."

[16] Amphibologia: a rhetorical term for ambivalence of grammatical structure, usually by mispunctuation. JS: "Agyrta: Mountebank."

[17] Compare Plautus, *Merc.* 1011: "suam quisque homo rem meminit." [Let each one be mindful of his own part.] Erasmus, *Ad.* 4.1.42.

Saluete ad vnum omnes florentes Academici,
Grati venistis Osunam; sed cuius magisterii,
Quales vnde, quas artes profitemini?
CRATINUS: Dicat pro se quisque, seorsim singuli.   130
EUBULUS: Tu qui primus es quam profiteris scientiam?
Vel vnde venis, e Peripato an a Stoâ?
Cuius sectator Platonis an Aristotilis?
Scotista, Thomista, realis, nominalis an quis alius?
POLUPRAGMATICUS: Nullius et omnium.
CRATINUS: Opinor Elius Hippias.   135
POLUPRAGMATICUS: Non sed illius e sorore nepos octuagesimus.
DESIDERIUS: Quâ polles arte potissimum?
POLUPRAGMATICUS: Mên rogas?
Grammaticus, Rhetor, geometres, pictor, alyptes,
Augur, scenobates, medicus, magus, omnia noui.
Vel si mauis Iesuita, vt dicam semèl.   140
EUBULUS: Mirus hic artifex.
POLUPRAGMATICUS: Fac periculum in Theologiâ,
Philosophiâ, Medicinâ, Staticâ, Sceneographiâ,
Politiâ, Thaumaturgiâ, fac in Vraniscophiâ,
Chyrosophiâ, Magiâ, Bial, Hartumin, Iedoni,
Notis, ignotis, licitis aut illicitis scientiis;   145
Solertem me dabo, senties qui vir siem.
CRATINUS: Quod nomen?
POLUPRAGMATICUS: Polupragmaticus.
DESIDERIUS: Erit forsan a consiliis mihi.
Inscribe nomen eius. Tu quis?
PANTOMAGUS: Medicus ego.
EUBULUS: Rationalis, Dogmaticus, Methodicus, Empericus?
PANTOMAGUS: Nullus horum, sed nouae medicinae assecla   150
Quam nuper docuit Diuus Philippus Aurelius
Theophrastus Paracelsus, ab Hohoffnein bumbast medicus.
DESIDERIUS: Hic est futurus Reipublicae necessarius.
EUBULUS: Quod nomen?
PANTOMAGUS: Pantomagus.

flourishing academics. Welcome to Osuna. But with whom have you studied, where do you come from, what sort of things, what arts do you profess?

CRATINUS: Let each one speak for himself, one at a time.

EUBULUS: You who are first, what knowledge do you profess? Or what school do you come from, the Peripatetic or Stoic? Are you a follower of Plato or Aristotle? Are you a Scotist, a Thomist, Realist, Nominalist, or something else?

POLUPRAGMATICUS: I am a follower of none and of all.

CRATINUS: Hippias of Elis, I suppose.[1]

POLUPRAGMATICUS: No, but the eightieth grandson of his sister.

DESIDERIUS: But in what especially are you an authority?

POLUPRAGMATICUS: Me? I am a grammarian, a rhetorician, a geometrician, a painter, a wrestling coach, augur, rope walker, physician, magician. I know it all.[2] Or if you prefer, I am a Jesuit. That sums it up.

EUBULUS: This man is a marvelous master.

POLUPRAGMATICUS: Test me on theology, philosophy, medicine, statics, scenography, politics, thaumaturgy; try uranoscopy, chirosophy,[3] magic, Bial, Hartumin, Jedoni,[4] the known, the unknown, licit or illicit sciences. I will prove myself an expert, and you will know what sort of man I am.

CRATINUS: What is your name?

POLUPRAGMATICUS: Polupragmaticus.

DESIDERIUS: Perhaps he will serve on my Privy Council. Write down his name. Who are you?

PANTOMAGUS: I am a physician.

EUBULUS: Rational, Dogmatic, Methodic, or Empiric?

PANTOMAGUS: None of those, but a follower of a new medicine which was taught recently by St. Philippus Aurelius Theophrastus Paracelsus von Hohoffnein Bombast, physician.[5]

DESIDERIUS: This man will be important to the republic.

EUBULUS: What is your name?

PANTOMAGUS: Pantomagus.

---

[1] JS: "A contemporary of Socrates. He was reputed to have excelled in all arts and crafts." See Plato, *Hippias Maior* and *Hippias Minor*. In both dialogues, Plato has Socrates expose the superficiality of Hippias' knowledge.

[2] JS: Juvenal's *Sat.* 3.76–77: "grammaticus rhetor geometres pictor aliptes / augur schoenobates medicus magus, omnia novit" [A grammarian, rhetorician, geometrician, painter, wrestling coach, augus, rope walker, physician, magician, he knows all.]

[3] OED: *statics*: science of weights and measures; *scenography*: drawing or painting in perspective; *thaumaturgy*: miracle working; *uranoscopy*: study of the heavens; *chirosophy*: science of the hand.

[4] JS: "Familiar spirits."

[5] What Pantomagus means to say is Philippus Aureolus Paracelsus, whose real name is Theophrastus Bombastus von Hohenheim.

EUBULUS: Quis tibi proximus?

LODOUICUS PANTOMETER: Lodouicus Pantometer, professor Matheseos.   155

EUBULUS: Quid potes?

LODOUICUS PANTOMETER: Caelorum motus exactè calleo,
    Et totius orbis terrae quenuis ferè angulum.

DESIDERIUS: Noui hoc hominum genus. Admittatur illicò.

CRATINUS: Instrumentorum illorum quem vsum habes?

LODOUICUS PANTOMETER: Vtor in Architecturâ, Gnomonice, Geodesiâ.   160

EUBULUS: Quis ille alter?

SIMON ACUTUS: Sophista perepateticus.
    Mihi proprium est syllogismis concludere.
    Retia sermonum doceo; qui contra me disputant
    Tacere cogo. Nomen Simon Acutus, homo Italus.

CRATINUS: Tu quis?

THEANUS: Rhetor si placet, auditores humanissimi,   165
    Non ita pridem fui, iam vero Theologus.

CRATINUS: Quid cum staterâ tibi?

THEANUS: Pondus verborum trutino,
    Affectus moueo, suadae medullam exerceo.

DESIDERIUS: Concionator opinor egregius; a sacris sis mihi.
    Finitimus oratori poeta. Sed quis es?   170

AMPHIMACER: Sum quicquid conor dicere, carmen erit.
    Scribo quosuis versus, carmen Elboicum
    Ad omnes numeros tricolos tetrastrophos,
    Dicolos distrophos, pedesque coriambos catalecticos.

DESIDERIUS: Ede nomen.

AMPHIMACER: Amphimacer enutritus in Alcada de las Heneras   175
    Literasque exhibeo serenitati tuae a dominâ
    Illustrissimâ Ducissâ de Medina Sydoniâ.

DESIDERIUS: Non curo literas: specimen artis exhibe.

EUBULUS: Who is that next to you?

LODOVICUS PANTOMETER: Lodovicus Pantometer, professor of mathematics.

EUBULUS: What do you do?

LODOVICUS PANTOMETER: I reckon exactly the motion of the heavens and almost any angle of the entire earth.

DESIDERIUS: I know this sort of man. Let him be admitted at once.

CRATINUS: What use do you have for those instruments?

LODOVICUS PANTOMETER: I use them in architecture, gnomonics, geodesy.[6]

EUBULUS: Who is that other man?

SIMON ACUTUS: A peripatic sophist. My job is to conclude syllogistically. I teach the snares of discourse; those who dispute with me, I drive to silence. My name is Simon Acutus, an Italian.

CRATINUS: Who are you?

THEANUS: If you please, most gentle listeners, not long ago I was a rhetorician, but now I am, in fact, a theologian.

CRATINUS: Why do you have those scales?

THEANUS: I weigh the weight of words, move the emotions, practice the marrow of persuasion.[7]

DESIDERIUS: An outstanding preacher, I suppose. You must serve as my chaplain. A poet next to the orator.[8] Who are you?

AMPHIMACER: I am one who will make a poem of whatever I try to say.[9] I write whatever verses you wish, a poem elbowic[10] in all meters: tricolic tetrastrophic, dicolic distrophic, and coriambic catalectic feet.

DESIDERIUS: Give your name.

AMPHIMACER: Amphimacer, nurtured in Alcada de las Heneras.[11] I have a letter for your highness from my mistress, the most illustrious Duchess de Medina Sydonia.[12]

DESIDERIUS: I don't care about the letter: give a sample of your art.

---

[6] OED: *gnomonics*: measuring or surveying with a dial; *geodesy*: land surveying.

[7] See Cicero, *Brutus* 15.59 and *De Senectute* 14.50.

[8] JS: Cicero, *De Oratore* 1.16.70: "Est enim finitimus oratori poeta." [For the poet is next to the orator.]

[9] Ovid, *Tristia* 4.10.25–26: "Sponte sua carmen numersos veniebat ad aptos, / Et quod temptabam dicere versus erat." [Of its own accord a poem came in fitting measure, and whatever I tried to say was verse.] Bensly: "To produce the effect of dropping into verse the final line of Amphimacer's speech is in the non-dramatic meter of 'dactylic pentameter.' "

[10] Burton apparently coined the Latin "elboicum" for the English "elbowic." OED: elbowic: "humorous. 1654. Gayton. *Fest. Notes* [1.3], Verses, which being above Hexameters, full sometimes, and sometimes over-makes, that rather sounding verse, we call Elbowick. 1727. Bailey II, 'Elboick,' a sentence or verse of a rude or ruffling quality, as it were hunching or pushing with the elbow."

[11] Amphimacer probably means "Alcala de las Heneras." JS: "The birthplace of Cervantes."

[12] JS: "Medina-Sydonia: the dukes of this Spanish town had long been famous."

AMPHIMACER: O Desideri Dux, vultus tuus emicat vt lux.
    Et vos o proceres, quorum sapientia, mores   180
    Splendent vt flores, quorum admiramur honores.
    Vos Maecenates date, nos erimusque Marones.
Per Iouem ex tempore.
DESIDERIUS: Ita videtur, vt, vt
    Admittatur. Sed gesticularis ille quis?
PEDANUS: Dicor, vocor, salutor, appellor, habeor, existimor   185
    Paedagogus, puerorum praefectus ab officio,
    Pedanus apud vulgus, praeceptor apud pueros,
    Per antiphrasin ludimagister, per periphrasin
    Maior iuuenum castigatorque minorum,
    Quod est tanquam, quasi, perinde, acsi diceres   190
    Gymnasiarcha, Pedotriba, vel Hipodidasculus,
    Magister, Magistellus, siue Magisterculus.
    Sed vtrum horum mauis accipe.
DESIDERIUS: Scribe Grammaticum. Sed qui reliqui?
EUBULUS: Nostrates, Angli, Galli, Germani, Itali.   195
DESIDERIUS: Vnà inscribantur omnes et gratuitò.
    Quod bonum faelix faustumque sit reipublicae:
    Ego Desiderius Osunae Dux authoritate meâ
    Admitto vos omnes vniversos et singulos,
    Dono vos immunitatibus et priuilegiis,   200
    Do vobis potestatem legendi, practicandi sedulò
    Suam facultatem, suum cuique Magisterium.
OMNES: Gratias habemus serenitati tuae.
DESIDERIUS: Conuiuentur, inde suum quisque cedat ad locum.
             [*Exit Dux et consiliarii.*]
SERUUS: Sedeatis si placet, paratum est conuiuium.   205
POLUPRAGMATICUS: Et quidni sedemus, primus locus erit meus.
THEANUS: Atqui per Iouem meus.
PANTOMAGUS: Et quidni meus?
AMPHIMACER: Μὰ Δία καὶ τοὺς ἄλλους Θεούς, primus ego.
POLUPRAGMATICUS: Scurra ineptissime.

AMPHIMACER: Oh Desiderius *Dux*,
      Your face shines as *lux*.
      In your wisdom, O *Proceres*,
      Mores shine as *flores*;
      We admire your *honores*.
      You be my Maecenas;
      I'll be your Marones.[13]
  Extemporaneous, by Jove!

DESIDERIUS: So it would seem. But, but, admit him. Who is that man waving?

PEDANTIUS: I am said, called, addressed, held, thought to be a schoolmaster, officially tutor of boys. I am Pedanus to the people, master to the boys. Through antiphrasis, I am ludimagister;[14] through periphrasis, leader of the young and castigator of minors—which is, just as, as if, as it were, so to speak a gymnasiarch, paedotribe, hypodidasculus, magister, magistellus, or magisterculus.[15] Take which ever of these you prefer.

DESIDERIUS: Write grammarian. But who is left?

EUBULUS: Some of our own people, Englishmen, Frenchmen, Germans, Italians.

DESIDERIUS: Enroll them together and freely. May this prove good, propitious and properous for the state:[16] I, Desiderius, Duke of Osuna, by the authority vested in me, do admit you one and all. I grant you immunity and privileges. I give to each of you the authority to read and to practice diligently the subject of which you are master.

ALL: Thank you, your serene highness.

DESIDERIUS: Let them feast together, then each one may retire to his own place.

              [Exit Duke and counselors.]

SERVANT: You may sit, please. The banquet is ready.

POLUPRAGMATICUS: Why don't we sit. I'll take the head of the table.

THEANUS: But that place is mine, by Jove.

PANTOMAGUS: Why not mine?

AMPHIMACER: By Zeus and all the other gods, I am first.

POLUPRAGMATICUS: Inept buffoon.

---

[13] Maecenas: a patron of literature in Augustan Rome. Marones: Vergil (Publius Vergilius Maro), one of the poets under Maecenas' patronage.

[14] *Antiphrasis*: a figure of speech by which words are used in a sense opposite to their proper meaning. "Ludimagister" is appropriately a school master, that is, the "magister" of the "ludus." But "ludus" can also mean, according to Cooper: "play in actes: mirth in woordes; sporte: game: pastime."

[15] These are Greek and Latin terms (the last two apparently coined diminutives) for school teacher.

[16] Bensly: A formula found in Latin documents and proclamations, expressing a wish or prayer for what follows. See also Erasmus, *Ad.* 3.6.100: "Bene sit ... Item in concionibus: Quod faustum felixque sit." [May it prove good ... Also in proclamations: may it prove prosperous and propitious.]

[*Concertatur de loco. Polupragmaticus dat alapam Pedano.*]
[*Intrat*] EUBULUS: Quis hic tumultus? Lapitharumne conuiuium?
POLUPRAGMATICUS: Nil mali, sed orta quaedam est contentio   210
    Inter peripateticum et medicum de vitae principio.
    Nos de Ideis, illi contendebant de Atomis.
AMPHIMACER [*potat*]: Quicunque vult meus esse frater, bibat semel
    bis ter quater.
EUBULUS: Hiccine ebrius?
POLUPRAGMATICUS: Non sed enthusiasmo quodam percitus.
EUBULUS: Hoccine philosophari? Non tam verum quam dictum vetus: 215
    Tam conuenire philosophis quam Horologiis.
    Vestrum est inter vos rem totam componere.
               [*Seruo loquitur*]
    Heus tolle ciathos. Suum quisque cedat in locum.

Scena Tertia
Cornutus. Sordidus. Rubicundus.   220

CORNUTUS: Amice Sordide, scio te virum politicum,
    Prudentem, ditem, si quem alium in hoc oppido.
SORDIDUS: Verum dicis.
CORNUTUS: Et bis praetorem.
SORDIDUS: Immo ter praetor fui.
RUBICUNDUS: Et senex es sexagenarius.
SORDIDUS: Diis gratia.
RUBICUNDUS: Et loquutus es non semèl coram ipso duce.   225
SORDIDUS: Ita sane.
CORNUTUS: Dic mihi tandem pro tuâ prudentiâ
    Num credas hanc nuper erectam Academiam
    Cessuram in rem nostram an in incommodum.
SORDIDUS: Spinosam Cornute quaestionem proponis mihi,
    Sed dicam quod saepe patrem audiui dicere,   230
    Conimbrae ciuem et tonsorem Academicum,
    Se plus lucratum fuisse illic, idque anno vnico
    Quam decem Osunae; credo cessuram in commodum.
RUBICUNDUS: Idem et ego.
SORDIDUS: Proferre possum rationes meas.

[*An argument breaks out over seats.*
Polupragmaticus slaps Pedanus. Eubulus enters.]

EUBULUS: What is this uproar? A Lapithean feast?

POLUPRAGMATICUS: No problem, but a certain disagreement arose between the peripatetic and the physician about the principle of life. We are arguing for primal forms, they for atoms.

[*Amphimacer makes a toast.*]

AMPHIMACER: Whoever wishes to be my brother, let him drink once, twice, three times, four times.[17]

EUBULUS: Is this man drunk?

POLUPRAGMATICUS: No, but roused with a certain enthusiasm.

EUBULUS: If this is what it means to be a philosopher, then there is truth to the old saying: As much agreement among philosophers as among clocks.[18] You settle this matter among yourselves.

[*He speaks to a servant.*]

Take away the cups. Let each one retire to his own place.

Scene three
Cornutus. Sordidus. Rubicundus.

CORNUTUS: Sordidus, my friend, I know you are a man as politic, wise, and wealthy as anyone in this town.

SORDIDUS: That's true.

CORNUTUS: And twice a judge.

SORDIDUS: No, I was judge three times.

RUBICUNDUS: And you're sixty years old.

SORDIDUS: Thank the gods.

RUBICUNDUS: And more than once you have spoken before the duke himself.

SORDIDUS: Certainly.

CORNUTUS: So tell me then in your wise opinion whether you believe this newly built university will be to our advantage or disadvantage.

SORDIDUS: You present me with a thorny question, Cornutus, but I'll say what I have often heard my father say. He was a citizen of Coimbra and a barber at the university. He said that he made more profit there in a single year than in ten at Osuna. I believe it will be to our advantage.

RUBICUNDUS: I do too.

SORDIDUS: And I can give my reasons.

---

[17] See *AM* Democritus (75): "The first pot quencheth thirst, so Panyasis the poet determines in Athenaeus; *secunda Gratiis, Horis et Dionyso*, the second makes merry; the third for pleasure; *quarta ad insaniam*, the fourth makes them mad."

[18] JS: Seneca, *Ludus de Morte Claudii*, 2.3.

RUBICUNDUS: Et ego meas.

CORNUTUS: Sed date mihi veniam   235
     Vobis dicendi quae sequentur incommoda.
     Primum vbi vili nunc vaenit lignum, ceruisia,
     Mox carae fruges, annona, cara omnia.
     Nam sunt gulones et potatores strenui.

SORDIDUS: Id nihil est. Abunde lucrabimur aliàs.   240

CORNUTUS: Sed qui demum oenopoli, pandochei.

RUBICUNDUS: Immo etaim omnes oppidani reliqui:
     Sartores, pistores, sutores, crepedarii,
     Pharmacopolae, tonsores, coci, lanei,
     Bibliopolae, architecti, et hoc genus hominum.   245
     Vbi nunc fere omnes aridâ reptent fame,
     Mox crescent in infinitum opulentiâ.

CORNUTUS: Sed non soluent scholares, non habent pecuniam.

SORDIDUS: Habent, sed nugis impendunt vt plurimùm.
     Si non soluunt, quorsum lex? In idem recidit: 250
     Diem des, duplum soluant, faenus optimum.

CORNUTUS: Sed ciues verberant.

RUBICUNDUS: Rarò, nugas agis.

CORNUTUS: Fures autem sunt, auferent ligna, poma, anates.

SORDIDUS: Tyrones, pueri.

CORNUTUS: Sed audi grauissimum.
     Periclitabitur, opinor, vxorum pudititia.   255

SORDIDUS: Leue vulnus, et contemnendum quod non nocet.
     Quid si voceris corniger? Quaestus vberimus.
     Sed habesne formosam aut nubilem filiam?
     Ducent indotatam.

RUBICUNDUS: Vultis dicam, quod sentio
     Et vobis clam? Credo nos omnes fuisse cornigeros   260
     Antequam scholares adirent hoc oppidum.

CORNUTUS: Verum perpetuas alent nobiscum inimicitias.
     Contemnent, irridebunt.

RUBICUNDUS: Oderint, irrideant,
     Contemnant, cornutum vocent. Deteriores non sumus.
     Me vocant nasulum, rubicundum, sordidum,   265
     Et vocent vsque, dum me vocent diuitem.

SORDIDUS: Mecastòr non dubito, quin intra annos decem
     Videre hanc nostram perpusillam vrbeculam
     Siuillae, Salamancae aut Cordubae similem
     Si me de rebus hisce consulentem velitis sequi–   270
     Soluant, inquam soluant. Quod reliquum est, eat.

CORNUTUS: Quando vos vultis, idem et mihi placet.

RUBICUNDUS: And I mine.

CORNUTUS: But give me a chance to tell you what disadvantages will follow. First, where now wood and beer are cheap, soon fruit and grain will be expensive. All things will be dear. These academics are gluttons and vigorous drinkers.

SORDIDUS: It's nothing. We'll make a large profit at something else.

CORNUTUS: But surely also the tavern owners and inn keepers.

RUBICUNDUS: And all the rest of the townspeople: the tailors, bakers, cobblers and shoemakers, the druggists, barbers, cooks, butchers, booksellers, builders, and people like this. Where now almost all are hungry, soon they will grow in infinite wealth.[1]

CORNUTUS: But scholars won't pay; they have no money.

SORDIDUS: They have money, but most often they spend it on trifles. And if they don't pay, what's the law for? It comes to the same thing. You give them a day to pay. They pay double; that's the best interest.

CORNUTUS: But they beat the citizens.

RUBICUNDUS: Rarely. You're being silly.

CORNUTUS: But they are thieves; they'll steal our wood, apples, ducks.

SORDIDUS: They're just boys, mere boys.

CORNUTUS: But I have heard a very serious thing. The virtue of our wives, I believe, will be tested.

SORDIDUS: A slight wound and what does no harm ought not to be feared. So what if they say you have horns? It's most profitable. Don't you have a pretty daughter of marriageable age? They will marry her without a dowry.

RUBICUNDUS: Do you want me to tell you privately what I think? I believe we were all wearing horns before the scholars came near this town.

CORNUTUS: In truth, they'll be constant trouble. They'll look down on us, make fun of us.

RUBICUNDUS: So let them hate us, make fun of us, mock us, say we have horns; we're no worse off. Let them call me little nosey, hot head, tight wad, and let them keep calling me those things, as long as they call me rich.

SORDIDUS: Good heavens, I don't doubt that within ten years we'll see our little village much like Seville, Salamanca or Cordova, if you'll just take my advice in these matters. Let them pay, I say, let them pay. Whatever else happens, it doesn't matter.

CORNUTUS: Since that's what you want, it's fine with me.

---

[1] Plautus (fragment apud Aulus Gellius, 3.3.5): "Major pars populi aridi reptant fame." [The greater part of the starving people stroll about in hunger.] Burton uses the quotation in *AM* pt. 1, sec. 2, mem. 3, subs. 15 (311), and renders it as "they almost starved a great part of them."

Scena Quarta
Staphila. Tarentilla. Camaena.

STAPHILA: Mecastor lege durâ viuunt mulieres,   275
    Et misera est inprimis vetularum conditio,
    Quibus est nix in capite et sulcus in genâ.
    Mihi quidem tres sunt dentes, capilli totidem
    Nec magìs video quam sereno die noctua.
    Sed quod dolet magìs suspecta sum veneficii.   280
    Olim cum fueram virgo ambiri a multis me memini,
    Sed iam a nullis rogor. Oblinam et pingam licet
    Chachinnantes reiiciunt. Nardoque perfundam caput,
    Vbicunque nauseant. Proh dii quid agerem?
    Dicuntque halitum quendam posticum exire a me clanculum.   285
    Nam vt quod res est dicam, ano meo non possum fidere
    Quin ad singulos quosque gressus ferè sibilet,
    Et a posterioribus exhalet quendam spiritum.
    Sed quid? Alia mihi ineunda est via
    Quam vt mendicem. Quiduis tentandum priùs.   290
    Lena futura sum; faueat Venus precor.
    Aedes conduxi in suburbanis hortulis
    Nactaque sum duas succi plenas adolescentulas,
    Alteram Polupisti nobilis e rure filiam,
    Ciuis alteram. Cedent, spero, in lucrum mihi.   295
    Nam cum cateruatìm huc accedant Academici,
    Lotrix insidiabor cum meis mercibus.
    Scholares sunt apti ad practicandum scio.
    Det Plutus vt sit illis pecuniarum satis.
    Experiemur vtrunque. Nam Romae fuimus   300
    Lisbonae, Siuillae, Cordubae, Valentiae,
    Sed ibi tot sunt numero meretrices, tam vili pretio
    Scortum vaenit, vt omninò lucrandum sit nihil.
    Vnaquaeque ferè domus lupanar Venetiis.
    Dedi operam incassum illic, sed eccum filiolas.   305
                   [Intrant]
TARENTILLA: Non est cerussa neque gipsum in hoc oppido,
    Nulli colores.
STAPHILA: Non refert. Non est eadem ratio
    Osunae ac alibi; variantur pro loco et homines.
    Non hic opus vnguentis pigmentis caeterisque
    Quibus fucum faciunt aulicae mulieres.   310
    Sunt hic tyrones rudes qui capiuntur illicò.
    Simulac puellam praetereuntem vident,
    Iurant Briseîn esse Atalantam aut deam Gnidiam,

Scene four
Staphila. Tarentilla. Camaena.

STAPHILA: Good heavens, women live under harsh conditions and the state of old women, with snow on their heads and wrinkles on their faces, is especially wretched.[1] I have only three teeth left and the same number of hairs, and I don't see any better than an owl on a clear day. But what saddens me more, I have been suspected of sorcery. I remember once when I was a young girl, I was solicited by many, but now, no one wants me. I could put on powder and rouge, but men would laugh as well as reject me. I could sprinkle my head with perfume, but they would get ill. Dear gods, what am I to do? People say that a certain rear wind escapes from me in secret. To put it bluntly, I can't trust my ass. At almost each and every step, it whistles and breathes forth a certain spirit from behind. But what can I do? I must find some way other than begging. Anything whatever should be tried first. I'll be a bawd, and I pray that Venus bless me. I have rented a house in a garden outside the city and found two juicy young girls. One is the daughter of Polupistos, a nobleman from the country; the other is the daughter of a citizen. I hope they'll turn a profit for me. When the academics come here in troops, I will lie in wait as a "laundress" with my "merchandise." I know scholars are primed to the deed; Plutus grant that they have enough money. We'll test both. We have been in Rome, Lisbon, Seville, Cordova and Valencia, but there were so many whores there and they sell at such a low price, almost nothing may be earned. In Venice nearly every house was a brothel. I worked in vain there. But look. The dear girls.

[*They enter.*]

TARENTILLA: There is no powder or makeup in this town, no colors.

STAPHILA: It doesn't matter. There aren't the same expectations in Osuna as elsewhere. Things vary according to the place and the people. There's no need here for perfume and makeup and the other things the women of court use. Here there are just rude children who are captured on the spot. As soon as they see a girl walking by, they swear she is Briseis, Atalanta, the goddess Aphrodite, or Venus as Euphranor once painted her.[2] These young academics don't know the harlot's art. They dare not look at a girl, except in the dark. Otherwise, they blush, pale, and their teeth chatter with fear.

---

[1] Plautus, *Mer.* 817: "Ecastor lege dura uiuont mulieres." [By heaven, women live under harsh conditions.]

[2] *Briseis*: The slave girl of Achilles, taken from him by Agamemnon. See Homer, *Il.*1. For Atalanta and the Calydonian boar-hunt, see Ovid, *Met.* 8.299ff; for Atalanta and the race with Hippomenes, see Ovid, *Met.* 10.560ff. OCD: *Euphranor*: an Athenean sculptor and painter, c. 364 bc. *AM* pt. 3, sec. 2, mem. 5, subs., 3 (211): "as Euphranor of old painted Venus."

Aut qualem olim Euphanor depinxit Venerem.
Nam quod ad artem attinet meretritiam,   315
Ne norînt quidem recentes Academici.
Nisi sit in tenebris, puellam non audent aspicere;
Secus rubent, pallent, praetimore dentes quatiunt.
CAMAENA: Abiiciemus ergo versicolores caligas
    Auratam bombicinamque supellectilem?   320
STAPHILA: Nihil minùs.
CAMAENA: Ego non abiiciam.
STAPHILA: Cum fuerint comitia vel concursus nobilium
    Tum sunt in vsu crines hyacinthini,
    Armillae, inaures, tyarae, plumaeque tremulae.
    Tunc incedetis auratis sandaliis;   325
    Vnguentis, oleis, emplaustris vtemini.
    Hic non opus.
TARENTILLA: Quid ergo faciendum velis?
STAPHILA: Indutae hic tanquam ciuis honesti filiae.
    Incedetis per omnes plateas die quolibet
    Ad macellum, ad forum; si scholaris exeat,   330
    Aliud agentes ite; si rimetur acuratiùs,
    Subrides aliquando; si propius accesserit,
    Erubesces. Si quid obscenum vrget, indignabere.
    O si ego iam qualis tu nunc es forem!
CAMAENA: Benè mones.
STAPHILA: Vos horum recordemini.   335
    Quod reliquum est, detur fortunae et mihi.

Scena Quinta
Polumathes. Philobiblos.

PHILOBIBLOS: Polumathes, Osunam venisti gratissimus.
    Tu, qui spectatas vbique terrarum Academias   340
    Vidisti, quid de Osunâ censes, quid de Andalusiâ?
POLUMATHES: Ducatus hic sane longè florentissimus,
    Vbique vitalis et perennis salubritas.
    Et quod aduertendum Cato iubet, nitent acolae.
PHILOBIBLOS: Pulchra sanè laus, sed haeccine ea regio   345
    In quâ tot olim floruerunt Arabes?
POLUMATHES: Ipsa. Nam cum per Europam saeuiret barbaries,
    In hunc se locum contraxit philosophia.
PHILOBIBLOS: At quae causa tam longae peregrinationis tuae?
POLUMATHES: Vt cum Pontani Supputio sapientem consulerem.   350
PHILOBIBLOS: Quasi per tot vrbes erranti non occurrat sapiens.

CAMAENA: Then do we throw away our fancy shoes and our gold and silk stuff?

STAPHILA: Of course not.

CAMAENA: I'll not throw them away.

STAPHILA: When councils meet or noblemen còme to town, then you put flowers in your hair, wear bracelets, earrings, a tiara, trembling feathers. Then put on your golden slippers, use your perfume, cream, and make-up. Now there is no need.

TARENTILLA: Then what do you want us to do?

STAPHILA: Dress as the daughters of honest citizens. Walk along the streets whenever you like, to the meat market, the forum. If a scholar should be there, go on about your business; if he should pay attention, smile; if he approaches you, blush. If he suggests something obscene, be indignant. Oh, if only I could be as you are now!

CAMAENA: That's good advice.

STAPHILA: You remember these things. Leave the rest to fortune and to me.

Scene five
Polumathes. Philobiblos.

PHILOBIBLOS: Polumathes, I'm very glad you have come to Osuna. You have visited the distinguished universities in all parts of the world. What do you think of Osuna, of Andalusia?

POLUMATHES: The duchy here is clearly the most flourishing by far; every-where there is vitality and perennial good health. And, something Cato encouraged people to notice, the farmers are prosperous.[1]

PHILOBIBLOS: Certainly pretty praise, but is this not the region where once so many Arabs flourished?

POLUMATHES: The very same. For while barbarism was raging through Europe, philosophy took refuge here.

PHILOBIBLOS: But what is the cause of your long peregrination?

POLUMATHES: So that, like Supputius in Pontano, I might consult a wise man.[2]

PHILOBIBLOS: Do you mean that while wandering through so many cities, you did not happen upon a wise man?

---

[1] Bensly: "The elder Cato in his *De re rustica* [1.1], in giving directions for buying a farm, says: you must be careful to notice how prosperous the neighbors are: Vicini quo pacto niteant, id animum advertito!"

[2] Bensly: Pontano, *Ant.* 86ff. Burton has borrowed heavily from the dialogue for this and several other scenes. In response to the question "Where have you been," Suppatius answers, "A sapientibus quaeritandis." [In search of a wise man.] He then describes his visits to several cities in Italy. *AM* Democritus (46): "When Supputius in Pontanus had travelled all over Europe to confer with a wise man, he returned at last without his errand, and could find none."

POLUMATHES: Ne vnus quidem.

PHILOBIBLOS: Incredibile.

POLUMATHES: Ita est.

PHILOBIBLOS: Quid ita?

POLUMATHES: Ob inopiam.

PHILOBIBLOS: Mira narras. Romae fuisti an apud Italos?

POLUMATHES: Vagatus per compita, plateas, diuersa vrbis loca,
 Obuiam fiunt peregrinantum greges incompositi,   355
 Faeneratores, causidici, lenones, lucro dediti,
 Rhetores passim, poetae, et id genus hominum,
 Sapientes vero nulli. Quod ad reliqua:
 Cardinalium ferè mulabus subtritus fueram,
 Et meretricum manus vix saluus euaseram.   360

PHILOBIBLOS: Abires itaque. Breuis inde traiectus in Graeciam.

POLUMATHES: Non audebam.

PHILOBIBLOS: Quî sic?

POLUMATHES: Ne si in Turcas inciderem,
 Damnarer ad remos.

PHILOBIBLOS: Cur non in Germaniam?

POLUMATHES: Vixi illic per menses aliquot, sed illorum ibi
 Frequenti compotatione obruitur ingenium.   365

PHILOBIBLOS: An apud Batauos fuisti?

POLUMATHES: Non, ob tumultus bellicos.

PHILOBIBLOS: An apud Gallos?

POLUMATHES: Vtique leues inueni et subdolos
 Magisque curantes corpus quam animam.

PHILOBIBLOS: An apud Anglos?

POLUMATHES: Dii boni, belluam vidi multorum capitum.
 Annus ipse non est adeo varius adeoque mutabilis   370
 Ac eorum ingenia.

PHILOBIBLOS: Vidistîn veterem Oxoniam?

POLUMATHES: Et instructam illorum bibliothecam, tum in eâ
 Mortuos multos inueni, sed catenis malè habitos,
 At viuum illic sapientem vidi neminem.

POLUMATHES: Not even one.

PHILOBIBLOS: Incredible.

POLUMATHES: But true.

PHILOBIBLOS: Why is that?

POLUMATHES: Because of dearth.

PHILOBIBLOS: What strange things you tell. Weren't you in Rome among the Italians?

POLUMATHES: I strolled along cross roads, city streets, through various parts of the city and met disorderly hoards of wanderers: usurers, advocates, pimps, money seekers, rhetoricians scattered about, poets, and men of that sort. But in truth, no wise men. And what's more, I was almost trampled by the Cardinal's mules and scarcely escaped safely the hands of whores.[3]

PHILOBIBLOS: And so you should have left. From there, it is just a brief passage into Greece.

POLUMATHES: I did not dare go to Greece.

PHILOBIBLOS: Why is that?

POLUMATHES: Lest, if I had fallen into the hands of the Turks, I be condemned to the galleys.

PHILOBIBLOS: Why not into Germany?

POLUMATHES: I lived there for some months, but all the drinking there is wearing out their wit.

PHILOBIBLOS: Were you in Holland?

POLUMATHES: No, because of their warlike riots.

PHILOBIBLOS: With the French?

POLUMATHES: I found them light and deceitful, caring more for the body than the mind.

PHILOBIBLOS: The English?

POLUMATHES: Good gods! I saw a many-headed monster. The year itself is not so varied and mutable as their wits.[4]

PHILOBIBLOS: Did you see dear old Oxford?

POLUMATHES: And its furnished library. I saw no living wise men there, but many dead ones, badly held with chains.[5]

---

[3] Pontano, *Ant.* 87: "Dum sic per urbem vagor, duo maxime periculosa contigere: nam et meretricum manus vix evasi, . . . et sacerdotum mulabus pene subtritus sum." [While thus I was strolling through the city, I happened on two great dangers, for I scarcely escaped the hands of whores and I was almost trampled by priests' mules.] JS: "Mules" refer to concubines. He quotes the *Fabyan Chronicle* (ca. 1494), 7.229.259, "Ye Cardynall made sharpe processe agayn prestys, yt noresshed Cristen-moyles [mules]."

[4] Pontano, *Ant.* 87: "Volui videre Genuam, quam ubi vidi, dii boni, beluam illam multorum capitum vidi; annus ipse neque tam varius, neque adeo mutabilis quam Genuensium civium sunt ingenia." [I wanted to see Genoa, which when I saw it, good gods, I saw a many-headed monster. The year itself is not so varied nor yet so mutable as the wits of the citizens of Genoa.]

[5] Pontano, *Ant.* 86–7: "Hinc Bononiam cum venissem, vivum illic sapientem inveni

PHILOBIBLOS: Doctos vbicunque viros vidisti sat scio.   375
POLUMATHES: Profecto paucos. Exulant artes, exulat philosophia.
  Iurisperiti inprimis quaestum vberem faciunt.
  Reliqui sordent.
PHILOBIBLOS: De Osunensibus hisce quid statuis?
POLUMATHES: Nondum contraxi familiaritatem Academicis,
  Verum, si vis, post mensem vnum aut alterum   380
  Quod petis dicam, at hâc lege interìm—
                    [*Susurrat*]
  Vt si tu quid obserues, communices mihi.
PHILOBIBLOS: Volo. Sed aurem admoue.
POLUMATHES: Cautum benè.

Scena Sexta
Polupragmaticus. Stephanio *cum seruo*.   385
Aequiuocus. Antonius.

POLUPRAGMATICUS: Laudo consilium paternumque animum.
  Qui filium cupis erudiendum bonis artibus
  Vt sis voti compos, dabo operam sedulò.
STEPHANIO: Ago grates. Habebis me nec ingratum nec immemorem.   390
  At si paternitati tuae placeat, quaeram hoc obitèr.
POLUPRAGMATICUS: Quod vis?
STEPHANIO: Quo sumptu sit opus, quo temporis spatio
  Priusquàm ad culmen conscendat artium?
POLUPRAGMATICUS: De sumptu dicam alibi; iam si velis omniscium
  Sicut ego, viginti annis opus existimo.   395
  Nam ego septem annos dabam grammaticae,
  Totidem rhetoricae, totidemque dialecticae,
  Sex musicae, sex metaphisicae, decem morum studio,
  Nouem politiae. At in mathesi annos quatuordecem.
STEPHANIO: Numerauit octuaginta. Quot annos natus es?   400
POLUPRAGMATICUS: Captus per deos!
AEQUIUOCUS: Implicitè non explicitè.
STEPHANIO: Capio. Sed quot annis informabis filium?
POLUPRAGMATICUS: Bono sis animo. Quot vis? Video quosdam igniculos.
  Nam multum pollicetur mihi bona indoles
  Quae elucet hoc adolescente secundum phisiognomos.   405
  Frontem habet elatam, Mercurialem lineam
  Habet conspicuam, quae iuxta Metaposcopos—

PHILOBIBLOS: I know well enough you have seen learned men somewhere.

POLUMATHES: Few, in fact. The arts are banished, philosophy banished. Lawyers, of course, are making lots of money, but the rest are held of no account.

PHILOBIBLOS: What so you think of the people of Osuna?

POLUMATHES: I am not yet that familiar with the academics, but if you wish, after a month or two, I'll answer your question. But meanwhile, this condition: [*He whispers*] If you observe anything, tell it to me.

PHILOBIBLOS: I will, but lend an ear.

POLUMATHES: Good advice.

Scene six
Polupragmaticus. Stephanio *with servant.*
Aequivocus. Antonius.

POLUPRAGMATICUS: I applaud your wisdom and paternal affection. I will work diligently so that you, who wish your son educated in the liberal arts, may have what you wish.

STEPHANIO: Thank you. You will find me neither ungrateful nor unmindful. But if you don't mind, Father, I would ask this in passing.

POLUPRAGMATICUS: What do you want?

STEPHANIO: How much will it cost, and how long will it take before he can reach the pinnacle of learning?

POLUPRAGMATICUS: I'll discuss the cost later. Now, if you want your son to know everything as I do, I calculate it will take twenty years. For I devoted seven years to the study of grammar, the same number to rhetoric, and the same to dialectic, six to music, six to metaphysics, ten to ethics, nine to politics. But to mathematics, fourteen years.

STEPHANIO: That's 80 years. How old are you?

POLUPRAGMATICUS <*aside*>: Caught, by god!

AEQUIVOCUS: Implicitly, not explicitly.[1]

STEPHANIO: I understand. But how long will you need to educate my son?

POLUPRAGMATICUS: Be of good courage. How long do you want? I see a certain spark. A natural ability, which shines in this youth according to his physiognomy, promises good things to me. He has a high forehead, an obvious Mercurial line, which together with the metoposcopy—and the

---

neminem, mortuos vero multos eosque in catenis habitos." [When I came to Bologna, I found no living wise man there. In truth there were many dead ones, and those held in chains.] He is referring to the books which were normally chained to their benches.

[1] Aequivocus is punning on explicit and implicit articles of faith. Deferrari: *fides explicita et implicita*: the explicit or unfolded faith and the implicit or unexplained faith.

Pilorumque color et, et ipse oculus
Magnum ostentant ingenium, bonamque memoriam.
STEPHANIO: Benè dicis.
POLUPRAGMATICUS: Audîn, docebo filium tuum   410
    Artem dicendi et disputandi tribus hebdabodis,
    Vno mense totius systema philosophiae
    Ad meam methodum.
STEPHANIO: Itane?
POLUPRAGMATICUS: Factum puta.
    Possem docere pro sex coronatis, pro decem,
    Pro quingentis, sed si vis filium tuum   415
    Instituendum breui, maiori opus industriâ,
    Et magnus labor magnam mercedem petit.
STEPHANIO: Mercedem quamuis impende; quid vis dabitur
    Modò sit ad vsus honestos et necessarios.
POLUPRAGMATICUS: Modò sit, inquis, quid interponis modò?   420
    Quasi nescirem quid esset necessarium
    Tot comitum, baronum, praeceptorque nobilium.
STEPHANIO: Ne succenseat paternitas. Viginti en minas.
    Vis aliud quid?
POLUPRAGMATICUS: Tu numerabis pecuniam.
    Quod reliquum est fidei committes meae.   425
    Breuique faciam vt cum Philippo laetabere
    Genuisse te filium quem fidei committes meae.
STEPHANIO: Benè dicis. Commendo natum meum tibi
    Erudiendum tam moribus quam scientiâ.
AEQUIUOCUS: Comisit ouem lupo.
STEPHANIO: Iubeo te valere.
POLUPRAGMATICUS: Nos te.
STEPHANIO: Fili vale.   430
                [Dat Aequiuoco pecuniam.]
    Heus serue.
POLUPRAGMATICUS: Tu sequere me intus puer.

color of his hair, and, and the eye itself, reveal great talent and a good memory.[2]

STEPHANIO: Well put.

POLUPRAGMATICUS: Listen, I will teach your son the art of speaking and disputation in three weeks, the entire system of philosophy in a month by my own method.

STEPHANIO: Is that so?

POLUPRAGMATICUS: Consider it done. Now, I am able to teach for six crowns, for ten, for 500, but if you wish your son taught quickly, the effort is greater. And great labor commands a great price.

STEPHANIO: Name any price. Whatever you wish. It will be given, provided that it be for honest and necessary uses.

POLUPRAGMATICUS: You say "provided that." Why did you say "provided"? As if I, the teacher of so many counts, barons and noblemen, would not know what was necessary?

STEPHANIO: Don't be angry, Father. Here are forty pounds. Do you want anything else?

POLUPRAGMATICUS: You pay the money, the rest you should commit to my trust. I'll see to it that soon, like Philip, you will be happy to have had a son you could commit to me.[3]

STEPHANIO: Well said. I commend my son to you to be instructed as much in character as in knowledge.

AEQUIVOCUS <aside>: He is entrusting the sheep to the wolf.[4]

STEPHANIO: I bid you good day.[5]

POLUPRAGMATICUS: And we you.

STEPHANIO: Goodbye, Son.

[He gives the money to Aequivocus.]

Come, servant.

POLUPRAGMATICUS: Follow me inside, young man.

---

[2] For Burton on physiognomy and metoposcopy, see *AM* pt. 1, sec. 2, mem. 1, subs. 4 (208–9).

[3] JS: " 'Philip': Father of Alexander the Great. King Philip, writing to Aristotle, is said to have expressed joy, not so much over the birth of his son as that he was born in the days of Aristotle, who he hoped might educate the boy."

[4] JS: Terence, *Eun.* 832. Erasmus, *Ad.* 1.4.10.

[5] Plautus, *As.* 296: "iubeo te saluere" [I bid you farewell.]

ACTUS SECUNDUS
Scena Prima
Polupistos. Dromo. Simon Acutus.
Amphimacer. Aequiuocus.

POLUPISTOS: Dromo, quod erat nomen istius hominis
    Cuius tam celebris fama est apud Academicos?
DROMO: Sesquipedale nomen habet sed omninò excidit.
POLUPISTOS: Potestne rem furto sublatam repertere?
DROMO: Ita ferunt, et locum indicare et numerum furum.   440
POLUPISTOS: Dii boni seruetis hunc hominem in salutem meam.
    Sed vbi habitat?
DROMO: Vidên, deambulantem Academicum,
    Roges eum.
      [*Intrat Simon Acutus cum duobus tyronibus legens ad eos.*]
POLUPISTOS: Tacè.
SIMON ACUTUS: Quoniam necessaria est. Crysiari ad categoriarum
rationem quae ab Aristotile tradita est, etc. Notate benè: quoniam   445
necessaria est. Id est, quia necessitas cogit me. Pauper fortasse fuit.
Crysioare. Id est, aurum rogare vel mendicare; verbum infinitui modi
a Graeco verbo Cecarrasoraomi. Ad Categoriarum rationem vel ad ra-
tionem Categoriarum, non refert. Categoriae sunt aues quaedam   450
Macedonicae rationales vt canes et equi: notate et hoc per viam. Et est
Graecum licet scribatur Latinis literis: notetur et illud valdè. Quae ab
Aristotile tradita, etc. Sic arbitrabar. Hic Aristotiles fuit valdè pauperibus munificus. Noui fontem eius nominis. Tu nihil notas?   455

ACT II
Scene one
Polupistos. Dromo. Simon Acutus.
Amphimacer. Aequivocus.

POLUPISTOS: Dromo, what was the name of that man whose fame is so cele-
brated among the academics?
DROMO: He has some sesquipedalian name, but it escapes me entirely.
POLUPISTOS: Isn't he able to recover stolen items?
DROMO: So they say, and to name the place and the number of thieves.
POLUPISTOS: Dear gods, preserve this man for my sake. But where does he live?
DROMO: Do you see the academic walking by? Ask him.
[*Simon Acutus enters with two young students; he is reading to them.*]
POLUPISTOS: Be quiet.
SIMON ACUTUS: "Quoniam necessaria est. Crysiari ad categoriarum rationem
quae ab Aristotile tradita est,"[1] and so forth. Note this well: "Quoniam
necessaria est": that is, because necessity forces me. Perhaps he was a
poor man. "Crysioare": that is, to ask or beg for gold. It is a verb in the
infinitive mood, from the Greek verb "cecarrasoraomi." "Ad categoriarum rationem" or "ad rationem categoriarum," it makes no difference.
Note this also by the way: categories are certain birds of Macedonia, with
a sense of reason, like dogs and horses. And, note this especially, it is
Greek, although written in Latin letters. "Quae ab Aristotile tradita," and
so forth. Just as I thought. This Aristotle was very generous to the poor.
I know the origin of his name.[2] Aren't you writing this down?

---

[1] Bensly: Simon Acutus is commenting on a Latin translation of Porphyrius's introduction to Aristotle's *Categories*. "Simon imagines that the vocative of the man's name to
whom Porphyrius addresses his work is a *verb* & derives it from the Greek χρυσός & the
Latin *orare*!"

[2] Bensly: "Simon suggests that Ἀριστοτέλης is derived from ἄριστος and τελεῖν, to
pay, because he was 'valde pauperibus munificus.'"

POLUPISTOS: Interpellabo. Salue, domine.

SIMON ACUTUS: Tu, salue, quicunque sis quoque.

POLUPISTOS: Nostîn magistrum quendam Polupragmaticum,
    Vbi habitet?

SIMON ACUTUS: Video quo tendis, sed maiorem nego.

POLUPISTOS: Quo tendam ego?

DROMO: Contendit forsan de viâ.

SIMON ACUTUS: Quaestio tua sumi potest duplicitèr—   460
    Primum vbi quaeritur ad hoc, num magistrum sciam.
    Dico quod sic. Sed an hunc, dico quod non sciam.

POLUPISTOS: Pace tuâ dicam. Hoc ego non intelligo.

DROMO: Pol nec ego.

SIMON ACUTUS: Sic explico; duplex est scientia: intuitiua, quae hic non
    intelligitur; vel discussiua, quae pendet a sensu; et sic scire est per   465
    causas scire. Vel sic, scio formalitèr, quatenus Ens in quantum Ens
    habet in mente nostra vnum conceptum omnibus communem,
    sicut habet Scotus in Metaphisicis. Sed non quidditatiue, quatenus
    Indiuiduationis Principium propriam habet entitatem, vel singu-   470
    larizetur per Accidentia secundum Diuum Thomam aliquid ad-
    dens, positiuum suum subiectum Indiuiduans non secundum esse
    cognitum, sed reale repraesentatiuum. Et sic non scio Magistralita-
    tem suam.

POLUPISTOS: Tu me homo adiges ad insaniam.

SIMON ACUTUS: Concludam syllogisticè.
    Omnis scientia Dianoetica fit a praecedente cognitione   475
    Sed non habeo praecedentem cognitionem. Ergò—

POLUPISTOS: Quorsum haec? Quid mihi cum scientiis?

SIMON ACUTUS: Per Iouem est Aristotilis Posteriorum liber I, caput I.

POLUPISTOS: Nugas agis.

SIMON ACUTUS: Quia tu non intelligis.

POLUPISTOS: Proh deum!

SIMON ACUTUS: Quid quaeris?

POLUPISTOS: Num scias hunc hominem.   480
    Responde ad rem quaeso, vel prorsùs tace.

POLUPISTOS: I'll interrupt. Good day, sir.

SIMON ACUTUS: Good day to you, whoever you are.

POLUPISTOS: Do you know a certain master, Polupragmaticus, where he lives?

SIMON ACUTUS: I see where you are tending, but I deny your major.[3]

POLUPISTOS: Where I am tending?

DROMO: Perhaps he is contending about the way.

SIMON ACUTUS: Your question can be taken two ways. First, if it is asked in this sense, whether I know a master, I say yes. If in the sense whether I know this master, I say that I do not know.

POLUPISTOS: May I speak, please. I don't get this.

DROMO: Good heavens, neither do I.

SIMON ACUTUS: I will explain it as follows. Knowledge is two-fold. Intuitive, which is not understood here, or discursive, which depends upon sense. And thus to know is to know through causes. Or thus: I know formally to the extent that being as being[4] has in our mind one concept common to all, just as Scotus holds in the *Metaphysics*. But not quidditatively to the extent that the principle of individuation[5] has its own essence or is particularized through accidents, according to St. Thomas, adding something and individuating its own subject not according to a known being, but according to an actual representative thing. And thus I do not know his Masterness.

POLUPISTOS: You, sir, are driving me insane.[6]

SIMON ACUTUS: I shall conclude syllogistically. All knowledge becomes dianoetic from a precedent cognition, but I do not have a precedent cognition.[7] Therefore—

POLUPISTOS: Is there no end to this? What does this knowledge have to do with me?

SIMON ACUTUS: By Jove, it's from Aristotle's *Posterior*, Book I, Chapter I.

POLUPISTOS: You are making a fool of me.[8]

SIMON ACUTUS: Because you don't understand.

POLUPISTOS: Dear gods!

SIMON ACUTUS: What are you asking?

POLUPISTOS: Whether you know this man. Answer what I ask, or just be quiet.

---

[3] Bensly: I.e., the major premise in a syllogism. See Shakespeare, *I Henry IV*, 2.4.489.

[4] Deferrari: "being, or more properly, a being, something having 'esse' either essential or existential, in some way, not necessarily actual."

[5] Deferrari: "principium individuale seu individuans seu individuationis, the individual and the specific principle, or the principle which makes a thing an individual, and that which gives it its nature and essence and thereby places it in a definite species."

[6] JS: Terence, *Ad.* 111: "tu homo adigis me ad insaniam."

[7] Bensly: " 'Omnis scientia Dianoetica' etc. is a Latin translation of the words at the very beginning of the first book of *Posterior Analytics*."

[8] Erasmus, *Ad.* 1.4.91: "nugas agere."

SIMON ACUTUS: Si non loquaris ad idem secundum idem et eodem
    tempore,
    Meum respondere non est necessarium.
    Respondebo tamen et ad vtramque quaestionem breuitèr.
    Scio per Intellectum speculatiuum, non practicum,   485
    Vel sic scio quatenus est in praedicamento Substantiae,
    Sed non quatenus est in praedicamento Vbi.
POLUPISTOS: Quid hoc ad rem? Non respondes mihi.
SIMON ACUTUS: Possem aliter
    Sed nolo. Nam quod octavo Topicorum dicit Aristotiles,
    Respondere vanae interrogationi non est necessarium.   490
POLUPISTOS: Ilicèt.
SIMON ACUTUS: Eo.

[Exit]

POLUPISTOS: Proh dii, qualis hic est homo?
DROMO: Opinor vel melancholicum vel morionem Academicum.
POLUPISTOS: Ita videtur, sed eccum appropinquantem alium.

[Intrat Amphimacer legens libro.]

AMPHIMACER: Conticuere omnes intentique ora tenebant.
    Ora tenebat. Os pro vultu. Elegans per Iouem.   495
    Inde toro pater Aeneas. Pater, ob Ascanium filium.
POLUPISTOS: Alloquamur. Nostîn magistrum Polupragmaticum?
AMPHIMACER: Nescio per charites.
POLUPISTOS: Nec aedes suas?
AMPHIMACER: Per mare, per terras, et per pia numina iuro.
POLUPISTOS: Ne iures.
AMPHIMACER: Testor humum, tum testor aquas; tum testor Olympum.   500
POLUPISTOS: Dromo, quid ait?
DROMO: De Olimpo loquitur.
AMPHIMACER: At vos qui tandem quibus aut venistis ab oris?
POLUPISTOS: Populares tui.
AMPHIMACER: At quae tanta fuit Osunam tibi causa videndi?
POLUPISTOS: Vt conuenirem hunc hominem, nostîn hospitium?
AMPHIMACER: Noui subiungamque descriptionem Topographicam.   505

SIMON ACUTUS: If you would not repeat the same things each time, my response would not be necessary. Nevertheless I shall respond to each question briefly. I know through the speculative intellect, not the practical, or thus I know in so far as it is in the predicate of substance, but not in so far as it is in the predicate of where.[9]

POLUPISTOS: What does this have to do with the matter? You are not answering me.

SIMON ACUTUS: I could otherwise, but I don't want to, for Aristotle says in Book 8 of the *Topics* that it is not necessary to respond to empty questions.

POLUPISTOS: Go away.

SIMON ACUTUS: I'm going.

[Exit Simon Acutus]

POLUPISTOS: Dear gods, what sort of man is he?

DROMO: I think he is either melancholy or an academic ass.

POLUPISTOS: So it seems. But look, another one is approaching.

[Enter Amphimacer reading a book.]

AMPHIMACER: "Conticuere omnes intentique ora tenebat."[10] "Ora tenebat": "os" for "vultus." Elegant, by Jove. "Inde toro pater Aeneas":[11] "Father," because he had a son, Ascanius.

POLUPISTOS: Let's speak to him. Do you know Master Polupragmaticus?

AMPHIMACER: I do not know, by the Graces.

POLUPISTOS: Nor his home?

AMPHIMACER: I swear by the sea, the lands and the pious spirits.[12]

POLUPISTOS: You need not swear.

AMPHIMACER: I call as my witness the earth, the waters, and Olympus.

POLUPISTOS: Dromo, what is he saying?

DROMO: He's talking about Olympus.

AMPHIMACER: But who are you or from what shores have you come?[13]

POLUPISTOS: We are your countrymen.

AMPHIMACER: But what was the great occasion of your seeing Osuna?[14]

POLUPISTOS: So that I might meet this man. Do you know where he lives?

AMPHIMACER: I know and I shall give a topographical description.

---

[9] Deferrari: "praedicamentum" is the predicate in logic, or one of the ten general classes of predicates and of being, the translation of Aristotle's term "kategoria." The ten predicates are: substantia, quantitas, qualitas, relatio, passio, actio, quando seu tempus, ubi seu locus, situs, habitus.

[10] Vergil, *Aen.* 2.1.

[11] Vergil, *Aen.* 2.2.

[12] Ovid, *Tristia*, 2.53: "Per mare, per terras, per tertia numina iuro." (Loeb) [I swear by the sea, the lands and the three spirits.]

[13] Vergil, *Aen.* 1.369: "Sed uos qui tandem? quibus aut uenistis ab oris." [But who are you? from what shores have you come?]

[14] Vergil, *Ecl.* 1.26: "Et quae tanta fuit Romam tibi causa uidendi." [And what was the great occasion of your seeing Rome?]

POLUPISTOS: Topograph: quid hoc?
AMPHIMACER: Poeticum exemplum capies?
   Regia Solis erat sublimibus alta columis,
   Clara micante auro, flammasque imitante pyropo,
   Cuius ebur nitidum fastigia summa tegebat,
   Argenti bifores radiabant lumina valuae.   510
   Haec est Topographica solis descriptio.
   Sed si vacet—
POLUPISTOS: O, non vacat, non vacat.
AMPHIMACER: Si non forte vacet, tum generose vale.
                  [Exit]
            [Intrat Aequiuocus]
POLUPISTOS: Dromo, quid suades?
AEQUIUOCUS: Quis quaerit Polupragmaticum
   Tam diluculò?
POLUPISTOS: Is sum. Estnè herus tuus domi?   515
AEQUIUOCUS: Domi non est, tuae scilicet, at est suae.
   Nam reuera nondum surrexit Iuppiter meus.
   Alcumenam suam Tarentillam nunc complexu fouet.
POLUPISTOS: Quando aderit?
AEQUIUOCUS: Ad pomeridianam tertiam.
POLUPISTOS: Interìm—vale.

                Scena Secunda   520
                Theanus. Pedanus.

THEANUS: Quid vis, Pedane?
PEDANUS: Vt chartae huic nomen apponas si placet.
THEANUS: Quid sibi vult?
PEDANUS: Testimoniales literae.
THEANUS: Fiet. Sed quam nunc vitae rationem inis?
PEDANUS: Rus eo docturus nobilis cuiusdam filios.   525
THEANUS: Tege caput.
PEDANUS: Bene est.
THEANUS: Ita volo. Tege caput,
   Pedane, et vbi primum rus adieris caue
   Vt sit gestus grauis, et, quam cito poteris,
   Vt sint vestes nitidae. Cauendum id vnicè:
   Sit vultus comis plerumque et blandus nisi sit in scholâ.   530
   Tum vero nasum corruga et frontem capera.
PEDANUS: Fiet.
THEANUS: Sed si vis insignis haberi grammaticus,
   Comparandi sunt libri plures in folio.

POLUPISTOS: Topograph: what's that?

AMPHIMACER: Will you take a poetic example? "The court of the sun stood high on lofty columns, with glittering gold and flaming bronze; its highest ceiling was covered with shining ivory; silver doors radiated with light."[15] This is a topographical description of the sun. But if there is time—

POLUPISTOS: Oh, there's no time, no time.

AMPHIMACER: If peradventure there is no time, then a noble goodbye.

[*Exit Amphimacer; enter Aequivocus*]

POLUPISTOS: Dromo, what do you suggest?

AEQUIVOCUS: Who is looking for Polupragmaticus so early?

POLUPISTOS: I am. Is your master at home?

AEQUIVOCUS: He is not at home, that is, not at your home, but he is at his home. For in truth, my Jupiter has not yet arisen and now holds Tarentilla, his own Alcmena, in fond embrace.[16]

POLUPISTOS: When will he be home?

AEQUIVOCUS: This afternoon at the third hour.

POLUPISTOS: Until then, goodbye.

Scene two
Theanus. Pedanus.

THEANUS: What do you want, Pedanus?

PEDANUS: That you sign this paper, please.

THEANUS: What is it about?

PEDANUS: It's a testimonial letter.

THEANUS: I'll sign it. But what sort of life are you now considering?

PEDANUS: I am going to the country to teach the sons of a certain nobleman.

THEANUS: Cover your head.

PEDANUS: It's fine.

THEANUS: I wish it so. Cover your head, Pedanus, and as soon as you arrive in the country, take care that your demeanor be serious and as soon as you are able that your clothes be elegant. You should also take care that your appearance be especially handsome and pleasing, except in the classroom. There, wrinkle your nose and frown.

PEDANUS: I'll do that.

THEANUS: If you wish to be considered important as a grammarian, you should purchase more books in folio.

---

[15] JS: Ovid, *Met.* 2.1–4.

[16] From Plautus, *Am.* 289–90: Mercurius: "meu' pater nunc pro huius uerbis recte et sapienter facit, / qui complexus cum Alcumena cubat amans, animo obsequens." [Mercury: According to this report, my father is now spending his time wisely and well. He is lying with Alcmena, holding her and loving her to his heart's content.]

PEDANUS: Habeo Calapinum et cum commento Virgilium.

THEANUS: Sic oportet. Sed si fueris ad mensam adhibitus,   535
Sit sermo plerumque de rebus philosophicis:
Quam diù viuant culex et apis, vel de Meteoris—
Sed in quibusuis sis supra modum Criticus.

PEDANUS: Attendo.

THEANUS: Inter confabulandum debes historiolam
Inserere aliquando, vel e graecis sententiam.   540
Δὶς καὶ τρὶς καὶ τὸ καλόν. Ἢ πίθι ἢ ἄπιθι.

PEDANUS: Enitar. Sed in scholâ quid agendum mones?
Virgamne suades an ferulam?

THEANUS: Non refert quam velis.
Nunc hanc, nunc illam.

PEDANUS: Sed quot plagas oportebat dare?

THEANUS: Erras, non est dicendum oportebat, sed oportuit.   545
Plebeio sex, tres tantum generosi filio
Nisi sis benè potus, iratus, vel melancholichus.

PEDANUS: Quot inquis dare debueram?

THEANUS: Erras iterum.
Dicendum est debui, non autem debueram.
Sed audi. Caue vt flagelles nobilis filium   550

PEDANUS: I have Calepino[1] and Vergil with a commentary.

THEANUS: And so you should. But if you are invited for a meal, let your conversation be especially philosophical: how long a gnat or bee lives, or about heavenly matters. In any conversation, you should be critical beyond measure.

PEDANUS: I'm listening.

THEANUS: You should insert into your conversations something historical, or a commonplace from the Greeks: "Good things twice and thrice,"[2] or "either drink or go away."[3]

PEDANUS: I'll try. But what do you advise doing in the classroom? Do you recommend the switch or the rod?[4]

THEANUS: It doesn't matter. Whichever you prefer. Sometimes one, sometimes the other.

PEDANUS: But how many blows should one give?

THEANUS: You've made a mistake. One ought not use the imperfect but the perfect tense of "should." Six to commoners, only three to the son of a nobleman, unless you are well drunk, angry or melancholy.

PEDANUS: But how many do you say I ought to give?

THEANUS: You've made another mistake. One should use the perfect not the pluperfect tense of "ought."[5] But listen. Beware of beating the son of a

---

[1] JS: "Ambrogio Calepino, an Augustinian monk (1435-1511), compiled a huge polyglot dictionary, issued at Reggio in 1502."

[2] Plato. *Philebus* 60a: "εὖ δ' ἢ παροι μία δοκεῖ ἔχειν, τὸ καὶ δίς καὶ τρὶς τὸ γεκαιλῶς ἔχον ἐπανοπολειν τῶ λόγῳ δειν." (Loeb) [I think the proverb "we ought to repeat twice and even thrice that which is good," is an excellent one.]

[3] Erasmus, *Ad.* 1.10.47.

[4] See Pontano, *Ch.* 35. Pedanus, a shade of a grammarian who has visited the classical authors in the underworld, says to Mercury: "At Iuvenalem nimis me graviter obiurgasse, quod dicerem oleagina virga pueros a me verberari solitos; oportuisse enim ferula illos percuti. Quocirca, Arcas Deus, monitos facias verbis meis grammaticos omnes ferula ut utantur." [But Juvenal scolded me quite harshly because I said I was accustomed to beat boys with an olive switch; they should have been hit with a rod. Therefore, Mercury, with my words you should warn all grammarians to use the rod.]

[5] Pontano, *Ch.* 35. While Pedanus is talking to Mercury, Theanus approaches and introduces himself as a "grammatista." He should have said, according to Pedanus, "grammaticus," [a grammarian], not "grammatista," [teacher of grammar]. Theanus then chides Pedanus for using the verb "addisce," [know this in addition], rather than "disce," [know this]. The two pedants then begin arguing about the proper use of verb tenses: "PED. Rursum peccasti, dicere enim, non dixisse oportebat dici. THEAN. Et tu rursum item peccasti, nam non oportebat, sed oportuit dicendum erat. PED. Prisciano caput fregisti, neque enim erat, sed fuit dicere debueras. THEAN. Prisciano pedes fregisti; debuisti enim, non debueras. PED. Immo debueras, non debuisti. THEAN. Immo debuisti, non debueras." [PED. You've made another mistake, for one ought to say "dicere," not "dixisse." THEAN. And you again have made a mistake, for one ought to say "oportuit," not "oportebat." PED. You have fractured Priscian's skull, for you ought not say "erat," but "fuit." THEAN. You've fractured Priscian's feet. "Debuisti" not "debueras." PED. On the contrary, "debueras" not "debuisti." THEAN. On the contrary, "debuisti" not "debueras."]

Nisi priùs impetratâ a matre veniâ.
PEDANUS: Quid ita?
THEANUS: Caue etiam. Sed alibi instituam.
Profecturum te nunc video. Benè vale.

Scena Tertia
Pantomagus solus.   555

Tanti eris aliis quanti tibi fueris,
Et qui se vilipendit vilipendetur ab aliis.
Ego ne quid ignoretis sum doctor medicus.
Sed cur medicus? Quia nobis ex furto viuere.
Solisque licet impunè hominem occidere.   560
Doctor Osunensis diuortor his aedibus,
Et apud Idiotas audio vir doctissimus,
Quod ad artes quibus vtor, incedo grauis,
Decentèr amictus, sicut videtis, annulis
Ornatus, et quoad barbam summè conspicuus.   565
Si quis me quaerat, duco in Musaeum statìm
Ornatum vitriolis, chartis, libris omnium generum,
Quos ego tamen omnino non intelligo.
Ornamenti causa stant secundum classes suas.
Huc vbi ventum de Naturâ Morbi rogo,   570
Discurro de Essatis Essentificatis localitèr emunctoralitèr,
De Anatron Embrionato, et minerali sulphere,
Subiungens diuersas opiniones diuersorum hominum,
Quid Auenziar, quid Rhases, et quid Mesue,
Quid Paracelsus. Miratur ille singularem peritiam, 575
Infinitamque lectionem quando reuera mihi

nobleman unless you first get permission from the mother.[6]
PEDANUS: Why is that?
THEANUS: Just beware. I'll instruct you another time. I see now that you are
about to leave. Goodbye.

Scene three
Pantomagus alone.

You will be of such worth to others as you are to yourself, and who holds
himself in low esteem will be so held by others.[1] I, lest you do not know, am
a physician. But why a physician? Because we alone are allowed to live by
theft and to kill human beings with impunity.[2] As the doctor of Osuna I am
lodged in these buildings and considered a most learned man among the un-
learned. I make use of this. I go forth to the arts with dignity, dressed properly, as you can see by my rings and very respectable beard. If anyone should
consult me, I lead him at once into my study equipped with little glasses,
charts, and books of all sorts, which by the way I don't understand at all. But
for the sake of decoration they stand there arranged according to their classes. I ask those who have come here about the nature of their illnesses; I discuss essatum essentificated[3] locally and emunctorially, embryonated anatron[4] and mineral sulphur, adding various opinions of various men, what
Avenzoar, what Rhases, what Mesue, what Paracelsus thought.[5] The patient
wonders at my particular skill and infinite reading, when in truth I know

---

[6] JS: "Professor Edward Bensly recalls in this connection a passage in Joseph Hall's
satires [*Virgidemiarum*, 2.6.12–14]. This book, a copy of which was in Burton's library (the
1598 edition) contains a satire describing the conditions under which a 'Gentle Squire'
hires a 'trencher-Chaplain' to instruct his sons. The last condition is: 'Last that he never
his yong master beat, / But he must aske his mother to define, / How many ierkes she
would his breach should line.'" See Kiessling, no. 746.

[1] Pliny, *Epistulae*, 1.3.15: "ut tibi ipse sis tanti, quanti videberis aliis" [As you are to
yourself, so you will be to others.]

[2] JS: See Pliny, *Naturae Historicae*, 29.12.18: "discunt periculis nostris et experimenta
per mortes agunt, medioque tantum hominem occidisse impunitos summa est." (Loeb)
[They learn from our dangers and gain experience through our deaths; only physicians
can kill human beings with complete impunity.]

[3] Rulandus: *Essatum Potentiale*: "the strength power and virtue which dwell in vegetable
and mineral things." OED: *essentificated*: made into an essence. Reference is given to
Paracelsus, 1660, *Archidoxis* 1.5.74: "Take Mercurie Essentificated, the which separate from
all Superfluites."

[4] Rulandus: *Anatron*: "Refuse of Vitrum (glass)." Also, "i.e., Baurac"; "i.e., Sagimen
(salt) of Vitrum (glass), or Salt of Alkali"; "Froth of Vitreum, Gall of Vitreum. The
German context terms it Sandiber, Gall of Glass."

[5] D-JS: Avenzoar, an Arabian physician of the twelfth century; Rhases, physician and
author of medical texts, first century; Joannes Mesue, Arabian physician and author of
medical texts, ninth century.

Sunt tantum peruulgati Receptus duo,
Quorum sacerdos alterum, anus alterum edocuit,
Compostî de Scammoneo vel Hellebero.
Hos alternatîm plerumque ministrare soleo.   580
De Emmatis, Emplaustris, Apophlegmatismis tamen
Loquor, de Iulapiis, Symplis, Electuariis,
De Dropace, Sinapismo, Opiatis, Topicis,
Suffitu et Suffumigatione, acsi Galenus forem.
Quibuscunque commendo victum salubrem,   585
Quando ego delectum ciborum non scio
Nisi quod flatulenta cogant crepitum.
Purgo plerumque singulos, nullâ ratione habitâ
Aetatis morbiue; nec prosum nec obsum, sed fores crepunt.

Scena Quarta   590
Antonius. Aequiuocus.

AEQUIUOCUS: Optatus mihi aduenis, Antonî. Quo tam dilicculò?
ANTONIUS: Ad publicas lectiones.
AEQUIUOCUS: Ad lectiones, quid ita?
ANTONIUS: Vt ediscam.
AEQUIUOCUS: Et quid edisces si diis placet?
    Quod sunt praedicabilia? Nugas hasce apagesis.   595
ANTONIUS: Has nugas vocas?

only two common remedies, one taught by a priest, the other by an old woman—mixtures of scammonia or helleborum.[6] I usually give these alternately, although I speak of emetics, emplastrums, apophlegmatismus,[7] of juleps, simples, electuary, or about dropax, sinapismus, opiates, topics,[8] perfuming and suffumigation—as if I were Galen.[9] I recommend to each one a healthy diet, although I know nothing of the selection of foods, except what forces gas. I often purge each one without account for age or disease. I neither help nor harm. But the doors creak.[10]

Scene four
Antonius. Aequivocus.

AEQUIVOCUS: I'm happy you have come for me, Antonius. Where to so early?
ANTONIUS: To the public lectures.
AEQUIVOCUS: To lectures, why is that?
ANTONIUS: So that I may learn.
AEQUIVOCUS: And what, if it please the gods, will you learn? That there are predicables?[1] Away with this nonsense.
ANTONIUS: You call this nonsense?

---

[6] Cooper: *scammonia*: "An hearbe the iuyce whereof corrected purgeth cholar, and is of apothecarics called 'Diagrydium,' of much vse in phisike." *Helleborum*: "An hearbe wherof be two kinds: 'Elleborus albus' in english Lingworte, the roote wherof is neesing pouder. 'Elleborus niger' the hearbe named beares foote, or terworte, or setteworte." See also *AM* pt. 2, sec. 4, mem. 2, subs. 1 (226–27) where Burton discusses "White hellebore, which some call sneezing powder, a strong purger upward...." and *AM* pt. 2, sec. 4, mem. 2, subs. 2 (230ff.), on "Black hellebore, that most renowned plant, and famous purger of melancholy...."

[7] Thomas: *emplastrum*: "A plaister or salue made of diuers things: a plaister of claie or waxe, to laie on a graffe, where the barke is gone." *Apophlegmatismus*: "A medicine, which kept or chewed in the mouth, draweth humors out of the head."

[8] Cooper: *dropax*: "An excellent oyntment made of pitch." Thomas: *sinapismus*: "A medicine, ointment, or salue made partly of mustard, seruing to raise blisters or wheals vpon the skin." Rulandus: *topic*: "A Medicament which is applied to the Skin after the manner of a Plaster."

[9] Galen of Pergamum, AD 129?–199. Cooper: "In phisike he was so excellent, as he may iustly seeme to be raysed by diuine prouidence, at that time to make perfecte that noble arte, and to confounde the many folde sectes and errours, with whiche as then it was defaced."

[10] The creaking door was a convention in classical comedy for announcing entrances. See for example Terence, *Ad.* 264; *Heaut.* 173, 613; *Eun.* 1029; Plautus, *Am.* 496; *Mil.* 270, 328, 410.

[1] OED: in Aristotelian logic, *predicable*: "The classes or kinds of predicates viewed relatively to their subjects, to one or other of which classes every predicted thing may be referred; the second intention of predicates considered in relation to subjects." Porphyry gives five predicables: genus, species, difference, property, accident.

AEQUIUOCUS: Nugas omnium nugacissimas.

ANTONIUS: Itane?

AEQUIUOCUS: Ita. Quid tibi cum genere et spetie?
    An tu filius et haeres idque patris vnicus?

ANTONIUS: Quid inde?

AEQUIUOCUS: Quid ergò tibi cum scientiis?
    Viderînt has tricas fratres natu minimi,   600
    Quos ad seruitutem nouercans Natura peperit,
    Vile vulgus, inopes, et id genus hominum
    Quos ad laborem damnauit tristis Horoscopus.

ANTONIUS: At quid vis interim faciam?

AEQUIUOCUS: Quid faciam rogas?
    En tibi pictas chartas et omne genus aleae.   605
    Hae Musae sunt studiis aptiores tuis—
    Da te mihi per dies aliquot discipulum modò.
    Dedocebo te mores istos, effingam de nouo,
    Et efficiam te peritissimum omnium artificem.

ANTONIUS: Artificem cuius artis?

AEQUIUOCUS: Artis potatoriae,   610
    Veneris, aleae, vt potare possis strenuè,
    Et cum decore fumum e naribus euomere,
    Obuios salutare, et ambire dominam.

ANTONIUS: At compotationes has interdixit seriò pater.

AEQUIUOCUS: Interdixit pater. Quid eris etiamnum puer?   615

ANTONIUS: Iussitque vt darem operam studiis noctes et dies.

AEQUIUOCUS: Non refert quid iussit, satis superque doctus es.

ANTONIUS: Egone doctus satis?

AEQUIUOCUS: Potes chartae nomen apponere.

ANTONIUS: Possum.

AEQUIUOCUS: Iterum dico, satis superque doctus es.

ANTONIUS: Sed Latinum vult pater.

AEQUIVOCUS: The most nonsensical nonsense of all.

ANTONIUS: Is that so?

AEQUIVOCUS: Yes, it's so. Why do you care about genus and species? Aren't you your father's only son and heir?

ANTONIUS: What of it?

AEQUIVOCUS: Then why do you need knowledge? These trifles are for younger brothers whom nature, like a stepmother, begets for servitude, or for the vile common folk, the poor, and that sort of man whom a sad horoscope condemns to labor.[2]

ANTONIUS: Then what would you have me do?

AEQUIVOCUS: You ask "what should I do"? Here, for you: cards and all sorts of dice. There are the muses more suited to your studies. Be my student for just a few days. I'll teach you those manners, I will form you anew and make you the most skilled master of all.

ANTONIUS: A master of what art?

AEQUIVOCUS: The art of drinking, lechery, and gambling so that you will be able to drink with diligence and with decorum to blow smoke from your nose, to greet those you meet, and court a mistress.[3]

ANTONIUS: But father strictly forbade drinking parties.

AEQUIVOCUS: "Father forbade." Will you always be a little boy?

ANTONIUS: He demanded that I study day and night.

AEQUIVOCUS: It doesn't matter what he demanded. You are learned enough and more.

ANTONIUS: I'm learned enough?

AEQUIVOCUS: You are able to write your name on a piece of paper.[4]

ANTONIUS: Yes, I can do that.

AEQUIVOCUS: So I say again. You are learned enough and more.

ANTONIUS: But father wants me to learn Latin.

---

[2] See *AM* pt. 1, sec. 2, mem. 3, subs. 15 (317), concerning the ignorance of the public: "Because they are rich, and have other means to live, they think it concerns them not to know, or to trouble themselves with it; a fitter task for younger brothers, or poor men's sons, to be pen and inkhorn men, pedantical slaves, and no whit beseeming the calling of a gentleman."

[3] *AM* pt. 2, sec. 3, mem. 2 (139): " 'If he can hawk and hunt, ride a horse, play at cards and dice, swagger, drink, swear,' take tobacco with grace, sing, dance, wear his clothes in fashion, court and please his mistress, talk big fustian, insult, scorn, strut, contemn others, and use a little mimical and apish complement above the rest, he is a complete (*Egregiam vero laudem* [a truly noble compliment]), a well-qualified gentleman; these are most of their employments, this their greatest commendation."

[4] Compare Chrysophilus in *Philomathes*, lines 4840–43, on the education of his son: "Sat ego peritum filium Aphronium reor / Si legere possit syngraphum et nomen suum / Peculiari scribere ita valeat modo / Nequis imitetur, scire quid plura expetat?" [I consider my son Aphronius experienced enough if he can read a promissory note and write his name in such a way that it can't be forged; why should he want to know more?] *The Christmas Prince*, ed. F. S. Boas and W. W. Greg (Oxford: Univ. Press, 1922), 158.

AEQUIUOCUS: Bene se res habet.   620
    Audi, hoc vbi memoritèr edidisceris:
    Qui nescit dissimulare nescit viuere.
    Ne quid vltra de Latinitate cogitaueris.
ANTONIUS: Quî demum tempus impendam?
AEQUIUOCUS: Etiamne rogitas?
    Tu sis sollicitus de cane venatico,   625
    De cantu et choreâ, venatione et aucupio,
    De lanistâ et dominâ, haec studia te magìs decent.
    Sed heus tu. Inuitor ego ad proximum Oenopolium
    Hâc nocte ad caenam; eris hospes meus.
    Aderunt puellae illic, combibones optimi, tibicines;   630
    Pergraecabimur vnâ, genio noctem addiximus.
    Ne quid haesites. Mecum ibis. Eris acceptissimus.
ANTONIUS: Quando ita suades, Aequiuoce, duc quo vis, sequar.

Scena Quinta
Polumathes. Theanus. Philobiblos.   635

THEANUS: Ambo peregrinantes studiosi?
POLUMATHES: Ambo sumus.
THEANUS: Sed quae causa apud nos morae tam diutinae?
PHILOBIBLOS: Discendi.
THEANUS: Quid est quod scire desideras?
POLUMATHES: Multa sunt in quibuscunque fere scientiis
    In quibus haereo, quae solui quamprimum cupio.   640
THEANUS: Roga quid vis modò sit in artibus.
    Nam per annos triginta nunc magister fui,
    Octies bursarius, bis subpraefectus collegii mei.
PHILOBIBLOS: Vir doctus proculdubiò.
POLUMATHES: Soluesne quod rogo?
THEANUS: Soluam si potero.
POLUMATHES: Tentabo priùs in grammaticâ.   645

AEQUIVOCUS: No problem. Listen, when you have memorized this you will be educated: Qui nescit dissimulare nescit vivere.[5] You will not need to know anything more about Latin.

ANTONIUS: Then how will I spend my time?

AEQUIVOCUS: You have to ask? You should worry about a hunting dog, about song, dance, hunting and fowling, about fencing, and about a mistress.[6] These studies are more suited to you. But listen. I am invited to a nearby tavern tonight for dinner. You will be my guest. Girls will be there, excellent drinking companions, lute players; we will party together and devote the night to pleasantry. Don't be undecided. You will come with me. You will be most welcome.

ANTONIUS: I'm persuaded, Aequivocus. Lead where you will; I will follow.

Scene five
Polumathes. Theanus. Philobiblos.

THEANUS: Are you both students from abroad?

POLUMATHES: Yes, we are.

THEANUS: Why are you staying here so long?

PHILOBIBLOS: To learn.

THEANUS: What is it you want to know?

POLUMATHES: In almost every field of knowledge there are many things about which I am uncertain and which I want to have resolved as soon as possible.

THEANUS: Ask whatever you want, only let it be in the arts, for I have been a Master of Arts for thirty years now, eight times a bursar, and twice subprefect of my college.

PHILOBIBLOS: A learned man, no doubt.

POLUMATHES: Will you answer what I ask?

THEANUS: I will answer if I am able.

POLUMATHES: First I will try grammar.

---

[5] [He who does not know how to dissemble does not know how to live.] JS: "This line occurs also in Burton's *Anatomy* [pt. 1, sec. 2, mem. 3, subs 15. (316)] and is said to have been a favorite maxim of the Emperor Frederic Barbarossa." "But when [the ignorant public] contemn learning, and think themselves sufficiently qualified, if they can write and read, scramble at a piece of evidence, or have so much Latin as that emperor had: '*Qui nescit dissimulare, nescit vivere*' [he who cannot dissemble cannot live], they are unfit to do their country service...."

[6] *AM* pt. 1, sec. 2, mem. 3, subs. 15 (320): "Let me not be malicious, and lie against my genius; I may not deny but that we have a sprinkling of our gentry, here and there one, excellently well learned.... But they are but few in respect of the multitude, the major part (and some again excepted, that are indifferent) are wholly bent for hawks and hounds, and carried away many times with intemperate lust, gaming, and drinking."

THEANUS: Quid a me scire cupis quae spectant ad pueros?
PHILOBIBLOS: Aquila non capit Muscas. Roga quid seriò.
POLUMATHES: Quod est summum bonum?
THEANUS: Bonum sacerdotium.
PHILOBIBLOS: Lepidè per Iouem.
POLUMATHES: Dubitatur de generatione meteorôn,
    Incremento Nili, et origine fontium,   650
    An mare per polos sit nauigabile?
PHILOBIBLOS: De sympathia ammonii et hydrangirii,
    Caphuri, crisocolli, et plumbi cinerii
    Infinisque aliis? Statue quid? Supersedebimus tibi.
THEANUS: Credendum est in his cum catholicâ ecclesiâ.   655
PHILOBIBLOS: Dissimulat, opinor; roga quid in artibus.
POLUMATHES: Quid censes de quadraturâ circuli?
PHILOBIBLOS: De volutâ Dinostrati?
POLUMATHES: Quid de contactus angulo diuidatur?
PHILOBIBLOS: Daturne minimus?
THEANUS: Legebam in Euclide ad pontem asininum semèl.
POLUMATHES: Qualis Arithmeticus?
THEANUS: Scio numerare pecuniam.   660

THEANUS: Why do you wish to learn from me those things which pertain to young boys?

PHILOBIBLOS: An eagle does not catch flies.[1] Ask something in earnest.

POLUMATHES: What is the highest good?

THEANUS: A good benefice.

PHILOBIBLOS: Witty, by Jove.

POLUMATHES: What is your opinion about the cause of meteors, the rising of the Nile, the origin of headwaters, whether the sea is navigable through the poles?[2]

PHILOBIBLOS: About the sympathy of ammonius and quick silver, camphor, chrysocolla,[3] grey lead[4] and other base things? What is your opinion? We yield to you.

THEANUS: In these matters one should follow the belief of the Catholic church.

PHILOBIBLOS: I think he is dissembling. Ask something about the arts.

POLUMATHES: What do you think about the squaring of the circle?

PHILOBIBLOS: About the curve of Dinostratus?[5]

POLUMATHES: How might the angle of contact be divided?[6]

PHILOBIBLOS: Is the least given?

THEANUS: I was reading once in Euclid about the Bridge of Asses.[7]

POLUMATHES: What sort of mathematician are you?

THEANUS: I know how to count money.

---

[1] Erasmus, *Ad.* 3.2.65.

[2] *AM* pt. 2, sec. 2, mem. 3 (36): "In Africa [I would] examine the fountains of Nilus, whether Herodotus, Seneca, Pliny, *lib. 5, cap. 9.* Strabo, *lib. 5,* give a true cause of his annual flowing." *AM* pt. 2, sec. 2, mem. 3 (38): "I would find out with Trajan the fountains of Danubius, of Ganges, Oxus." *AM* pt. 2, sec. 2, mem. 3 (35): "Whether the sea be open and navigable by the Pole Arctic, and which is the likeliest way, that of Bartison the Hollander, under the Pole itself, which for some reasons I hold best: or by *Fretum Davis* [Davis Strait], or Nova Zembla."

[3] Thomas: *chrysocolla*: "A kinde of minerall founde like sand in the veines of brasse, silver or gold: one kinde of it is called 'Boras,' with which the Goldsmithes soulder gold."

[4] Rulandus: *Plumbum Cinereum*—Grey Lead "is the German Bismuth. It differs from the black and white species, and is, as it were, a metal by itself. It is more noble than Lead, but inferior to Silver, and has a middle position between both."

[5] Dinostratus or Deinostratus, a Greek mathematician, fl. c. 350 BC. "He is known chiefly for his study of the quadratix, a curve already invented by one Hippias, very likely Hippias of Elis. This curve enabled him to square a circle." David Eugene Smith, *History of Mathematics* 1 (Boston: Ginn and Company, 1923), 92. Burton mentions the squaring of the circle in *AM* pt. 2, sec. 2, mem. 4 (97).

[6] OED: *angle of contact*: the angle between a curve and its tangent at any point, or the infinitesimal angle between two consecutive tangents at that point; also called the angle of contingence of curvature.

[7] JS: "In *Euclid,* Book I, Prop. 5. Equivalent to saying, 'A bridge difficult for stupid young things to cross.'" The diagram somewhat resembles a bridge. It is this proposition which beginning students usually find "difficult to cross."

POLUMATHES: De triplici terrae motu quid existimas?
De stellâ nouâ sublunaris an aetherea?
PHILOBIBLOS: Nouam Ramerus induxit hypothesîn
Nouam Tycho Brahe, nouam Fracastorius,
Nouam Haelisens Roeslin, nouam Patritius,   665
Nouam Thaddeus Hagesius ab Hagecke medicus.
THEANUS: Domine saluum fac, quaenam haec incantatio?
POLUMATHES: Hi omnes excludunt elementum igneum.
THEANUS: Iterum.
POLUMATHES: Hos omnes Maginus perstringit, qui de nupero
Sphaeram nouam effinxit vndecimam.   670
Hic peccat contra Mathematica principia,
Ille optica, at ille philosophica.
Cui credendum? Quid statius? Obnixè a te rogo.
THEANUS: Quod supra nos nihil ad nos.
POLUMATHES: Neque curas Astronomiam?

POLUMATHES: What do you think about the three-fold motion of the earth?[8] About the new star, is it sublunar or ethereal?

PHILOBIBLOS: Ramerus has introduced a new hypothesis, Tycho Brahe a new one, Fracastorius a new one, Haelisens Roeslin a new one, Patritius a new one, Thaddeus Hagesius, the physician from Hagecke, a new one.[9]

THEANUS: Heaven help us. What is this incantation?

POLUMATHES: They all exclude the element of fire.[10]

THEANUS: Again.

POLUMATHES: Maginus,[11] who recently identified a new sphere, the eleventh, censures all of them; one errs in mathematical principles, another in optics, another in philosophy. Whom should we believe? What do you think? I ask you in earnest.

THEANUS: What is above us does not concern us.[12]

POLUMATHES: So you are not concerned with astronomy?

---

[8] See *AM* pt. 2, sec. 3, mem. 3 (52–53) on the "triple motion" of the earth.

[9] *AM* pt. 2, sec. 3, mem. 3 (56–57): "But to avoid these paradoxes of the earth's motion ... our latter mathematicians have rolled all the stones that may be stirred: and to solve all appearances and objections, have invented new hypotheses, and fabricated new systems of the world, out of their own Daedalian heads. Fracastorius will have the earth stand still. ... Nicholas Ramerus will have the earth the center of the world, but movable. ... Tycho Brahe puts the earth the centre immovable. ... Helisaeus Roeslin censureth both." *AM* pt. 2, sec. 2, mem. 3 (52): "Keplerus, Patricius, and some other neoterics have in part revived this opinion; and that every star in heaven hath a soul, angel, or intelligence to animate or move it, etc." JS: "Fracastorius: Hieronymus Fracastro (1484–1553), astronomer, geologist, physicist, poet, and physician." "Helisaeus Roeslin: Helisaeus (Eliseo) Roeslin, German astronomer and scholar of the sixteenth century, lived at Frankfort, and, among other things, wrote *Theoria nova coelestium Meteoron* (Strassburg, 1578)." "Patricius: Franciscus Patricius, or Patrizi (1529–1597), lived at Caieta, Italy, and wrote several works on history, mathematics, and astronomy mentioned in *The Anatomy of Melancholy* ('Digression of Air')." "Thaddeus Haggesius: According to a note in *The Anatomy*, Thaddeus Haggesius wrote a book on *Metoposcopy*, about 1578."

Burton owned a copy of Brahe's *Learned: Tico Brahae, his, astronomicall, conjecture, of the new and much admired * which appered in the yeare 1572* and Roeslin's *Theoria nova coelestium metewrwn* [sic] *in qua ex plurimum cometarum phoenomenis ... afferuntur, ... super quibus cometa anni M. D. LXXVII. novo motu.* ... Kiessling, nos. 203 and 1356.

[10] *AM* pt. 2, sec. 2, mem. 3 (48): "P. Nonius Saluciensis and Kepler take upon them to demonstrate that no meteors, clouds, fogs, vapours, arise higher than fifty and eighty miles, and all the rest to be purer air or element of fire: which Cardan, Tycho, and John Pena manifestly confute by refractions, and many other arguments, there is no such element of fire at all."

[11] D-JS: Joannes Antonius Maginus, an Italian mathematician of the sixteenth and seventeenth centuries. *AM* pt. 2, sec. 2, mem. 3 (50): "Maginus makes eleven heavens, subdivided into their orbs and circles, and all too little to serve those particular appearances." In a marginal note, Burton adds, "In Theoricis planetarum; three above the firmament, which all wise men reject." Burton owned a copy of Maginus's *Ephemerides coelestium motuum ... ab anno Domini 1598.* Kiessling, no. 996.

[12] Erasmus, *Ad.* 1.6.69.

THEANUS: Non omnino; caput mihi calendarium,   675
    Nasus Iudex, venter Horologium.
    Diis gratia, scio prandendi cubandique tempora,
    Dies festos, et quid opus Astronomiâ?
POLUMATHES: Quid profiteris?
THEANUS: Quicquid animo collibitum est meo.
PHILOBIBLOS: Dic mihi, medice, quod est morborum initium?   680
THEANUS: Non sum medicus.
PHILOBIBLOS: Dic mihi, iuridice,
    Quid arbitreris de Papionani lege Arithmeticâ.
    Expone nobis legem Falcidiam si poteris.
THEANUS: Non sum iurista.
PHILOBIBLOS: Sacerdos proculdubiò.
THEANUS: Quidni sacerdos?
POLUMATHES: Habes itaque linguarum peritiam.   685
    Praefert Hebreae Belgicam Goropius, Punicam
    Alter, Graecam Apollinaris; interpone iuditium.
THEANUS: Nil mihi cum linguis; quid opus tantâ scientiâ?
    Scio Missam celebrare, legere et scribere
    Et concionari possum, cum ad vicem meam venit.   690
POLUMATHES: O virum miserum indignum et stolidum!
THEANUS: Cur sic exclamas?
POLUMATHES: Miseresco tui.
THEANUS: Ego tui.
POLUMATHES: Sapientum octauus.
PHILOBIBLOS: Merum pecus.

Scena Sexta
Tarentilla. Amphimacer.   695

TARENTILLA: Inter omnes eos qui me simul ambiunt,
    Scholares, oppidanos, rusticos, aulicos,
    Vnus est qui se poetam nominat—
    Homo rudis et qui ridetur ab omnibus.
    Hunc ego quum non curem, nam quid mihi cum eo   700
    Qui non habet argentum, vanâ spe lacto tamen,
    Eò quod omnem nostram exhilaret familiam,
    Cantilenis rithmis, et fabulis suis—
    Sed eccum venit; prae me feram melancholicam.

THEANUS: Not at all. My head is a calendar, my nose a judge, my stomach a
   clock. Thanks to the gods, I know when to eat and sleep and I know the
   festival days so what need is there for astronomy?
POLUMATHES: What do you profess?
THEANUS: Whatever pleases me.[13]
PHILOBIBLOS: Tell me, physician, what is the source of disease?
THEANUS: I am not a physician.
PHILOBIBLOS: Tell me, judge, what decision would you render about the ar-
   ithmetical law of Papionanus? Explain to us, if you can, the Falcidian
   law.[14]
THEANUS: I am not a lawyer.
PHILOBIBLOS: A priest, no doubt.
THEANUS: And why not a priest?
POLUMATHES: And so you have a talent for languages. Goropius prefers Bel-
   gian to Hebrew, another prefers Punic, Apollinaris prefers Greek.[15] Put
   forth your judgment.
THEANUS: Languages are nothing to me. What need is there of such knowl-
   edge? I know how to celebrate Mass, to read and write, and I can preach
   when it comes my turn.
POLUMATHES: O wretched, unworthy and stupid man.
THEANUS: Why do you exclaim such things?
POLUMATHES: I pity you.
THEANUS: And I you.
POLUMATHES: The eighth wise man.[16]
PHILOBIBLOS: A mere goat.

Scene six
Tarentilla. Amphimacer.

TARENTILLA: Of all those who are courting me now, scholars, townsmen, rustics, courtiers, there is one who calls himself a poet. He's a hick, and
   everyone makes fun of him. Although I don't like him—what do I need
   with a man who has no money—I do tease him with vain hope because he
   amuses our household with his songs, poems and stories. But look. Here
   he comes. I'll pretend I'm melancholy.

---

[13] Plautus, *Am.* 191: "utquomque animo conlibitum est meo." [Whatever pleases me.]
[14] JS: "Falcidian Law: P. Falcidius, Roman tribune under Augustus, 40 BC. The law
related to proportionate inheritance." "Papinianus: A Roman jurist under Septimus
Severus, c. AD 212."
[15] D-JS: Joannes Goropius, a Dutch physician and scholar of the sixteenth century. The
"other" and this particular Apollinaris are unidentified.
[16] Erasmus, *Ad.* 1.8.90.

AMPHIMACER: Haeccine Tarentilla? Sic est. Compellabo magnificè.   705
   Salue pulchricoma nympha et roseum fulgens iubar,
   Virginum decus, honor aetatis tuae,
   Formâ proceritate et candore animi—
               [*Haeret*]
TARENTILLA: Haeresne? Iuno Lucina, fer opem.
AMPHIMACER: Quae mulierum genus superas faeminarum,   710
   Cuius a vertice et nigricantibus oculis,
   Tale quiddam spirat ac ab aureâ Venere.
TARENTILLA: Quorsum haec? Quasi me ne norîs quidem.
AMPHIMACER: Ne norîm, meae delitiae, mea rosa, meum suauium?
   Quid agis? Quid reluctaris? Da mihi basium.   715
   Tantisper da suauiolum, dum basia restant
   Ex animâque tuâ dum spiritus in mea labra
   Influit inque iecur mulgenti dulcia philtra.
   Quod apud Theocritum Venus Adonidi,
   Serenissima Tarentilla, id ego tibi.   720
TARENTILLA: Ne sis molestus.
AMPHIMACER: Quaeso ne frontem capera.
TARENTILLA: Non vacat nugis tuis nunc operam dare.
AMPHIMACER: Nugis? Attamen hae nugae pondera vocis habent.
   Liceat deosculari manum aut calceamentum tuum.
   Quid an grauaris dolere dentium?   725
   An forte furtiuum vereris osculum
   Vt sempèr ferè ori admoueas manum.
TARENTILLA: Osculum et basium, et nil praeter osculum.
AMPHIMACER: Viri amantis osculum, apud volentem puellam
   Tacitae petitionis obtinet locum, apud nolentem   730
   Precationis. Achilles Tatius, liber primus.
TARENTILLA: Quorsùm venis? Quid ergo vis? Quid petis?

AMPHIMACER: Could this be Tarentilla? Why, so it is. I'll address her in high style. Hail, pretty-haired nymph and shining rosy splendor, most beautiful of maidens, honor of your age in form, stature and purity of mind—[1]

[*He hesitates.*]

TARENTILLA: Are you stuck? Juno Lucina, bring help![2]

AMPHIMACER: You who surpass the image of feminine women, from whose head and black eyes such a something breathes forth as if from golden Venus.

TARENTILLA: What is this? You act as if you didn't even know me.

AMPHIMACER: Would I not know you, my dearest, my rose, my sweetness? What are you doing? Why do you resist? Give me a kiss.[3] Just give me a little kiss while your kisses remain, and from your soul a spirit flows onto my lips and, as it milks a sweet love potion, into my liver. According to Theocritus, as Venus to Adonis, so, dearest Tarentilla, I to you.

TARENTILLA: Don't be bothersome.

AMPHIMACER: I beg you, don't frown.

TARENTILLA: I don't have time now to listen to this nonsense.

AMPHIMACER: Nonsense? And yet this nonsense holds the weight of words.[4] Let me kiss your hand or your heel. What, do you have a toothache? Or perhaps you fear a furtive kiss that you almost always put your hand to your mouth.

TARENTILLA: A kiss, a kiss, and nothing but a kiss.

AMPHIMACER: "The kiss of a lover to a willing wench is a silent wooing, to an unwilling one is but an humble petition." Achilles Tatius, Book I.[5]

TARENTILLA: Why have you come here? What do you want? What are you looking for?

---

[1] Throughout the scene, Amphimacer's words "in high style" addressed to Tarentilla are a medley of familiar phrases from the classical love poets, Plautus, and Terence. See *AM* pt. 3, sec. 2, mem. 3 (157) on the "Symptons or Signs of Love-Melancholy": "All the gracious elogies, metaphors, hyperbolical comparisons of the best things in the world, the most glorious names; whatsoever, I say, is pleasant, amiable, sweet, grateful, and delicious, are too little for her."

[2] Terence, *And.* 474; *Ad.* 487. Bensly: "Tarentilla invokes the aid of Juno Lucina (prayed to in cases of difficult child-birth) for the poet, that he may have an easy *delivery* of his verses."

[3] Catullus 5.7: "Da mihi basia mille." [Give me a thousand kisses.]

[4] JS: Ovid, *Heroides* 3.4: "lacrimae pondera vocis habent" (Loeb) and *Fasti* 1.182 "dictaque pondus habent." Bensly: "Lacrimae pondera vocis habent" occurs again in Ovid, *Epistulae ex Ponto* 3.1.158. [Tears hold the weight of words.]

[5] JS: This translation "is taken from the text of Robert Burton's brother, William Burton. This translation was done in 1597." Burton owned a copy of Achilles Tatius, *De Clitophontis & Leucippes amoribus lib. VIII. Longus Sophistae de Daphnides & Chloes amoribus lib. IV. Parthenius Nicaeensis de amotoriis affertibus lib. I. Omnia nunc primus simul edita Graece ac Latine.* It was a gift from his brother William. Kiessling, no. 4.

AMPHIMACER: Non ego diuitias Arabum, rubriue lapillos
    Aequoris insignes cupio, nec quicquid Iberus
    Amne Tagus rutilante vehit, populosque superbos   735
    Sceptigera domitare manu, etc. Sed vnicum basiolum.
TARENTILLA: Si te donarem basio, quid subires causâ meâ?
AMPHIMACER: Tuus, o regina, quod optas explorare labor; mihi
    Iussa capessere fas est. Quid vis impera.
TARENTILLA: Impero silentium.
AMPHIMACER: Audi poema priùs   740
    Quod hesternâ nocte de te composui.
TARENTILLA: Recita.
AMPHIMACER: Da mihi te facilem, dederisque in carmina vires,
    Ingenium vultu statque caditque tuo.
TARENTILLA: Hoccine poema?
AMPHIMACER: Prologus. Attendas. Incipio.
    Te Tarentillâ non est formosior illa.   745
TARENTILLA: Quaenam illa? Si diis placet.
AMPHIMACER: Tacên, obsecro.
    In totâ Osuna non est te pulchrior vna.
    Si digitos spectes, digiti sunt consule digni,
    Siue oculos, oculi sunt tanquam sydera caeli.
TARENTILLA: Tam bonus in versu quam Mulciber est in a horshewe.   750
AMPHIMACER: Frons sursum a dorso, dorsum stat fronte deorsum,
    Crus quasi thus, pes velut aes, mamma est quasi flamma.
TARENTILLA: Poetarum facilè princeps. At cur mamma quasi flamma?
AMPHIMACER: Vt stipulam flamma exurit, sic me tua mamma.
TARENTILLA: Perge.
AMPHIMACER: Est vmbelicus medio velut aequore ficus,   755
    Inter se partes septem nectuntur vt artes.
TARENTILLA: Si vis vel non vis debes commedere Stockfishe.
AMPHIMACER: Laudaremnè genas, currentes corpore venas,
    Candida colla nitentia coctum lac velut ollâ?
    Quod reliquum est, versu non possum dicere, cum tu   760
    Tantam praecellas quantum inter Cynthia stellas.
TARENTILLA: Cum faciam vitulum pro frugibus, ipse venito.

AMPHIMACER: "I desire not the riches of Arabia, the rare stones of the Red Sea, nor anything the Iberian Tagus carries in its glowing waters, to rule a proud people with a sceptered hand," etc.[6] I just want one little kiss.

TARENTILLA: If I were to give you a kiss, what would you do for me?

AMPHIMACER: "Your task, O Queen, is to decide what you desire, mine to do your bidding."[7] Order what you will.

TARENTILLA: I order silence.

AMPHIMACER: First hear a poem I wrote last night about you.

TARENTILLA: Read it.

AMPHIMACER: "Give yourself easily to me and you will have given strength to my song. My inspiration both stands and falls upon your look."[8]

TARENTILLA: This is a poem?

AMPHIMACER: The prologue. Pay attention. I begin:
"She is not more lovely than you, Tarentilla."

TARENTILLA: Who is this "she," for heaven sake?

AMPHIMACER: Be quiet, I beg you.
"In all of Osuna, there is no one more beautiful than you.
Look at your fingers, they are fingers worthy of a consul,[9]
Or your eyes, they are like the stars in the sky."

TARENTILLA: As good at verses as Vulcan is at horseshoes.

AMPHIMACER: "From front to back and back to front,
Legs like incense, feet like bronze, breasts like flames."

TARENTILLA: Easily the prince of poets. But why "breasts like flames"?

AMPHIMACER: Just as flames ignite straw, so your breasts me.

TARENTILLA: Go on.

AMPHIMACER: "The navel in the middle is like a fig tree in water;
The seven parts among themselves are bound like the seven arts."

TARENTILLA: Whether you want to or not, you should eat stockfish.

AMPHIMACER: "Should I praise your cheeks, the veins running through your body,
Your white neck shining like cooked milk in a jar?
What is left of you, I cannot describe in verse.
You surpass other women, as Cynthia[10] does the stars."

TARENTILLA: "When I sacrifice a heifer for the harvest, come yourself."[11]

---

[6] JS: Palingenius, *Zodiacus Vitae*, 5.1-4.

[7] JS: Vergil, *Aen.* 1.76–77.

[8] JS: Ovid, *Fasti*, 1.17–18: "Da mihi te placidum, dederis a carmina viris / ingenium voltu statque caditque tuo." (Loeb) [Give yourself willingly to me and you will have given strength to my song. My inspiration both stands and falls upon your look.]

[9] Bensly: "This is a ludicrous perversion of Vergil [*Ecl.* 4.3], 'Si canimus silvas, silvae sint consule dignae.' " [If we sing of the forest, let the forest be worthy of a consul.]

[10] The goddess Diana; the moon.

[11] Vergil, *Ecl.* 3. 76–77: "Phyllida mitte mihi: meus est natalis Iolla; / cum faciam vitula

Interìm ad Anticeras, nisi me modo spreueris, ito.
               [*Exit*]
AMPHIMACER: Ipse venito cum faciam, etc. Id est, quando eo cubitum.
   Capio, mi Tarentilla. At cur, Interim ad Antyceras?   765
   Id est, ut sis facetus et ingeniosus sicut semper es.
   Benè monet, et hoc sedulò praestitero.

Scena Septima
Polupragmaticus. Polupistos.
Aequiuocus. Dromo.   770

POLUPRAGMATICUS: Torquem inquis aureum die Veneris ad primum
   gallicinium.
   Hoccine totum?
POLUPISTOS: Me miserum! Vix totius demidium.
   Amisi gemmas inestimabiles vtique et inumerabiles.
POLUPRAGMATICUS: Quae summa totius?
POLUPISTOS: Decem opinor myriadas.
AEQUIUOCUS: Cognatus meus est; mentitur tam egregie—   775
POLUPISTOS: Praeter paternum amnulum et torquem illum aureum,
   Qui fuit aui, abaui, ataui, abataui nonagesimi.
   Pondo talentis ter centum, catenis octodecem.
DROMO: Praeter haec suffurati sunt duos equos Frisios,
   Comederûnt capones tres, gallum gallicareum   780
   Oua centum, duo farta, tres ingentes artocreas.
POLUPRAGMATICUS: Mira narrat. Os hinc sublinam probè.
DROMO: Par caligarum ab Hedione nostro et ligulas nouas,
   Vas lactis demoliti.
POLUPISTOS: Tacên, verbero.
POLUPRAGMATICUS: Ludos hic miros faciam.
AEQUIUOCUS: Patellâ dignum operculum.   785
POLUPRAGMATICUS: Quid petis?
POLUPISTOS: Peto fures capi si possis efficere.

Meanwhile, unless you really hate me, go to Anticyra.[12]

[*Exit*]

AMPHIMACER: "Come yourself when I sacrifice," etc. That is, when I go to bed. I understand, my Tarentilla. But why "meanwhile to Anticyra"? That is, so that you may be as witty and clever as you always are. Good advice, and I will tend to it right away.

Scene seven
Polupragmaticus. Polupistos.
Aequivocus. Dromo.

POLUPRAGMATICUS: A golden necklace, you say, on Friday at dawn. Is this all?

POLUPISTOS: O wretched me! Scarcely half of the whole. I have lost jewels surely priceless and countless.

POLUPRAGMATICUS: What is the total value?

POLUPISTOS: About a hundred thousand, I think.

AEQUIVOCUS <*aside*>: He must be a cousin. He lies so outstandingly well.

POLUPISTOS: Besides, there was my father's ring, and a golden necklace which belonged to my grandfather, great-grandfather, great-great-grandfather, great-great-great-grandfather all the way to the 90th generation. It weighs 300 talents and has 18 chains.

DROMO: Besides those, they have stolen two Frisian horses, they have eaten three capons, a cock, 100 eggs, two stuffed puddings, three large meat pies.

POLUPRAGMATICUS <*aside*>: What strange things he tells. I'll make a proper fool of him for this.

DROMO: A pair of boots and new buckles from our Hedio and a dish of spilled milk.

POLUPISTOS: Quiet, scoundrel.

POLUPRAGMATICUS <*aside*>: I'll have fun with this.

AEQUIVOCUS <*aside*>: A lid worthy of the pot.[1]

POLUPRAGMATICUS: What do you ask?

POLUPISTOS: I ask that the thieves be captured, if you can bring it about.

---

pro fugibus, ipse venito." [Send Phyllis to me: it is my birthday, Iollas; when I sacrifice a heifer for the harvest, come yourself.]

[12] Cooper: "an yle ouer agaynst the mountayne Deta of Thessalie where the herbe Elleborus groweth, which purgeth melancholy." See *AM* pt. 2, sec. 4, mem. 2, subs. 2 (230). Erasmus, *Ad.* 1.8.52: "Naviget Anticyras." Horace, *Sat.* 2.3.164–166: "non est periurus neque sordidus: immolet aequis / hic porcum Laribus: verum ambitiosus et audax: / naviget Anticyram." [He who is not false or foul, let him sacrifice a pig to the benevolent gods; he who is ambitious and bold, let him sail to Anticyra.]

[1] LS: Proverb: patellae dignum operculum [like to like].

POLUPRAGMATICUS: Si posses. Si vis, terram suo mouebo de loco,
　　Lunam e caelo, ciebo grandinem et tonitrua.
　　Arte meâ faciam vt mus loco dimoueat
　　Quod quadringenta boum iuga non trahant.　　　　　790
POLUPISTOS: O illustrem artificem!
DROMO: O execrandum carnificem!
AEQUIUOCUS: Boues pictos aut mortuos herus intelligit.
POLUPRAGMATICUS: Possum, si libet, vnius ope herbeculae
　　Fugare totum exercitum, seras quaslibet
　　Aperire; ope huiusce quem vides annuli　　　　　795
　　Prandere apud Batauos, caenare in Italia.
AEQUIUOCUS: Non eodem die, et sic verum est totum, quod ait.
POLUPISTOS: O admirandam peritiam!
DROMO: O execrandam inscitiam!
POLUPRAGMATICUS: Si vis huc in medium proferam, idque statìm
　　Vmbram Agamemnonis, aut Achillis animam.　　　　800
POLUPISTOS: Virum proculdubiò doctissimum.
DROMO: Sapientum octauum.
POLUPRAGMATICUS: Nil me latet non quid agatur apud Inferos,
　　Colocynthropiratas, aut Madagascar accolas.
AEQUIUOCUS: Scilicet in genere, sed non in spetiè.
POLUPISTOS: Iupiter ipse nihil potest maius.
DROMO: Hic impostor nihil minus.　　　　　805
POLUPRAGMATICUS: Quid Iuno in aurem insusurret Ioui,
　　Musicam accire flammamque e pugnis excutere.
POLUPISTOS: Deus bone, homo homini quid interest!
DROMO: Stulto intelligens.
POLUPRAGMATICUS: Possum in medio aere arcem extruere,
　　Quod fuit et quod futurum, ad vnguem praedicere.　　810
AEQUIUOCUS: Testis ego sum praedixisse quidem, sed falsò omnia.
DROMO: Pol hoc periclitabor. Quo fui natus in loco?
POLUPRAGMATICUS: Tuguriolo fortasse.
DROMO: Mentiris per Iouem.
　　Quoties enim matrem meam audiui dicere
　　Me natum fuisse simul et genitum in scrobe.　　　　815
　　Sed quod fatum me manet?
POLUPRAGMATICUS: Volam manus et frontem inspiciam.
　　In fronte distorta martialis, liniola—
　　Diuulsa, crassa, cruciformis, solarem intersecans
　　Biothonandum ostendit. Sed cedo manum.

POLUPRAGMATICUS: "If you can." If you wish, I shall move the earth from its place, the moon from the sky, I'll produce hail and thunder. By my art I can have a mouse move what four hundred yoke of oxen could not drag.

POLUPISTOS: O distinguished master!

DROMO <aside>: O detestable villain!

AEQUIVOCUS <aside>: My master means pictures of oxen, or dead ones.

POLUPRAGMATICUS: I can, if I want, with the aid of a single herb, put an entire army to flight or open any door. With this ring which you see, I can breakfast among the people of Holland and dine in Italy.

AEQUIVOCUS <aside>: But not on the same day, so all that he says is true.

POLUPISTOS: O admirable skill!

DROMO <aside>: O detestable stupidity!

POLUPRAGMATICUS: If you wish, I shall bring forth right here and now the shade of Agamemnon or the soul of Achilles.

POLUPISTOS: No doubt a very learned man.

DROMO <aside>: The eighth wise man.

POLUPRAGMATICUS: Nothing is hidden from me, not what is done among the dead, the Colocynthrian pirates, or the inhabitants of Madagascar.

AEQUIVOCUS <aside>: That is, in general, not in particular.

POLUPISTOS: Jupiter himself can do no more.

DROMO <aside>: This impostor, nothing less.

POLUPRAGMATICUS: I know what Juno whispers in the ear of Jupiter.[2] I can call forth music, dispel the flame from battle.

POLUPISTOS: Dear god. What a difference between man and man.

DROMO <aside>: What a difference between intelligence and stupidity.[3]

POLUPRAGMATICUS: I can build a castle in the air and predict exactly what was and what will be.

AEQUIVOCUS <aside>: Indeed, I have witnessed his predictions, but all have been false.

DROMO: By heavens, I'll test him. In what place was I born?

POLUPRAGMATICUS: In a cottage, perhaps.

DROMO: You lie, by Jove, for often I have heard my mother say that I was born and begot in a ditch. But what fate awaits me?

POLUPRAGMATICUS: Let me see your hand and your forehead. On the forehead, the line of Mars is distorted, divided, thick, cruciform, intersecting the line of the sun. It shows death. But give me your hand. Here a pale

---

[2] JS: Plautus, *Trin.* 208: "sciunt quod Iuno fabulatast cum Iove" [They know what Juno says to Jove.]

[3] Terence, *Eun.* 232: "Di immortales homini homo quid praestat, stulto intelligens quid interest." [Immortal gods, what a difference man from man, what a difference intelligence from stupidity.]

Hic a Rascettâ descendens Saturnina pallida—   820
Quid semicirculus in mensali! Signum homicidii.
POLUPISTOS: Rem tenes.
POLUPRAGMATICUS: Diuulsum thenar salacem et furem.
Caue ut dolatas posthâc conscendas arbores,
Ne demissum lapsus per funem repentè concidas
Cadendo collum frangas. Noli altum sapere.   825
POLUPISTOS: Rubet, pallet, scrupulum iniecisti homini.
DROMO: Ego te per deos.
AEQUIUOCUS: Vìn sceleste quid agis?
POLUPISTOS: Liceat hoc vnum interrogare si vacet.
Vbi nunc isti fures sunt aut quid agant?
                    [*Oculo speculum adiacet.*]
POLUPRAGMATICUS: Sunt, sunt, sunt, in hoc ipso temporis articulo,   830
In Campo Calatraue prope de La Pante Pagum.
Toleti cras pernoctabunt, ad signum Solis, foro veteri.
POLUPISTOS: Beasti. Sed quâ demum potes arte reducere?
POLUPRAGMATICUS: Confide, reducam vèl e faucibus Erebi,
Faciamque, si vis, vt seorsìm singuli   835
Cum capistris in manu domum tuam adeant.
POLUPISTOS: Siccine ais?
POLUPRAGMATICUS: Factum puta. Sed quid interìm dabis?
POLUPISTOS: Cape has viginti minas.
DROMO: Dabitur per Iouem.
Os tibi longè non abest ab infortunio.
AEQUIUOCUS: Quid tu facies?
DROMO: Faciam.
POLUPISTOS: Etiamnè furcifur?   840
POLUPRAGMATICUS: Bellè. Cape hoc vnguentum et hunc puluerem.
Inunge postes omnes circa aedes tuas,
Sepelito scriptum hoc ad ingressum vestibuli,
Tum circum circa sternes hunc puluerem.

saturnine descending from the rascetta—a semicircle in the mensal!⁴ A
sign of murder.

POLUPISTOS: You've got it right.

POLUPRAGMATICUS: A divided thenar, a braggart and a thief. Beware hereafter of climbing hewn trees, lest sliding down a rope you are suddenly dis-
membered or, in falling, you break your neck. Do not aspire to high
places.⁵

POLUPISTOS: He blushes and pales; you've made him anxious.⁶

DROMO: And I you, by god.

AEQUIVOCUS: What are you doing? Looking for trouble?

POLUPISTOS: Let me ask this one thing, please. Where are those thieves now;
what are they doing?

POLUPRAGMATICUS [*He looks in a glass.*]: They are, they are, they are at this
very moment in the Calatrave Field near the district De La Pante. Tomorrow they will sleep in Toledo, at the Sign of the Sun in the old market.⁷

POLUPISTOS: That delights me. But how can you bring them back?

POLUPRAGMATICUS: Trust me, I will bring them back even from the jaws of
hell. And if you wish, I'll have them come to your house, one by one,
with halter in hand.

POLUPISTOS: Do you say so?

POLUPRAGMATICUS: Consider it done. But what will you give?

POLUPISTOS: Take these 40 pounds.

DROMO: It is given, by Jove. Your face is not far from misfortune.⁸

AEQUIVOCUS: Will you be the cause?

DROMO: I'll be it.

POLUPISTOS: Is that so, knave?

POLUPRAGMATICUS: Rightly said. Take this ointment and this powder. Anoint
all the posts around your house, bury this inscription near the door to
the entrance, then sprinkle this dust around in a circle.

---

⁴ *AM* pt. 1, sec. 2, mem. 1, subs. 4 (209): "Chiromancy hath these aphorisms to foretell
melancholy. Taisnier, *lib. 5, cap. 2,* ... thus has it: 'The saturnine line going from the
rascetta through the hand to Saturn's mount, and there intersected by certain little lines,
argues melancholy; so if the vital and natural make an acute angle' (Aphorism 100). ...
Thaddaeus Haggesius, in his *Metoposcopia,* hath certain aphorisms derived from Saturn's
lines in the forehead, by which he collects a melancholy disposition." Burton owned a
copy of Taisnier. Kiessling, no. 1566.

⁵ Bensly: Romans 11.20, *Vulgate*: Noli altum sapere, sed time. A. V. translation: Be not
high minded, but fear.

⁶ JS: Terence, *Ad.* 227–28: "timet: / inieci scrupulum homini." [He's frightened: make
him anxious.]

⁷ See *AM* pt. 2, sec. 1, mem. 1 (6), for Burton on those who "make fire that not burn,
fetch back theives with stolen goods, show absent faces in a glass."

⁸ JS: Plautus, *Bacch.* 595: "ne tibi hercle hau longe est os ab infortunio." [Nor, by
Hercules, is your face far from misfortune.]

POLUPISTOS: Sed quando faciam?
POLUPRAGMATICUS: Die et horâ Mercurii   845
  Proximè sequenti. Fures vltro domum venient.
POLUPISTOS: Cum bonis?
POLUPRAGMATICUS: Cum bonis, at hoc obitèr caue.
  Ne tu vel seruulorum tuorum quispiam
  Per tres ante horas et nouem scrupulos
  Mingat, cacet, vel e postico sibilet.   850
  Nullus sit faetor. Si sit, labor erit irritus.
  Ludetisque operam.
POLUPISTOS: Curabo diligentèr omnia.

POLUPISTOS: When do I do this?

POLUPRAGMATICUS: The day and hour of Mercury, next following. The thieves will come to your home of their own accord.

POLUPISTOS: With the goods?

POLUPRAGMATICUS: With the goods. But see to this also. Neither you nor any of your household servants, for three hours before and within a nine hundred foot square, should make water, go to stool, nor break wind. If this should happen, your work will be for nothing. You will have wasted your time.

POLUPISTOS: I will tend to all diligently.

ACTUS TERTIUS
Scena Prima
Aequiuocus. Antonius. 855

ANTONIUS: Deum immortalem, quantus ignis in me aestuat;
Venas totumque cor incendens flammis furentibus
Vt videar mihi pro verbis flammam emittere;
Non apud Aetnam ita furit Enceladus gigas,
Adeo Camaena mea coquit et formae decus. 860
Cuius tantus est splendor et lepos vt vix putem
Esse aut fuisse aliquam cum quâ conferri queat.
Quae de Helenâ et Cytherea poetae ferunt
Vana sunt, prae hac sordent; vna omnibus
Praecellit, aureum pomum quae ferret dignissima. 865
AEQUIUOCUS: Ascultabo hic quid secum mussitet Antonius.
ANTONIUS: Quid hic referam nigricantes oculos,
Lacteam ceruicem, aut auream caesariem,
Turgentes mammas; deos deasque omnes reor
Naturamque posuisse in hâc quod pulchrum fuit. 870
Nam non vt reliquae videntur mulieres aulicae,
Quae fucatae cerussâ, purpurissâ aut stibio,
Se cingunt, poliunt, curaturâ reddunt amabiles,
Soli vestae debentes aut arti quod pulchrum habent.
At in hâc genuinae formae gratia et verus color, 875
Simplex, sincera, clara, diuina, elegans—
Tam suauitèr arridet, bellè canit, concinnè tripudiat
Vt spectatores ferè omnes adigat ad insaniam.
Me quod attinet ita mulieres omnes deleuit ex animo
Vt quo me vertam nesciam; ita iactor, crucior miser. 880

ACT III
Scene one
Aequivocus. Antonius.

ANTONIUS: O immortal god, such a fire burns in me; my veins and heart so
completely rage with furious flames that I seem to myself to emit flames
for words. My Camaena and the beauty of her body seeth even more
than the raging giant Enceladus at Etna.[1] So great is her beauty and
charm that I scarcely think there is or has been anyone who can compare
with her. What the poets tell of Helen or Venus are but empty things;
they seem paltry before her; she alone surpasses all, most worthy of the
golden apple.

AEQUIVOCUS <aside>: I will listen here to what Antonius mutters to himself.

ANTONIUS: How shall I tell of her dark eyes, her milky-white neck, or golden
hair and swelling breasts. I believe that all the gods and goddesses and
nature have given to her what was beautiful. She is not as other women
seem, those women of court who are painted with white powder, rouge,
or eye shadow and who fortify, polish, and render themselves lovable by
design, owing what beauty they have only to clothing or to art. But in her
there is the grace of genuine beauty, of true color, simple, sincere, clear,
divine, and elegant. She laughs so sweetly, sings so beautifully, dances so
pleasingly that she drives to madness almost everyone who sees her. As
for me, she has so driven from my mind all other women that I know not
where to turn. Thus I am tormented and tortured, wretch that I am.[2]

---

[1] Cooper: *Enceladus*: "A gygaunt, the sonne of Terra, which was stryken with the
lightening of Jupiter, and buried under the hill Aetna."

[2] Antonius's complaint is again a medley of commonplace expressions from the
classical lyric and comic poets. See, for example, Plautus, *Cist.* 206–10: "iactor, crucior,
agitor, / stimulor, uorsor / in amori' rota, miser exanimor, / feror, differor, distrahor,
diripior, / ita nubilam mentem animi habeo." [I am tormented, tortured, tossed about,
aroused, turned upon love's wheel, wretch that I am, I am out of my mind, I am driven

AEQUIUOCUS: Quo me vertam? Quid faciam? Caudex, stipes, asinus—
    Et dignus qui iactere et cruciere et sis miser.
ANTONIUS: Quid interim suades?
AEQUIUOCUS: Quid uis?
ANTONIUS: Vt amicâ fruar.
    Hoc precor effice, et emancipatum do me tibi.
AEQUIUOCUS: Mitte suspiria, et stolidas hasce querimonias.   885
    Ad custodem vetulam rectâ te proripias;
    Huic aurum des; muneribus agendum, non suspiriis.
    Hanc si feceris tuam, facilem inuenies aditum.
ANTONIUS: Benè mones. Sed quî cum puellâ me geram?
AEQUIUOCUS: Mitte pathicas querelas, meum cor, meae delitiae.   890
    Iacta te filium et haeredem patris vnicum
    Iuratoque te ducturum, si secus frui non poteris.
ANTONIUS: Quid egone iurem hoc?
AEQUIUOCUS: Securè et liberè.
    Sed heus, linguâ iures oportet, non autem animo.
    Iuro te ducturum me. Id est, in altero saeculo.   895
    Numquamne audiuisti me sic iurantem aut tutorem tuum?
    Fac imitere, simulacque armillas dabis
    Aut monile, aut quod fatuae virgines volunt.
ANTONIUS: Armillas inquis et monile, sed vnde pecunias?
    Illud est quod me nunc torquet maximè;   900
    Quid comminiscar, aut quam tendam fabricam
    Vt pecunias emungam? Hoc doce.
AEQUIUOCUS: Opportunè memoras.
    Scribe literas ad matrem tuam quam ocyssimè.
    Dic te aegrotum febricitasse per menses aliquot,
    Febremque tuto iures, sed amoris reserues tibi;   905
    Apud pharmacopolas et medicos insumpsisse pecuniam.
    Haec citò fieri cures. Alio me auocant negotia.
                          [*Exit*]
ANTONIUS: Ago tibi gratias, scribamque ad matrem illicò.
    Quae credula quum sit, et supra modum misericors
    Plorabit statìm, et o mî Antonî puer,   910
    Mî filî Antonî, suauis puer, neque dormiet, scio,
    Ingemiscens ad haec, dum miserit pecuniam.

AEQUIVOCUS: "Where shall I turn? What shall I do?" Blockhead, fool, ass. You deserve to be tormented and tortured. You should be wretched.

ANTONIUS: What then do you suggest?

AEQUIVOCUS: What do you want?

ANTONIUS: To enjoy my mistress. I pray you, bring this about and I give myself, surrendered, to you.

AEQUIVOCUS: Stop the sighing and those snivelling complaints. Right away you should go to the old woman who guards her. You should give money to her. These matters are accomplished with presents, not with sighs. If you win over the guardian, you will find the entrance easy.[3]

ANTONIUS: Good advice. But how should I act with the girl?

AEQUIVOCUS: Forget the pathetic complaints, "my heart," "my delight." Just mention that you are your father's only son and heir. If nothing else works, swear that you will marry her.

ANTONIUS: How should I swear this?

AEQUIVOCUS: Securely and freely. But listen, you should swear with your tongue, not with your mind. "I swear I will marry you." That is, in some other lifetime. Have you never heard me or your tutor swearing in this way? Do the same and at the same time give her bracelets or a necklace or whatever things foolish girls want.

ANTONIUS: You mention bracelets and a necklace, but where do I get the money? That is what really tortures me now. What should I invent, what story should I tell to come up with some money? Teach me this.

AEQUIVOCUS: It's appropriate that you mention it. As quickly as you can, write a letter to your mother. Say that you have been burning with fever for some months. You can safely swear to the fever, but keep the "of love" to yourself. Say that your money has been spent for medicine and physicians. Take care that you do this quickly. Business calls me elsewhere.

[Exit Aequivocus]

ANTONIUS: I thank you and I will write to my mother immediately. Since she is trusting and very kindhearted, right away she will cry, "O, my little boy, Antonius, my son, Antonius, sweet boy." And I know she won't sleep for worrying about this until she sends me the money.

---

on, scattered about, pulled asunder, torn apart, I have so beclouded a mind.] Burton quotes this passage from Plautus in *AM* pt. 3, sec. 2, mem. 3 (143), "Symptons or Signs of Love-Melancholy."

[3] Terence, *Heaut.* 300–301: "nam disciplinast eis demunerarier / ancillas primum ad dominas qui adfectant viam" [It is a rule for men who are trying to reach a mistress to first reward the maid.]

Scena Secunda
Pantomagus et patientes.

RUSTICUS: Haec est ni fallor Pantomagi domus.   915
HOSPES: Et haec hora pomeridiana tertia.
RUSTICUS: Paulisper expectabimus.
HOSPES: Eccum venit.
PANTOMAGUS: Qui primus venit fit prior; cuius hoc lotium?
RUSTICUS: Aegroti.
PANTOMAGUS: Sed cuius aetatis, sexus, quod nomen habet?
RUSTICUS: Annon patet ex vrinâ?
PANTOMAGUS: Nihil minùs.   920
RUSTICUS: Vxoris est.
PANTOMAGUS: Vbi dolet?
RUSTICUS: Lecto.
PANTOMAGUS: Non intelligis?
    In miseriacis hic dolor, saeuit calor hypocondriis,
    Et in regione conuulsus Epigastricâ.
RUSTICUS: Non capio.
PANTOMAGUS: Per partes vmbelicales tumor,
    Ingens etiam diaphaeresis apud Haemorroides.   925
RUSTICUS: Committo rem totam et salutem suam fidei tuae.
    Ego planè rudis. Quod videtur consules.
PANTOMAGUS: [Scribit]
    Hunc habe Receptum, adi Pharmacopeum meum.
    Habitat in viâ Iacobeâ ad signum bouis.
              [Succedit alius.]
    Ostendit haec vrina cruciatum Artheriticum   930
    Affectu quodam Ischiadico, sed vbi dolet?
HOSPES: Afficior aliquandò mirâ quadam vertigine,
    Pedes labuntur, impingo in parietes caput.
PANTOMAGUS: Tu plus aequo potas, et ille est morbus tuus.
    Ieiunandum est tibi per tres dies continuos.   935

Scene two
Pantomagus and patients.

RUSTIC: Unless I'm mistaken, this is Pantomagus' house.

THE FRIEND: And this the third hour.

RUSTIC: We'll wait for a little while.

THE FRIEND: Look, he's coming.

PANTOMAGUS: First come, first served. Whose urine is this?

RUSTIC: A sick person's.

PANTOMAGUS: But of what age, sex, what's his name?

RUSTIC: Can't you tell from the urine?[1]

PANTOMAGUS: Not at all.

RUSTIC: It's my wife's.

PANTOMAGUS: Where is she sick?

RUSTIC: In bed.

PANTOMAGUS: Don't you understand? There is this pain in the meseraic, the heat of hypocondriasis rages, and there are convulsions in the epigastric region.[2]

RUSTIC: I don't get it.

PANTOMAGUS: There is a swelling through the umbilical region, even great diaphoresis at the hemorrhoids.

RUSTIC: I leave this whole thing and my wife's health up to you. It's clear that I don't know anything. You do what you think is best.

PANTOMAGUS [*He writes*]: Take this prescription to my apothecary. He lives on the Jacobean Way near the sign of the ox.

[*Another patient approaches.*]

This urine shows a painful arthriticum affected by a certain sciatica, but where does it hurt?

THE FRIEND: Sometimes I'm afflicted with a certain strange dizziness; I stagger and bump my head on walls.

PANTOMAGUS: You drink too much. That's your problem. You must abstain for three consecutive days.

---

[1] JS: "Burton is here satirizing the water-prophets of his time, who claimed the ability to diagnose all ailments from looking at the urine. An interesting volume, published at London in 1637, by Dr. Thomas Brian, bears this title: *The Pisse-Prophet, or, Certain pisse-pot lectures. Wherein are newly discovered the old fallacies, deceit, and jugling of the Pisse-pot Science, &c.*"

[2] See *AM* pt. 1, sec. 2, mem. 5, subs. 2 (377) on hypochondriacal melancholy: "Most agree that a hot liver is in fault. 'The liver is the shop of humours, and especially causeth melancholy by his hot and dry distemperature. The stomach and meseraic veins do often concur, by reason of their obstructions, and thence their heat cannot be avoided, and many times the matter is so adust and inflamed in those parts, that it degenerates into hypochondriacal melancholy,' Guianerius, *cap. 2, tract. 15*, holds the meseraic veins to be a sufficient cause alone. The spleen concurs to this malady, by all their consents, and suppression of hemrods."

HOSPES: Illud non placet.

PANTOMAGUS: Nec potandum.

HOSPES: Illud minùs.

PANTOMAGUS: Dic decem credos, quinque paternosters, tres Auemarias
  Quolibet die ter. Deîn hoc suspende ad collum tuum.

HOSPES: Fiet.

PANTOMAGUS: Cuius hoc lotium?

                    [*Succedit alter.*]

OPPIDANUS: Meum.

PANTOMAGUS: Quid cruciat?

OPPIDANUS: Vxor, vxor, annon potes mederi vxori malae?   940

PANTOMAGUS: Non insanit?

OPPIDANUS: Et me ferè adigit ad insaniam.
  Vt neque dies neque noctes pacatus agere valeam.
  Sed et totam strepitu suo impedit viciniam.
  Clamores eius sunt supra Galli cantum aut horologium.

PANTOMAGUS: Quomodo afficitur?

OPPIDANUS: Rixatur, clamat, dentitonat,   945
  Hinnifremit, titionatur, iaculatur pelues et patinas,
  Candelabratur, me et ancillas delumbat fustibus.

PANTOMAGUS: Mira narras.

OPPIDANUS: Si quid potes, quaeso, fer opem.

PANTOMAGUS: Illine lumbos suos bis vel ter quercino baculo.
  Remedium ad hoc non habetur excellentius.   950

                    [*Succedit quartus generosus.*]

  Cuius haec?

GENEROSUS: Mea.

THE FRIEND: That would not be pleasing.

PANTOMAGUS: You must not drink.

THE FRIEND: That would be less pleasing.

PANTOMAGUS: Say ten Credos, five Paternosters, three Ave Marias three times on whatever day pleases you. Then hang this from your neck.

THE FRIEND: That I'll do.

PANTOMAGUS: Whose urine is this?

[*Someone else comes forward.*]

TOWNSMAN: Mine.

PANTOMAGUS: What is troubling you?

TOWNSMAN: My wife, my wife. Can you cure my unfortunate wife?

PANTOMAGUS: Is she mad?

TOWNSMAN: And nearly driving me mad. I have no peace night or day. She even upsets the entire neighborhood with her noise. Her shouts are louder than a rooster's crow or a clock.

PANTOMAGUS: In what way is she afflicted?

TOWNSMAN: She quarrels, shouts, grinds her teeth, neighs like a horse, smoulders like a firebrand, throws pots and pans, glows like a candlestick and lames me and the serving girls with her walking stick.[3]

PANTOMAGUS: Strange things you tell.

TOWNSMAN: If you can do anything, I beg you for help.

PANTOMAGUS: An oaken cudgel to her loins two or three times a day. There is no better remedy.

[*A fourth gentleman comes forward.*]

Whose is this?

GENTLEMAN: Mine.

---

[3] Pontano, *Ant.* 57: "Memor es, hospes, beluae illius quam dux Poenorum Hannibal vidit in somnis, silvas, agros, villas, oppida quaque incederet cuncta vastantem? Haec illa est belua, nequaquam tamen ut illa somnium, sed historia et vera quidem belua. Cives quidem coeteri aut horologium aut galli cantum secuti e somno cubilibusque excitantur, at viciniam nostram Euphorbiae clamores ne videre quidem somnum noctibus patiuntur, quasi dies agere quietos valeamus. Clamat, inclamat, frendit, dentitonat, hinnifremit, rixatur, furit; veru, pelves, patinas iaculatur, titionatur, candelabratur: novis enim vocibus novus beluae huius furor exprimendus est, atque utinam exprimi plane posset! ancillas alias delumbat fustibus, alias mutilat gladio, has unguibus excaecat, illas pugnis exossat." [Friend, do you remember that monster whom Hannibal, the leader of the Carthaginians, saw in his sleep, the one that destroyed every forest, field, village, town it approached? This woman is that monster, and by no means one of dreams but of fact and indeed a true monster. Other people in our town awake to the sound of a clock or rooster's crow. But the shouts of Euphorbia do not allow our neighborhood sleep even at night, as if we have the strength to spend a quiet day. She shouts, screams, gnashes her teeth, grinds her teeth, neighs like a horse, quarrels, rages. She throws the roasting spit, pots, pans. She smoulders like a firebrand, glows like a candlestick—the new furor of this monster must be expressed in new words, but would that she were able to be expressed. She lames some serving girls with her walking stick, others she maims with a knife; she puts out the eyes of some with her nails, she breaks the bones of others with her fists.]

PANTOMAGUS: Quomodo tecum se res habet?

GENEROSUS: Oculi, aures, stomachus malè se habent
    Si placet; et sum supra modum melancholicus.

PANTOMAGUS: Si consultum vis oculis, advocatum posthac ne videris,
    Auribus autem, si domi mulierem non habueris.   955
    Ad stomachum: caue ne deuores ferrum aut chalibem
    Fragmenta ollarum, lapides aut paleas.
    Nam praeterquam quod durae concoctionis sunt, stomacho nocent.
    Ad melancholiam: si ad diem vis esse hilaris vinum bibe,
    Si ad mensem porcum occide, si ad annum, vxorem ducito.   960
    Cuius hoc lotium?

[Succedit Ancilla.]

ANCILLA: Herae.

PANTOMAGUS: Vbi aut quid dolet?

ANCILLA: Cruciatur prolis procreandae desiderio.

PANTOMAGUS: Cruciaturne prolis procreandae desiderio?
    In hoc morbo vulgaris medicina parum valet.
    Sunt hic multi studentes, multi Academici,   965
    Inter quos proculdubiò reperiatur aliquis
    Eius naturae concors, a quo forsan concipiat.

ANCILLA: Hos dudum fratres monachosque expertae fuimus.

PANTOMAGUS: At hoc variis modis et saepè tentandum fuit.

ANCILLA: Veremur ne sola multitudo nobis nocuerit.   970

PANTOMAGUS: Itane? Salutem dices herae tuae meo nomine,
    Eamque me visurum fortasse die crastino,
    Laturumque Diasatirion quod sit in rem suam.

ANCILLA: Gratus aderis.

PANTOMAGUS: Herusne domi?

ANCILLA: Non.

PANTOMAGUS: Bene est.

[Exit Ancilla]

    Vos autem curate vos, et si quid malè fuerit   975
    Hic me consulite, aut vestram accersite me domum.

[Exeunt]

    Valete. Sic damnum aliorum est lucrum mihi
    Et fama mea ex Idiotarum infortuniis;
    Sic efflorescam faxit Aesculapius.

PANTOMAGUS: So how are things with you?

GENTLEMAN: My eyes, ears, and stomach are pretty bad, thank you, and I am more melancholy than I should be.

PANTOMAGUS: If you want advice about your eyes, hereafter do not see a counsellor. About the ears: if there is a woman at home, there should not be. As to the stomach: take care not to eat iron or steel fragments of jars, stones or straw for they are hard to digest and harm the stomach.[4] As for the melancholy, if you wish to be merry for a day, drink wine; if for a month, kill a pig; if for a year, take a wife. Whose urine is this?

[*A maid servant comes forward.*]

MAID: My mistress's.

PANTOMAGUS: Where or why does she hurt?

MAID: She is tortured by her desire for pregnancy.

PANTOMAGUS: She is tortured by her desire for pregnancy? For this affliction of the common people there is little need for medicine. There are many students, many academics here. No doubt among those someone of agreeable nature may be found, someone by whom she could perhaps conceive.

MAID: Not too long ago we tried both friars and monks.

PANTOMAGUS: But you ought to have tried in many ways and at many times.

MAID: We are worried that the sheer number may be harmful.

PANTOMAGUS: Is that so? Give my best to your mistress and say that I will visit her, perhaps tomorrow, bringing an aphrodisiac which may prove useful in her affairs.

MAID: You will be welcome.

PANTOMAGUS: Is the master at home?

MAID: No.

PANTOMAGUS: Good.

[*Exit the maid.*]

All of you, take care of yourselves, and if anything becomes troublesome, consult me here or call me to your home.

[*They leave.*]

Goodbye. And so the loss of others becomes gain to me and my fame comes from the misfortune of simple folks. Aesculapius,[5] bring it to pass that thus I may flourish.

---

[4] Pontano, *Ant.* 93: "Capuam ingressus obvium habui qui, quod physicum profiteri me crederet, consuluit quid oculis maxime conferre ducerem. Respondi: 'Si causidicum advocatumque nunquam videres.'—'Quid auribus?'—'Si nullam domi mulierem habueris.'—'Quid stomacho?'—'Si nunquam in mensa cum sacerdote cardinale accumbueris.'" [Traveling to Capua I met a man who, because he believed I had said I was a physician, asked what I would consider especially useful for the eyes. I responded, "If you never see an advocate or a counsellor." "For the ears?" "If you have no woman at home." "For the stomach?" "If you never dine with a Cardinal."]

[5] Cooper: *Aesculapius*: "The sonne of Apollo and Coronis and was called the god of Phisicke, and honoured in the fourme of a serpent."

ANTONIUS: Nisi me fallit animus bonum refert nuncium.
   Nam aedipol venit hilarior, mouet ocyùs,
   Et me quamprimum vidit exiliuit animo.
   Quae noua?
STAPHILA: Ita me deus amet optima.   985
ANTONIUS: Non sum apud me, cedo quî succedit negotium?
STAPHILA: Quin tu cesses vestem meam trahere.
   Trita est et lacerabitur cito.
ANTONIUS: Dic sedulò
   Vt se res habet; caue ne fingas aliquid.
STAPHILA: Non per Iouem, sed tu stes tamen proprius   990
   Ne quis ascultans nos interìm audiat.
ANTONIUS: Narra iam. Proh quam faetantem habet haec anus halitum!
STAPHILA: Quo abis?
ANTONIUS: Asculto.
STAPHILA: Dico te perditè amare eam
   Et alloqui velle.
ANTONIUS: Quid illa?
STAPHILA: Rubet faciem
   Subrisitque sibi ad nomen tuum.
ANTONIUS: Coniectura optima.   995
   Non recusauit munus?
STAPHILA: Non.
ANTONIUS: Et id non malum.
STAPHILA: Dico te tandem emoriturum idque subitò,
   Nisi potiaris saltem precio vel precario.
ANTONIUS: Hem. Quid tum ipsa?
STAPHILA: Erubuit iterùm,
   Sed ne time, totus sermo placuit.   1000
ANTONIUS: Vno verbo expedi.
STAPHILA: Attende. Decreuimus
   Iturum te cras ad aedes.
ANTONIUS: Subaudi tuas.
STAPHILA: Ita.
ANTONIUS: Illudis.
STAPHILA: Crede si lubet.
ANTONIUS: Ad horam quotam?
STAPHILA: Ad horam antemeridianam vndecimam.
   Sed quod signum amoris remittes, quod symbolum?   1005
ANTONIUS: Post salutem dabis hanc catenulam—
   Et sudarium hoc auro intertextum meo nomine.

Scene three
Antonius. Staphila.

ANTONIUS: Unless my mind deceives me, she is bringing good news. By heaven, as she comes she is more cheerful, she moves more quickly, and her spirit leaps up now that she has seen me. What's the news?

STAPHILA: The best, god love me.

ANTONIUS: I'm beside myself. Tell me. How did it go?

STAPHILA: Stop pulling at my dress. It's worn and will tear soon.

ANTONIUS: Tell me right away how things stand. Don't make up anything.

STAPHILA: Good heavens, I wouldn't do that, but you should stand nearer just in case someone listening should hear us.

ANTONIUS: Now tell me. <Aside> Dear god, what a foul breath this old woman has!

STAPHILA: Where are you going?

ANTONIUS: I'm listening.

STAPHILA: I said that you were dying for love of her and wanted to speak to her.

ANTONIUS: What did she say?

STAPHILA: She blushed and smiled to herself at the mention of your name.

ANTONIUS: A very good sign. She did not refuse the gift?

STAPHILA: No.

ANTONIUS: That's not bad either.

STAPHILA: At length I said that you would die immediately if you could not win her, at least by gifts or prayers.

ANTONIUS: Indeed. Then what did she do?

STAPHILA: She blushed again, but don't worry. The entire conversation went well.

ANTONIUS: In a word, explain.

STAPHILA: Pay attention. We have decided that you should go to the house tomorrow.

ANTONIUS: Am I to understand, to your house?

STAPHILA: That's right.

ANTONIUS: You're joking.

STAPHILA: Believe it if you like.

ANTONIUS: At what time.

STAPHILA: At eleven in the morning. But what sign of love will you bring, what token?

ANTONIUS: As a greeting you will give her this necklace—and handkerchief embroidered with my name in gold.

STAPHILA: Not nearly enough. Send your money purse. And I will wrench this ring from you whether you like it or not.

ANTONIUS: It's a gift from my mother. But take it.

STAPHILA: Now what are you giving me?

STAPHILA: Nimis exile munus, mittes crumenam tuam.
   Volenti nolenti extorquebo hunc annulum.
ANTONIUS: Matris donum. Sed habe.
STAPHILA: At quid das mihi?   1010
ANTONIUS: Iterumne tibi? Habe.
STAPHILA: Do tibi gratias.
   Sed Antonî virum te praebe. Bellum erit arduum.
ANTONIUS: Missa istaec fac. Ad horam praescriptam adero.

Scena Quarta
Polupistos. Dromo.   1015

POLUPISTOS: Vt dii illum perduant sceleratum hominem
   Qui primùm nobis hanc cudit Magiam,
   Zoroastem, Artesium, aut quemlibet alium.
   Vnquamne quisquam ita ludificatus fuit?
   Cape hoc unguentum, fures vltro domum venient.   1020
DROMO: Here praedixîn ego hoc antea?
POLUPISTOS: O credulam stultitiam seramque paenitentiam.
DROMO: Et modò nil praeter admirandam peritiam.
POLUPISTOS: Herumne illudis? Scelus? Abi in malam crucem.
               [*Exit Dromo*]
   Quasi solstitialis herba paulispèr fui.   1025
   Repentè exortus sum, repentè occidi.
   Sed quid agam, quam rationem, quam inibo viam?
   Nobilis a naturâ, laborare nequeo.
   Aut suffurandum, aut emendicandum est mihi.
   Furem certa manet crux, mendicum infamia.   1030
   Quibus querar? Amicis? Habebunt ludibrio.
   Popularibus? Illudent. Ignotis? Nihil dabunt.
   Dicamne me miserum? Dedignor, abominor.
   Mille supersunt modi, et mille sequar.
   Restat adhuc domi supellex, praediolum;   1035
   Hoc ego vendam. Est Osunae medicus
   Qui pro certo lapidem habet philosophicum.
   Hunc conducam, et huius vnius operâ
   Quicquid habeo domi, tripodes, trigas—
   Aes, cuprum, stannum, ferrum, plumbum, chalibem,   1040
   Et supellectilem omnigenum circa aedes meas
   Transmutabo in aurum; boues etiam et oues,
   Vehiculares equos pullos et asinos,
   Vnà cum Ephippiis, plaustris, curribus.
   Vertam in aurum, et sic fauente Mercurio   1045
   Fortunam et opes recuperabo pristinas.

ANTONIUS: More for you? Take this.

STAPHILA: Thank you. But, Antonius, prove yourself a man. It will be a harsh battle.

ANTONIUS: Never mind about that. I'll be there at the appointed hour.

Scene four
Polupistos. Dromo.

POLUPISTOS: May the gods destroy that accursed man, Zoroaster, Artesius,[1] or whoever it was who first hammered out this magic. Has anyone ever been made such a fool? "Take this ointment; the thieves will come to your home of their own accord."

DROMO: Didn't I warn you, Master?

POLUPISTOS: O credulous stupidity and late-learned penitence!

DROMO: And just a little while ago, nothing but "admirable skill."

POLUPISTOS: Are you mocking your master? Scoundrel? Go to hell.[2]

[Exit Dromo.]

For a little while, I was like a summer plant. Suddenly I sprang up, unexpectedly I died.[3] But what am I to do, what reason, what way will I find? A nobleman by nature, I am unable to work. Either I must steal or I must beg. A sure gallows awaits a thief, disgrace a beggar. To whom can I complain? To friends? They'll have a good laugh. To my countrymen? They'll mock me. To strangers? They won't help. Shall I call myself wretched? I disdain, I detest that. A thousand means remain, and I will pursue a thousand. I still have the household furnishings, a small estate. I'll sell this. There is in Osuna a physician who undoubtedly has a philosopher's stone. I'll see him, and by his help alone, whatever I have at home, three-legged pots, three-horse carts—brass, copper, tin, pewter, iron, lead, and all the other stuff around my house I will change into gold. Even the cows and sheep, the carriage horses, colts and asses, along with saddles, tumbrels, and carts I will turn into gold. And so, with Mercury favoring me, I will regain my former fortune and wealth.

---

[1] Cooper: *Zoroaster* or *Zorastes*: "A kynge of the Bactrians in the tyme of Ninus, and was before the warre of Troy .400. yeres. He first, as Plinie writeth, inuented magicall artes, and was in many other things excellently well learned, whereof he lefte bookes written behynde him." Artesius was a hermetic writer of the twelfth century. (D-JS) Burton mentions him only once in the *Anatomy of Melancholy* (pt. 2, sec. 1, mem. 1), in the section "Unlawful Cures rejected."

[2] A frequent expression in Roman comedy. See, for example, Terence, *And.* 317; Plautus, *Cas.* 977; *Poen.* 271; *Ps.* 335, 8461.

[3] Plautus, *Ps.* 38–39: "Quasi solstitialis herba paulisper fui: / repente exortus sum, repentino occidi." [For a little while I was like a summer plant: suddenly I sprang up, unexpectedly I died.]

Scena Quinta
Pedanus. Philobiblos. Theanus.

PEDANUS: Salue, vir Academice.

PHILOBIBLOS: Salue, vir humanissimè.

PEDANUS: Salutis tuae causâ ambulare te puto.   1050

PHILOBIBLOS: Rern tenes.

PEDANUS: Et tu beatus qui tali frueris otio
    Et tam faelici Academicorum consortio—
    Ad institutionem docta familiaritas multùm valet.

PHILOBIBLOS: Sed vnde tu?

PEDANUS: Pueris edocendis rure operam eloco
    Vbi non vrbanam sed villaticam Palladem colunt.   1055
    Nactus nunc otium visendi matrem Academiam;
    Vt latine loquamur, me tibi occurrisse gaudeo.
    Nobis enim doctis vtilis ac iucunda est exertitatio.

PHILOBIBLOS: Nobis doctis. Profecto tu es asinus, sed bone vir
    Multum te laudo quod nec in viâ vis otio marcescere.   1060

PEDANUS: Honestè quidem domine loqueris, sed incongruè
    Et quamprimum corrigas moneo.

PHILOBIBLOS: Satìs pro imperio.

PEDANUS: Nam vide splendesco, liquesco, tabesco et verba huiusmodi
    Respuunt casum illum.

PHILOBIBLOS: Ciceronem authorem habeo.

PEDANUS: Mentiris, garris, caecutis, non intelligis.   1065

PHILOBIBLOS: Oportet peregrinum iniuriam pati, secùs.

PEDANUS: Quid malum? Nonne te pudet tam barbarè loqui?
    Vbi tu gentium legisti iniuriam pati? Quo libro?

Scene five
Pedanus. Philobiblos. Theanus.

PEDANUS: Hello, sir academic.

PHILOBIBLOS: Hello, most gentle man.

PEDANUS: It occurs to me that you are taking a walk for the sake of your health.

PHILOBIBLOS: That's right.

PEDANUS: And you are fortunate to enjoy such leisure and the happy consortium of fellow academics. Learned acquaintance profits much one's instruction.

PHILOBIBLOS: Where are you from?

PEDANUS: I hire out in the country to teach young boys, where they worship Pallas not of the city but of the town. Now I have found leisure to visit my Alma Mater. I'm glad to have run into you so we may speak in Latin, for it is a useful and pleasant exercise for us learned men.

PHILOBIBLOS: "Us learned men"? Surely you are an ass, but, my good man, I do praise you for not wanting to grow slack through idleness, even when on a stroll.

PEDANUS: Indeed, my lord, you speak honestly but unsuitably, and I suggest you correct that as soon as possible.

PHILOBIBLOS: Imperiously spoken.[1]

PEDANUS: For you see, "splendesco," "liquesco," "tabesco" and verbs of this sort reject that ending.[2]

PHILOBIBLOS: I follow Cicero as my author.

PEDANUS: You speak falsely, babble, you are almost blind, you don't understand.

PHILOBIBLOS: Even so, one should endure the mistakes of a foreigner.

PEDANUS: What in the devil's name? Aren't you ashamed to speak so barbarously? Where in the world have you read "iniuriam pati"? In what book?[3]

---

[1] Terence, *Phorm.* 196: "Sati' pro imperio" [Imperiously spoken.]

[2] Pontano, *Ant.* 87: While relating his adventures in search of a wise man, Suppatius says that in Florence he met a certain petty schoolmaster who took exception with him because "cum inter loquendum excidisset ut dicerem *'ocio illic marcescere homines,'* quod huiusmodi verba *'splendesco, tabesco, liquesco'* casum illum respuant." [during our conversation it slipped out that I said, 'Quickly men grow slack there.' The schoolmaster replied that *splendesco, tabesco, liquesco* and verbs of that sort rejected that ending.] Suppatius then quotes from Cicero and Vergil to demonstrate how misinformed the schoolmaster was.

[3] Pontano, *Ant.* 88. After leaving Florence, Suppatius traveled to Rome where he encountered a certain grammarian. When Suppatius mentions having previously endured the mistakes of the schoolmaster, the grammarian replies: " 'Quid malum? non te pudet senem loqui latine nescire? ubi tu gentium reperisti *iniuriam patior*?'—'Atqui, inquam, apud Ciceronem in Philippica tertia': *'aequo animo belli patitur iniuriam, dummodo repellat periculum servitutis',* et in Laelio: *'is in culpa sit qui faciat, non qui patiatur iniuriam.' "* ["What in the devil's name? Aren't you ashamed that you, a grown man, do not know how to speak Latin? Where in the world have you found 'iniuriam patior'?" I said, "In Cicero's Third

PHILOBIBLOS: Non contendo nec enim vltra vacat ob negotium.
PEDANUS: Quo vadis?
PHILOBIBLOS: Ad consulendum medicum.
PEDANUS: Comes ero.   1070
  Sed quâ de re?
PHILOBIBLOS: An ad distillationem frictio sit vtilis.
PEDANUS: Absurdè et stolidè, non est dicendum frictio sed fricatio
  Quia nomen primae coniugationis quod tum vel itum habet
  In supino praeter caeterorum legem et ordinem
  Desinit in atio, (attendis?) non itio vel ictio.   1075
PHILOBIBLOS: Mirus hic homo.
                    [*Intrat Theanus.*]
THEANUS: Quid an Pedanum meum video?
  Is ipse est. Pedane, auspicato aduenis; vt vales?
PHILOBIBLOS: Sic me seruauit Apollo.
                    [*Exit*]
THEANUS: Vnde venis, quid agis?
  Nouus mihi quispiam videris tam veste nitidus.
PEDANUS: Pancraticè, athleticè, basilicè, commodè,   1080
  Glisco, glisco, glisco.
THEANUS: Laetor ita me dii ament.
  Sed quid tibi nobiscum nunc negotii?
PEDANUS: Ad visitandos amicos, et coemendos libros
  Doctosque consulendos.
THEANUS: Sed quem nunc locum geris?
PEDANUS: Eundem quem ante, nisi quod sit paulò auctior.   1085
  Nam et ego paedagogus iam et capellanus simùl;
  Quouis Sabbato bis concionem habeo.

PHILOBIBLOS: I don't want to argue with you, nor is there time. I have other things to attend to.

PEDANUS: Where are you going?

PHILOBIBLOS: To consult the physician.

PEDANUS: I'll come with you. But why are you consulting the physician?

PHILOBIBLOS: To ask whether friction may be useful in distillation.

PEDANUS: Absurd and foolish. One ought to say not "frictio," but "fricatio" because a noun of the first conjugation which has "tum" or "itum" in the supine, contrary to the law and order of the others, ends in "atio," not "itio" or "ictio." Are you paying attention?[4]

PHILOBIBLOS <aside>: This is a strange man.

[*Enter Theanus.*]

THEANUS: What, do I see my Pedanus? It is he himself. Pedanus, you have come at a fortunate moment. How are you?

PHILOBIBLOS: Thus Apollo has saved me.[5]

[*Exit Philobiblos.*]

THEANUS: Where have you come from, how are you doing? You seem someone new to me, you are so elegantly dressed.

PEDANUS: Heartily, athletically, royally, pleasantly I grow, I grow, I grow.

THEANUS: I am pleased. May the gods so favor me. But why have you come here?

PEDANUS: To visit friends, to buy books, and to consult learned men.

THEANUS: But what position are you holding now?

PEDANUS: The same as before, only slightly increased for I am now both a pedagogue and a chaplain at the same time. On any Sunday, I give a sermon twice.

Phillip: 'One must endure the misfortune of war calmly so long as he repels the threat of slavery.' And in Laelius: 'He may be at fault who commits an injury, but not he who suffers an injury.' "]

[4] Pontano, *Ant.* 88–89. Suppatius, still discussing his adventures in Rome, says: "Adieram medicum, sciscitaturus an distillationi frictio esset utilis. Aderat forte grammaticus audacia tam importuna ... obiurgare me statim coeperit quod *fricatio* non *frictio* diceretur; nomina enim quae a primae coniugationis verbis deducerentur supinum habentibus in *itum* vel in *ctum* praeter coeterorum verborum legem exire in *atio*, non in *itio*, nec in *ctio*: itaque *fricatio* non *frictio* dicendum esse." [I was going to inquire whether friction would be useful in distillation. By chance a bold and very rude grammarian was nearby. Right away he began to rebuke me because "fricatio" not "frictio" is proper, for nouns derived from first conjugation verbs, having a supine in "itum" or in "ctum," contrary to the rules of other verbs, end in "atio," not in "itio" nor in "ctio." And so, one must say "fricatio," not "frictio."]

Burton's Pedanus adds another mistake. He speaks not of nouns derived from first conjugation verbs but of nouns of the first conjugation. Nouns, of course, are not conjugated.

[5] Bensly: "An appropriate quotation from Horace [*Sat.* 1.9.78] where Horace playfully ascribes to Apollo, the patron of poets, his escape from the bore who had attached himself to him, when strolling on the Via Sacra in Rome."

THEANUS: Mira loqueris?

PEDANUS: Et praelector praeterea sum proximo in oppidulo.

THEANUS: Ditesces illico. Sed iam non vltra curas grammaticam?

PEDANUS: Vel maximè. Et opportunè nunc in mentem venit.   1090
  Sunt ibi quaedam quae me valdè sollicitum tenent.

THEANUS: Quaenam ea?

PEDANUS: Opinor esse magicum in Grammaticâ.

THEANUS: Dii meliùs!

PEDANUS: Ita dico; haec sibi quid volunt:
  Arx, stridens, rostris, spinx, praester, torrida, seps, trix,
  Et alibi vim, rauim, tussim, sitim, maguderim, amussim?   1095
  Inspexi Catholicon, Mammatrectum, et vocabularios
  Et non inuenio; opinor esse exorcismum aliquem.

THEANUS: Longè erras, et ostendam tibi errorem tuum alibi.

PEDANUS: Pace tuâ liceat interrogare hoc vnicum:
  Quo pede prius Helena Troianum littus appulerît?   1100
  Et quot vini cados Aeneae Acestes dederit?

THEANUS: Do you speak of marvels?

PEDANUS: And moreover, I give lectures in the next little town.[6]

THEANUS: You will be rich before long. But are you no longer interested in grammar?

PEDANUS: More than ever, and opportunely it has just come to mind. There are certain things there which truly worry me.

THEANUS: What things?

PEDANUS: I think there is magic in grammar.

THEANUS: Dear gods!

PEDANUS: So say I. What do these words mean: arx, stridens, rostris, spinx, praester, torrida, seps, trix, and elsewhere vim, rauim, tussim, sitim, maguderim, amussim? I have looked in the Catholicon, Mammotrectus and the vocabularies and have not found them.[7] I think there has been an exorcism.

THEANUS: You are quite wrong, but I shall explain your mistake to you some other time.

PEDANUS: Please, may I be permitted to ask this one thing? With which foot did Helen first touch the shore of Troy?[8] How many jars of wine did Acestes give to Aeneas?[9]

---

[6] Cooper: *praelector*: A reader to others. Bensly: the position Pedanus acquired "is that of 'lecturer,' that is *preacher* in a parish who was independent of the incumbent & supported by the contributions of the parishioners. They were especially to be found in towns and were as a rule puritans in their ecclesiastical views, playing an important part in the political and religious stir of the first half of the 17th century."

[7] JS: "The *Mammotrectus super Bibliam* was a famous Biblical glossary in the fifteenth century, compiled by Joannes Marchesinus. In the *Colloquies* of Erasmus it is sometimes referred to as the Mammothreptus, and Erasmus speaks slightly of the book. The earliest printing I have noted is that by George Husner, at Strassburg, in 1473. The *Catholicon* was likewise a dictionary, done by Joannes Balbus de Janua, and issued by Gutenberg, at Mainz, in 1460. It was compiled in 1286. The Latin words, beginning with arx (tower), are either 'mixed i-stems,' or Greek derivatives, with which the pseudo-grammarian had some difficulty."

[8] Pontano, *Ch.* 34. Pontano's Pedanus tells Mercury that while talking to the shade of Vergil, he asked: "equidem et illud percuntari volui, dextrone an sinistro priore pede e navi descendens Aeneas terram Italiam attigisset; ad quod Poeta ipse respondit satis se compertum habere neutro priore pede terram attigisse, sed sublatum humeris a remige, cui nomen esset Naucis, atque in litore expositum iunctis simul pedibus in arenas insiliisee; idque ex ipso remige habere se cognitum." [And indeed I wanted to question him whether Aeneas on descending from his ship had first touched the Italian shore with his right or left foot. To that the poet himself responded that he knew with certainty that Aeneas had first touched the shore with neither foot, but was carried on the shoulders of a sailor whose name was Naucis and placed on the shore. He jumped to the sand on both feet at the same time. And Vergil learned this from the sailor himself.]

[9] Pontano, *Ch.* 33. Pontano's Pedanus also asked Vergil "quot vini cados decedenti e Sicilia Aeneae Acestes dedisset, errasse se respondisse; neque enim cados fuisse, sed amphoras; ea enim tempestate cadorum usum in Sicilia nullum fuisse; partitum autem amphoras septem in singulas triremes accessisseque aceti sextariolum, idque se compertum habere ex Oenosio, Aeneae vinario." [how many jars of Sicilian wine Acestes had

THEANUS: Ne quid vltra iam quaeres. Tu mihi caenam dabis;
    Quod reliquum est inter caenandum disceptabimus.

Scena Sexta
Antonius. Camaena.   1105

ANTONIUS: Haec est hora quam statuit anus, sed Camaenam video.
    Ascultabo hic quales sermones secum habeat.
CAMAENA: O quam ego misera, insana et stulta olim fui.
    Quae sic amorem, et tam saepè execrata indignissimè,
    Omnesque puellas tanquam non sanae mentis habui,   1110
    Quae saltèm amarent, Medeam, Scyllam, aut Mynois filiam.
    Agnosco errorem et iam cano Palinodiam;
    Maior vis est fateor aligeri dei
    Quam vt resisti possit ab imbelli mulierculâ.
    Experior iam sero misera. Antonii siquidem mei   1115
    Ita coquit venusta forma, et vultus elegans
    Adeoque vrit vt si non ipsius complexu fruar,
    Statutum sit vitam finire ferro aut laqueo.
    Quare te Iunonem, Venerem et Cupidinem precor,
    Vt vel nos Hymenis iungatis optatissimis   1120
    Aut me morti dedatis; non possum hanc flammam pati.
ANTONIUS: Non possum me continere quin salutem et alloquar.
    Salue, mea Charis, mea Venus, meae delitiae.
    Immortalem vitam agere inter mortales me facis.
CAMAENA: Euge Antonî, salue ab imo calce ad summum verticem.   1125
    Cur tam tristis? Quid palles? Doletne quidquam? Dic sodes.
ANTONIUS: Hei mihi.
CAMAENA: Per deos te oro, animule mî,
    Ne quid me celes obsecro.
ANTONIUS: Iura silentium.
    Daque fidem te nulli commissuram vsquam gentium.

THEANUS: Don't ask anything more now. Dine with me tonight and we will discuss the rest at dinner.

Scene six
Antonius. Camaena.

ANTONIUS: This is the hour the old woman set, but I see Camaena. I will listen here to what she says to herself.

CAMAENA: Oh, how sad, silly, and foolish I was once. So often and without cause I cursed love and all girls, or at least those girls who were in love, like Medea, Scylla, or the daughter of Minos.[1] I must have been out of my mind. I recognize my error and I sing my palinode.[2] I confess that there is a greater force to the winged god than can be resisted by a weak woman. Now at last, poor me, I am being put to the test. Indeed, the handsome body and elegant face of my Antonius torture and inflame me to such a degree that, if I could not enjoy his embrace, I would resolve to end my life by iron or rope. Therefore I pray to you, Juno, Venus, and Cupid, to either join us in happy marriage, or let me die. I am not able to endure this passion.

ANTONIUS: I can't contain myself, I must speak to her. Hello my darling, my Venus, my sweet. You make me a god living among mortals.[3]

CAMAENA: Wonderful Antonius, greetings from head to foot. Why are you so sad? Why are you pale? What is bothering you? Please tell me.

ANTONIUS: Woe is me.

CAMAENA: I beg you by the gods, my darling, not to hide anything from me.

ANTONIUS: Swear silence. Promise you will tell no one, ever, in the entire world.

---

given Aeneas. Vergil responded that he had made a mistake for it was not jars but amphorae. At that time, jars were not used in Sicily. But seven amphora were distributed to each ship along with a pint of vinegar. Vergil learned this from the vintner of Aeneas.]

[1] Cooper: *Medea*: "She intertained yᵉ aduentourous Jason commyng to Colchos to wyn the golden fleese, and beynge rauyshed with the loue of his goodly personage, taught hym howe to escape all those daungers, that of necessitie he must aduenture to wynne his purposed enterpryse. After all whiche thynges atchieued, she ranne awaye with Jason." See Ovid, *Met.* 7.1–424. Cooper: *Scylla*: "A lady, daughter of Nisus king of the Megarenses, whiche for loue of Minos, hir fathers ennemy, stale a purple hear from hir fathers head, whiche caused him to be vanquisshed. But she being forsaken of Minos, threwe hir selfe into the sea, & was transfourmed into a byrde of hir name." See Ovid, *Met.* 8.1–151. The daughter of Minos could be either Ariadne, "A lady the wyfe of Theseus whom he forsoke, not withstandinge she had saued his lyfe" (Cooper) or Phaedra, "The wyfe of Theseus, and stepmother to Hippolytus," (Cooper) who fell in love with her stepson.

[2] Erasmus, *Ad.* 1.9.59. Cooper: *palinodia*: "A contrary songe: a retractation: a recantation: a revokyng of that one hath spoken or written."

[3] Erasmus, *Ad.* 1.5.99: "deum esse; deum facere" [To make a god of someone.]

CAMAENA: Habe fidem. Angeronam me dices aut Harpocratem.   1130
ANTONIUS: Paucis dicam. Perdite tè amo. Semper mihi formosissima,
    At nunc supra modum visa es pulcherima,
    Et tua forma ita semper obuersatur mihi
    Vt si non expleam amorem, derepentè periam.
    Iube quiduis, posce quoduis, nummos, gemmas, opes.   1135
    Denegare nec possum nec volo. Hoc vnum supplex peto
    Vt mihi vitam dones, cum sit in manu tuâ.
    Aut mihi nunc acquiesce, aut hac sicâ me interfice.
CAMAENA: O indignum facinus et singularem impudentiam!
    Tu me audes sollicitare de stupro!   1140
    An me venalem putas meretriculam,
    Aut cum scorto publico te verba facere?
    Nec mei rationem habes, canis impudens.
    Ni fidem dedissem, proh quantas turbas darem.
ANTONIUS: Quaeso ne me male capias, serenissima.   1145
    Voueo, do fidem, iuro, sancteque polliceor
    Per Premam, Premundam, Hymeneum et reliquos
    Coniugales deos, me ducturum te in vxorem statim;
    Haeres sum, et patris idem filius vnicus.
    Ne repelle, Camaena. Regiam vitam ages.   1150
CAMAENA: Dii te perduânt cum hac procacitate tua.
ANTONIUS: Quo fugis? Audi verbum vnicum.
CAMAENA: Non audio.
                   [*Exit*]
ANTONIUS: Non possum non admirari mulierum versutiam
    Quae cum viris tam bellè dissimulare didicerint
    Ac si omnes eâdem edoctae essent in scholâ.   1155
    Scio Camaenam me perdite amare sed quam bellè tegit.
    Sic est ingenium muliebre, et his plerumque moribus,
    Vt quanto plus petant tanto opponant se fortiùs,
    Quo magis exoptent, eò reluctentur plus et negent.
    Nam cogi volunt nolentes, reluctantes petunt.   1160
    Sed ad eam me conferam intus vt reconciliem mihi.

CAMAENA: I promise. You will call me Angerona or Harpocrates.[4]

ANTONIUS: Let me say just a few things. I love you desperately. I always thought you were beautiful, but now to me you seem most lovely, and I esteem your loveliness such that if I could not satisfy this love, I would suddenly die. Order what you wish, demand what you will: money, gems, wealth. I cannot deny you, nor do I want to. This only as your servant I beg: give life to me, since it is in your hand. Now, either assent to me or kill me with this dagger.

CAMAENA: O unworthy crime and singular impudence! You dare solicit me. Either you consider me a prostitute for sale or you think you are talking to a common whore. You have no care for me, you impudent dog. If I had not given my word, by god what a disturbance I would make.

ANTONIUS: I beg you, my dearest, don't misunderstand me. I vow, I pledge my faith, I swear, I promise solemnly by Prema, Premunda, Hymen,[5] and the other conjugal gods that I will marry you at once. I am an heir, my father's only son. Don't reject me, Camaena. You will live a royal life.

CAMAENA: May the gods destroy you for your bold, shameless impudence.

ANTONIUS: Where are you going? Hear just one word.

CAMAENA: I'm not listening.

[Exit Camaena]

ANTONIUS: I can't help but admire the wiliness of women who know how to lie so beautifully to men. It is as if they had all been taught in the same school.[6] I know Camaena loves me desperately, but she hides it so well. So is the nature and especially the character of women that the more they want something, the more strongly they set themselves against it; the more they desire, the more they resist and deny it. I know that they want those who don't want them, they seek those who are reluctant.[7] But I'll go inside to her to reconcile myself.

---

[4] LS: *Angerona*, the goddess of suffering and silence. *Harpocrates*, Egyptian god of silence, represented with his finger on his mouth; according to others, a Greek philosopher who enjoined silence respecting the nature of the gods.

[5] *AM* pt. 3, sec. 4, mem. 1, subs. 3, (355): "For all intents, places, creatures, they assign gods: . . . Prema, Premunda, Hymen, Hymenaeus, for weddings; . . . " In *AM* pt. 2, sec. 1, mem. 3 (12) Burton mentions Prema and Premunda along with Priapus and "bawdy gods."

[6] Terence, *Hec.* 203: in eodemque omnes mihi videntur ludo doctae ad malitiam [It seems to me that all women have been taught mischief in the same school]. Erasmus, *Ad.* 2.8.50: "eodem in ludo docti" [taught in the same school.]

[7] A similar idea is expressed in Terence, *Eun.* 812-13: "Novi ingenium mulierum / Nolunt ubi velis, ubi nolis cupiunt ultro" [I know the character of women. They are unwilling when you are willing; when you are unwilling, they want all the more.]

Scena Septima
Polumathes. Simon Acutus.

SIMON ACUTUS: Quid est quod scire desideras?

POLUMATHES: Scire volo

Quid arbitreris de concentu Pithagorico.   1165

SIMON ACUTUS: Scire te vellem inprimìs concentum esse duplicem,
Actiuum et Passiuum, Vocalem et Rithimicum. Vocalis quae proce-
dit ab arteriis et diaphragmate. Rithimica quae fit ab aequilaterâ
vocum collisione, iuxta proportionem coriambicam continuam su-
perpartientem submultiplicem.   1170

POLUMATHES: Quorsum haec?

SIMON ACUTUS: Elucescet illico. Haec autem proportio fit vel secundum quantitatem vel qualitatem. Quantitatiuè, idque ad mensuran-
tis benè placitum, vt enim numerus numerans a numerante fluat
in numeratum, sic mensura a mensurante in rem mensuratam, per   1175
quandam sympathiam et Apotomen Harmonicam. Tu non olfacis
responsionem meam?

POLUMATHES: O caelum, o terras, o maria Neptuni, sapit hic?

SIMON ACUTUS: Vel secundum qualitatem et sic quoad Euphoniam vel
gratiam. Rursus in Euphonia sex occurrant consideranda: longitudo,   1180
breuitas, pondus, et leuitas, filorum tenuitas, et oris ingenuitas.

POLUMATHES: Fleat Heraclitus an rideat Democritus?

SIMON ACUTUS: Concludam determinando metaphisicalitèr
Et ad mentem philosophi.

POLUMATHES: Facesse in malam rem, asine.   1185

SIMON ACUTUS: Non intelligis fortasse?

POLUMATHES: Nimis altùm sapis?

Quid? Egone vt feram huiusmodi ineptias?
Nec patiar, nec feram, nec inultus sinam.
                    [*Exit*]

SIMON ACUTUS [*Canit solus*]:

Personatus ego,   Esse merum pecus,

Scene seven
Polumathes. Simon Acutus.

SIMON ACUTUS: What is it that you wish to know?

POLUMATHES: I want to know what you think about Pythagorean harmony.

SIMON ACUTUS: I want you to know in the first place that harmony is of two
   sorts: active and passive, vocal and rhythmic. Vocal comes from the
   arteries and diaphragm, rhythmic from the equilateral concussion of
   voices together with the choriambic continuous superparticular submul-
   tiple proportion.

POLUMATHES: What is this?

SIMON ACUTUS: It will become clear immediately. Moreover, this proportion
   becomes either quantitative or qualitative. Quantitatively, according to
   what is pleasing to the measurer, for as the number numbering by the
   numberer flows into the numbered, thus measure by the measurer flows
   into the thing measured, through a certain sympathy and harmonic
   apotomen.[1] Do you get a whiff of my response?

POLUMATHES: O sky, o lands, o sea of Neptune![2] This man is wise?

SIMON ACUTUS: Or there is quality, and this with respect to euphony or
   grace. Again, in euphony, six things occur which must be considered:
   length, brevity, weight and lightness, thinness of strings, and natural
   condition of the mouth.

POLUMATHES: Would Heraclitus weep or Democritus laugh?[3]

SIMON ACUTUS: I shall conclude by determining metaphysically and philo-
   sophically.

POLUMATHES: You should be hanged, you ass.

SIMON ACUTUS: Perhaps you don't understand.

POLUMATHES: Are your thoughts too lofty? What? That I should endure in-
   eptitude of this sort! I will not suffer it, I will not bear it, and I will not
   permit it to go unavenged.[4]

[Exit Polumathes]

SIMON ACUTUS [*sings alone*]:

I impersonate   So I clothe myself.

---

[1] JS: "In Pythagorean music, a semitone, expressed by the vibration ratio 2187/2048;
but in the mind of this philosopher it comes to mean nothing."

[2] Terence, *Ad.* 790: "O caelum, o terra, o maria Neptuni."

[3] JS: "In [*AM* Democritus (59)], Burton enlarges upon the Latin, 'Fleat Heraclitus, an rideat Democritus,' in this fashion: 'Would this, think you, have enforced our Democritus to
laughter, or rather made him turn his tune, alter his tone, and weep with Heraclitus?' "

[4] Bensly: Cicero, *In L. Catilinam Oratio* 1.5.10: "Nobiscum versari iam diutius non
potes; non feram, non patiar, non sinam." [Now you will remain with us no longer; I will
not endure it, I will not suffer it, I will not allow it.]

Sic meipsum tego,   Et qui credit secùs.   1190
Vosque meae vestes,   Fallitur hiho, hiho,
Este mihi testes,   Fallaturque semper, io.

You, my vesture,	Is merely a sheep.
Be my attestor.	He is deceived, hiho, hiho.
Who otherwise believes	May he always be, io.

ACTUS QUARTUS
Scena Prima
Pantomagus. Polupistos.   1195

PANTOMAGUS: Attendas, duae sunt rationes vertendi rerum speties.
    Altera breuis, sed quae plus habet periculi,
    Et hanc artifices curtationem vocant;
    Altera longa, sed quae longè tutissima,
    Et hanc longationis verbo exprimunt.   1200
POLUPISTOS: Dic bonâ fide, tune hanc longationem tenes?
PANTOMAGUS: Exactè et ad vnguem.
POLUPISTOS: Quibus expensis opus?
PANTOMAGUS: Mille coronatis.
POLUPISTOS: Non refert de pecuniis
    Modò fiat aliquando, et confidas arti tuae.
PANTOMAGUS: Confidam? Dubitas?
POLUPISTOS: Sed quibus interim opus?   1205
PANTOMAGUS: Habere primum debemus specus subterraneos,
    Furnellos rectos, apertos, clausos, patulos
    De vitris arboreis, et de Mercurio philosophico
    Ad exertitium maiores et minoris operis.
POLUPISTOS: Praegnans animus aurum parturit mihi.   1210
PANTOMAGUS: De rege Antimonii et luto sapientiae,
    Et ad artem pertinentes aquas duodecem.

ACT IV
Scene one
Pantomagus. Polupistos.

PANTOMAGUS: Pay attention. There are two methods for changing the species of things. One is brief but more risky, and so the masters call this curtation; the other method takes a long time, but it is safer by a long way, and this is called longation.

POLUPISTOS: Tell me, in good faith, do you understand this longation?

PANTOMAGUS: To the very letter.[1]

POLUPISTOS: How much will it cost?

PANTOMAGUS: A thousand crowns.

POLUPISTOS: The money doesn't matter, just as long as it is done and you have confidence in your art.

PANTOMAGUS: I have confidence. Do you have doubt?

POLUPISTOS: But meanwhile, what needs to be done?

PANTOMAGUS: First we need to have a subterranean cave, a proper stove, open, closed, broad, made of crystallized wood and philosopher's mercury for the practice of greater and lesser works.

POLUPISTOS: His pregnant mind gives birth to my gold.

PANTOMAGUS: From the king of Antimonium and clay of wisdom, for the art of the twelve waters.[2]

---

[1] JS: Erasmus, *Alc.* 425. In Erasmus' colloquy, Lalus relates the story of a gentleman named Balbinus, deceived by a certain unnamed alchemist. The alchemist tells Balbinus, "duplicem esse huius artis viam: alteram, quae dicitur longatio, alteram, quae dicitur curtatio. . . . altera quae breuior est, sed plusculum habet periculi; altera quae longior est, sed eadem tutior." [There are two paths for this art; one is called longation, the other is called curtation. . . . One way is shorter, but more risky; the other way is longer, but safer.] Balbinus later says to the alchemist, "dic mihi bona fide, longationem tenes exacte?" [Tell me in good faith, do you understand longation well?] The alchemist replies, "ad vnguem." [To the letter.]

[2] JS: "An Oxford manuscript of the thirteenth century bears the title, 'On the Twelve

POLUPISTOS: His paratis quaenam est auri confectio?
PANTOMAGUS: Scire debes quod fumus albus, citreus, rubeus,
    Leo viridis, Almagra, et mortis immunditia,   1215
    Limpidum, sanguis, educa, et terra faetida,
    Azar, Ozizambe, Azinabam, Dautin, Euticen,
    Almazidor, Vffi, Tuffi, Marchoni, Tincar, et laton
    Cum Borregor et Azon, sale et anatron;
    Iuxta praeceptum Caleb filii Ezegid Medoia,   1220
    Sunt ingredientes ex quibus fit aurum purissimum.
POLUPISTOS: Vt hoc verbum Auri exhilerat cor meum.
PANTOMAGUS: Iam tu iurabis per praesidem Mercurium,
    Ne cui vnquam secretum hoc dixeris.
POLUPISTOS: Mên times? Egone quid dixero? Iuro Iouem—   1225
PANTOMAGUS: Credo. Sed numera pecuniam.
POLUPISTOS: Quam?
PANTOMAGUS: Rogas?
    Ad fornacem philosophicum praeparandum benè,
    Ad mercandos carbones, ollas, vitra, patinas.
POLUPISTOS: Quantum vis?
PANTOMAGUS: Numera quadringentos aureos.

POLUPISTOS: Is there some confection of gold when these things have been prepared?

PANTOMAGUS: You ought to know about Fumus Albus, Citrinus and Rubeus, Leo Viridis, Almagra, and the impurity of Mors, about Limpidum, Sanguis, Educa and Terra Faetida,[3] Azar, Ozzizambe, Azinabam, Dautin, Euticen, Almazidor, Uffi, Tuffi, Marchoni, Tincar, and Laton along with Borregor and Azon, Salt and Anatron;[4] according to the precepts of Caleb, son of Ezegid Medoia,[5] these are the ingredients from which is made the purest possible gold.

POLUPISTOS: My heart leaps at the mention of the word gold.

PANTOMAGUS: Now you will swear by guardian Mercury that you will never tell this secret to anyone.

POLUPISTOS: You don't trust me? Why would I tell? I swear by Jove.

PANTOMAGUS: I believe you. But count out the money.

POLUPISTOS: For what?

PANTOMAGUS: You need ask? For preparing well the philosopher's furnace, for buying charcoal, jars, glasses, plates.[6]

POLUPISTOS: How much do you want?

PANTOMAGUS: Count out 400 gold pieces.

Waters of the Secret River,' and, like many another ancient work of alchemy, is attributed to Aristotle."

[3] Rulandus: *Fumus Albus* is "Mercury, the Soul and the Tincture, Heavenly Water, the Quintessence of Venus; this smoke conducts the colour of the gold by a dry process into the height." *Fumus Citrinus* "is Yellow Sulphur." *Fumus Rubeus* "is Orpiment. It is also called Gold because it is bright." *Leo Virdis* "is the Ore of Hermes, Glass, and Vitriol, also the Blood from Sulphur, the first Mercury of Gold, altered by means of the Lunar Body. It is also Green Water which dissolves the living lime. The green is that which is perfect upon the stone, and can easily be made into gold." *Almagra* "is a copper bolus, or laton. . . . A red soil or clay, used as a lubricant by wheelwrights. Also a lotion." *Mors* "is called Death or Corruption. The body dies when the soul departs. The colour goes, the spirit or water is extracted. When it returns to it, it awakes, becomes living, bright, henceforth immortal." *Sanguis*, blood "is Orpiment, that is, the Stone which is not yet perfect, the Philosophical Water which gives life and unities." *Educa* is unidentified. *Terra Faetida* is sulphur.

[4] JS: "*Almagra* = red earth; *Almazidor* = verdigris; *Tincar* = borax, *Laton* = brass; *Azon* is probably azoth, or mercury; *Anatron* = saltpeter; *Tuffi* = a porous stone, or, perhaps, *tutia* = zinc oxide. . . . According to *Dictionnaire Mytho-Hermetique* (Paris, 1758), *uffituffi* is the odor emanating from 'Sages' Mercury,' and *Azinibam* is the sediment of the Pure Matter of the Sages."

[5] Unidentified

[6] Erasmus, *Alc.* 246: "Vt rem in pauca conferam, conuenit inter eos, vt negocium adgrederentur clam. . . . vtrinque iurantum est de silentio, quod faciunt, qui mysteriis initiantur. Iam ilico numeratur pecunia, vnde artifex mercaretur ollas, vitra, carbones reliquaque quae ad instruendam officinam pertinent." [To make a long story short, they reach an agreement to undertake the business in secret [and] each swears an oath of silence, like those initiated into the mysteries. Then the money is counted out for the alchemist to buy pots, glasses, charcoal, and other things needed to furnish the workshop.]

POLUPISTOS: Habe quingentos.

PANTOMAGUS: Probè curabuntur omnia. 1230

[Exit Pantomagus]

POLUPISTOS: Dii immortales, homo homini quid interest!
    Quam verè prudens hic, quam cordatè loquitur.
    Me quod attinet, statìm ac hoc aurum habuero,
    Princeps ero, et aedes aedificabo magnificas;
    Immo totas ciuitates mihi cognomines 1235
    Cum suis Theatris, balneis, et peristiliis,
    Gerontotrophiis, pedotrophiis, et nosocomiis.
    Nec tam priuatis quam publicis operibus
    Illustre nomen erit et decus meum.
    Alpes complanabo, et siluam Hyrciniam, 1240
    Desiccabo deinde Paludem Moeotidem,
    Proiiciendo in eam montes Hyberboreos.
    Desertum Lop et Zin prata erunt vberima,
    Mons Atlas frugifer, et arena Libica
    Producet sumptu meo decuplum, centuplum. 1245
    Loquuntur Idiotae et vulgus hominum
    De Ponte Traiani, et stupendis operibus
    Romanorum, Theatris et Mausoleis tumulis,
    At haec si ad nostra conferantur opera,
    Nulla futura. De viuo saxo pontes condam duos, 1250
    In ornamentum Europae et stuporem Oceani.
    Primus erit a Caleto ad Dorobornium,
    Alter ad fretum et fauces Euxini maris,
    Vbi Xerxes olim traiecit exercitum.
    Faciamque piscinam de mari mediterraneo, 1255
    Cum infinitis aliis quae nunc in mentem non veniunt.
    Hoc solum addam, si cui vestrum praebibero
    Siue sit ex auro, argento, aut gemma poculum,
    Cyathum ebibens secum domum auferat.
    Atque haec fient a pecuniis, et auro nouo. 1260
    Regali fastu viuam luxuque splendido—
    Delicatè agens et ditescens supra omnem fidem.

Scena Secunda
Polupragmaticus. Simon Acutus.

POLUPRAGMATICUS: Ambitus terrae secundum Eratosthenem 1265
    Est quadraginta mille stadiorum et dimidii,
    Cum sesquiplâ, octauâ superpartiente sesquidecimâ.

POLUPISTOS: Take 500.

PANTOMAGUS: All will be properly cared for.

[*Exit Pantomagus*]

POLUPISTOS: Immortal gods, what a difference there is among men![7] How truly prudent this one is, how wisely he speaks. As for me, as soon as I have this gold, I will be a nobleman, and I will build magnificent buildings. Indeed, whole cities will be named for me, along with their theaters, baths, peristyles and nursing homes, orphanages, and hospitals. Not so much by private as by public works will my name and fame be great. I will level the Alps and the Hercynian Woods and dry the Maeotian Fen by casting the Hyperborean mountains into it.[8] The desert Lop and Zin will become fertile meadows, the Atlas mountain will bear fruit, the Libyan sands will produce at my expense ten times, a hundred times. The unlettered and common people speak of the Trajan bridge, the amazing works of the Romans, the theaters and the tomb of Mausolus, but if these are compared to my works, they will be nothing. I will build two bridges of living stone to the honor of Europe and bafflement of the ocean. The first will stretch from Calais to Dover, the other to the channel and entrance of the Black Sea where Xerxes once led his army. I will make the Mediterranean a fish pond and do countless other things, which now don't come to mind. But let me add this: if any of you should have a drink with me, you will take your drinking cup home with you, whether it be of gold, silver or studded with gems. These things will be done with money and with new gold. I will live in regal pride and splendid luxury, at ease and growing rich beyond belief.

Scene two
Polupragmaticus. Simon Acutus.

POLUPRAGMATICUS: The circumference of the earth, according to Eratosthenes, is 40,000 and a half stadia, times one and a half sesquidecimal eights.[1]

---

[7] Terence, *Eun.* 232: "homini homo quid praestat." *Phorm.* 790: "vir viro quid praestat." [What a difference there is among men.]

[8] JS: In [*AM* Democritus (97)], "Burton speaks of draining the 'Maeotian Fenns' and cutting down 'those vast Hercynian Woods.' " See also *AM* Democritus (99): "In every so built city, I will have public walks, theatres, and spacious fields allotted for all gymnics, sports, and honest recreations, hospitals for all kinds, for children, orphans, old folks, sick men, madmen, soldiers, pest-houses, etc."

[1] JS: "Eratosthenes: A mathematician and astronomer, born at Cyrene, 270 B.C. He taught that the circumference of the earth equalled 250,000 stadia." OED: *stadium*: "An ancient Greek and Roman measure of length, varying according to time and place, but most commonly equal to 600 Greek or Roman feet, or one-eighth of a Roman mile."

SIMON ACUTUS: Quis hic qui de caelis tam magnifice loquitur?
    Secum supputat. Attendam.
POLUPRAGMATICUS: Ascultat hic aliquis.
    Secundum Alfraganum lunae concaui semediameter   1270
    Semidemetientes triginta tres terrae continet
    Cum quadruplâ sesquialterâ, duplâ sesquitertiâ.
SIMON ACUTUS: Interpellabo. Salue, vir grandistrepe.
POLUPRAGMATICUS: Simon Acute, quid agis?
SIMON ACUTUS: Te rebar Tichonem illum celebrem
    Tam sublimina fulminabas.
POLUPRAGMATICUS: Ego te vulgarem Academicum.   1275
SIMON ACUTUS: Sed quorsum hic tam insanus habitus?
POLUPRAGMATICUS: Ne roges.
    Sed quae fama tua iam?
SIMON ACUTUS: Hoc ipsum a te volo.
    Quî fiam illustris, dynastis, heroibus, ipso duci
    Aequè ac tu notus familiaris et socius.
POLUPRAGMATICUS: O Simon, Simon rem petis arduam,   1280
    Magni laboris opus. Quia sic ardes, tamen
    Docebo te ad famam viam compendiosissimam.
    Disputandum est frequentèr in scholis publicis
    Magno impetu.
SIMON ACUTUS: Hoc feci et cessit infaelicitèr.
POLUPRAGMATICUS: Agendum in Theatris, in publicis comitiis 1285
    Perorandum, vbi te tota Academia, tota regio
    Tum possit videre, tum proloquentem audiat,
    Aut coram ipso Duce.
SIMON ACUTUS: Orator sum valdè tenuis.
POLUPRAGMATICUS: Non refert quis sis. Saltem amicum habeas
    Cuius opera vtaris, tu tantum proferes.   1290
    Benè vestitus, super omnia viris illustrissimis
    Associare te debes.
SIMON ACUTUS: Haec forsan praestare potero.
POLUPRAGMATICUS: Vel sic. Cude suppositiones, orationes, epistolas
    Pralectiones, animadversiones, quicquid in buccam venit.
    Prosa an versu non refert, bis anno quolibet,   1295
    Et ad Francofurtanas plerumque nundinas.

SIMON ACUTUS: Who is this speaking so magnificently about the heavens? He is reckoning with himself. I'll listen.

POLUPRAGMATICUS: Someone is listening. According to Alfraganus[2] the semi-diameter of the crescent moon contains thirty-three half measures of the earth times four once and a half, twice three and a half.

SIMON ACUTUS: I'll interrupt. Hello, most eloquent sir.

POLUPRAGMATICUS: Simon Acutus, what are you doing?

SIMON ACUTUS: I was thinking that you were the famous Tycho,[3] you were thundering such lofty things.

POLUPRAGMATICUS: And I was thinking you were a common academic.

SIMON ACUTUS: But why this crazy appearance?

POLUPRAGMATICUS: Don't ask. But what about your reputation?

SIMON ACUTUS: This is the very thing I want from you. How may I become well-known, and like you, a friend and ally to notables, rulers, important men, and the duke himself?

POLUPRAGMATICUS: Oh, Simon, Simon, you seek a difficult thing. It is a work of great labor, but since you are so ardent, I will teach you the very shortest road to fame. One must declaim frequently and with great force in the public schools.

SIMON ACUTUS: I have done this, but it yielded unfortunate results.

POLUPRAGMATICUS: You must go to the theater, speak in public meetings where the entire university, the whole region, can see you and hear you speak. Or go before the duke himself.

SIMON ACUTUS: I'm rather a feeble orator.

POLUPRAGMATICUS: It doesn't matter what you are. At the very least you should have a friend whose work you will use, merely presenting it. Dress well, and above all, you should associate yourself with the most famous people.

SIMON ACUTUS: Perhaps I can do those things.

POLUPRAGMATICUS: Or try this. Hammer out suppositions, speeches, letters, lectures, differing opinions, whatever comes to mind.[4] It doesn't matter whether it is prose or verse, and you should do it most often, twice every year, at the Frankfurt Fair.[5]

---

[2] JS: "Alfraganus: Arabian astronomer, ninth century."

[3] Tycho Brahe.

[4] Cicero, *Att.* 7.10. Erasmus, *Ad.* 1.5.72. See also Erasmus, *Mor.* 142: "At meus ille scriptor quanto delirat felicius, dum nulla lucubratione, verum vtcunque visum est animo, quicquid in calamum incidit, vel somnia sua, statim literis prodit." [But my writer is far more happily deluded as he writes without thought, putting down on paper whatever he likes, whatever pops into his head, even his dreams.]

[5] See *AM* Democritus (23–24) for the opinions of Democritus Jr. on the publications of contemporary authors. On page 24, Burton mentions trading at Frankfurt. According to Ilan Rachum, ed., *The Renaissance: An Illustrated Encyclopedia* (New York: Mayflower, 1979), the importance of Frankfurt "was in its two annual fairs, held in April and

SIMON ACUTUS: Laboriosum nimis hoc, at enitar tamen.

POLUPRAGMATICUS: Hoc obitèr. Si scriptoris cuiuspiam mentionem
    feceris
    Epitheton adiicias. Mulus mulum scabit.

SIMON ACUTUS: Intelligo.

POLUPRAGMATICUS: Vel edas alienum opus tuo nomine   1300
    Cum notis quibusdam vel adiectiunculis.

SIMON ACUTUS: Inhonestum.

POLUPRAGMATICUS: Librumque inscribes heroi alicui,
    In cuius laudem insurges supra omnem fidem,
    Licèt ille bardus sit. Obsequium amicos parit.

SIMON ACUTUS: Prudentèr hoc.

POLUPRAGMATICUS: Operumque tuorum scribe ipse catalogum   1305
    Vitamque tuam praefiges.

SIMON ACUTUS: Hoc esset vanissimum.

POLUPRAGMATICUS: At hoc crebrô fit. Si quem norîs scriptorem
    celebrem
    Huic te opponas; quicquid ait nega–
    Conuelle, carpe, explode, sugilla, exibila.

SIMON ACUTUS: Hoc ambitiosum.

POLUPRAGMATICUS: Vel nouam sectam institues   1310
    Habebisque statìm sectatores innumeros.

SIMON ACUTUS: Opinor.

POLUPRAGMATICUS: Nostîn paradoxum absurdum aliquod?
    Explosum renouabis, aut fingas aliud de nouo:
    Moueri terram, stellas et lunam incoli et huiusmodi.

SIMON ACUTUS: Ridiculum.

POLUPRAGMATICUS: Vtcunque, defendes per Iouem.   1315
    Qui possit vel ausit, carpat opus tuum.

SIMON ACUTUS: That's a lot of work, but I'll try nevertheless.

POLUPRAGMATICUS: This also: if you make mention of some writer, add an epithet. Mule scratches mule.[6]

SIMON ACUTUS: I understand.

POLUPRAGMATICUS: Or publish the work of someone else in your name with certain notes or additions.[7]

SIMON ACUTUS: That's dishonest.

POLUPRAGMATICUS: Dedicate your book to some powerful man in whose praise you will surge beyond belief, even if he is dull. Flattery produces friends.[8]

SIMON ACUTUS: This is prudent.

POLUPRAGMATICUS: Write a catalogue of your works, and preface it with an autobiography.

SIMON ACUTUS: This is quite vain.

POLUPRAGMATICUS: And this especially: if you know of some famous writer, oppose him. Whatever he says, deny it. Tear him to pieces, reproach him, rebuke him, scorn, whistle, or hiss him out of the place.

SIMON ACUTUS: This is ambitious.

POLUPRAGMATICUS: Or found a new sect. You will immediately have many followers.

SIMON ACUTUS: I'll think about it.

POLUPRAGMATICUS: Do you know some absurd paradox? Revive one that has been rejected or make up something new: that the earth is being moved; that the stars and moon are inhabited; or something of this sort.[9]

SIMON ACUTUS: This is ridiculous.

POLUPRAGMATICUS: Whatever it is, you will defend it, by Jove. Let whoever will or dare attack your work.[10]

September, which attracted merchants from all over Europe. They made Frankfurt the capital of the publishing industry."

[6] JS: Ausonius, *Idyll* 12. Erasmus, *Ad.* 1.7.96. LS: A proverb, "mutuum muli scabunt." See also Erasmus, *Mor.* 142: "Illud autem lepidissimum cum mutuis epistolis, carminibus, encomiis sese vicissim laudant." [But most charming is when they praise each other by turns in letters, poems, eulogies.]

[7] Erasmus, *Mor.* 142: "Sed magis etiam sapiunt, qui aliena pro suis edunt." [But even wiser are those who publish another's work as their own.]

[8] JS: Terence, *An.* 68: "obsequium amicos, veritas odium parit." [Flattery produces friends, truth produces hatred.] Erasmus, *Ad.* 2.9.53.

[9] *AM* Democritus (78): "Copernicus, Atlas his successor, is of opinion the earth is a planet, moves and shines to others, as the moon doth to us. Digges, Gilbert, Keplerus, Origanus, and others, defend this hypothesis of his in sober sadness, and that the moon is inhabited: if it be so that the earth is a moon, then are we also giddy, vertiginous and lunatic within this sublunary maze." See also *AM* pt. 2, sec. 2, mem. 3 (53–54).

[10] Erasmus, *Mor.* 142: "Quid enim est negocii, treis illos doctos, si tamen ea legerint, contemnere?" [What does he care if three learned men contemn his work, if in fact they even read it.]

SIMON ACUTUS: At qui defendam si quis in me scripserit?
POLUPRAGMATICUS: Contemnes, irridebis, cuiuscunque sit ordinis,
    Qui sugillarit doctum et generosum opus tuum;
    Et licet ei dignus, quod aiunt, praestare matellam   1320
    Non sis, vilipendes infra iram tuam. Tu leo leporem?
    Ac si te penes omnis esset ars, omnis eruditio.
SIMON ACUTUS: Hoccine totum quod vis?
POLUPRAGMATICUS: Concludo breuitèr.
    Si vis insignis et primus haberi philosophus,
    Par est vt sis acutus, ferox, audax, impudens,   1325
    Leno, parasitus, vanus, vulpes, simia,
    Redargutor superbus, iactator omniscius,
    Irrisor, sublimiloquus, omnium horarum homo.
    Ditesces ita, et inclaresces quam ocyssimè.
                  [*Exit*]
SIMON ACUTUS: Rectè suades. Dabo operam pro virili meo,   1330
    Et pro eo quo sum imbutus ingenio,
    Producam ex hoc capite nonem Tomos illicò.
    Dicam libro primo lunam esse habitabilem,
    Idque leporibus et ceruis. At quid inquis ita?
    Quoniam cum indefessi latrent ad lunam canes,   1335
    Probabile est videre illic currentes lepores.
    Secundus aget de Thaumaturgicis operibus,
    Tertius de Zilphis, pigmeis, et spiritali animâ,
    Quartus de subpolaribus et politiâ Antipodum,
    Quintus de condelamitis, ragadibus et morbo gallico,   1340
    Sextus de Erebo et arcanis quisbusdam magicis,
    Nonus contra Vallam de reciprocatione sui et suus,
    De rebus aliis admirandis libris in reliquis.
    Audactèr desputabo, contradicam liberè.
    Vos auditores parate saltem versiculos,   1345
    Praefigendos in laudem authoris et operis;
    Reliqui ad coemendum parate pecunias
    Prostabunt Francofurti proximis nundinis.

SIMON ACUTUS: But if someone does criticize me, how will I defend myself?

POLUPRAGMATICUS: You will disregard or ridicule anyone who attacks your learned and noble work, no matter what rank he holds. Although, as they say, you may not be worthy to hold his chamber pot,[11] you will hold him in slight esteem, not worth your anger. Would you a lion attack a hare? Act as if you were in possession of every art, all learning.

SIMON ACUTUS: Is this all you suggest?

POLUPRAGMATICUS: I conclude briefly. If you want to be distinguished and considered a first-rate philosopher, you must be sharp, fierce, bold, impudent, a pimp, a parasite, vain, a fox, an ape, a haughty defender, one who tosses about all knowledge, a scoffer, a speaker of lofty things, a man for all seasons.[12] Thus will you grow rich and become famous most quickly.

[Exit Polupragmaticus]

SIMON ACUTUS: You make a good argument. I will try to the best of my ability and with whatever wit I have; I will produce nine tomes off the top of my head. In the first book, I will say that the moon is inhabited by hares and deer. And why, you ask? Because, when dogs bark unwearyingly at the moon, it is probable that they see hares running there. The second book will deal with thaumaturgical works. The third will be about sylphs, pygmies,[13] and the spiritual soul. The fourth about subpolar regions and the government of the Antipodes. The fifth will be about condyloma, rhagades,[14] and the French pox. The sixth about Erebus and some arcane magic. The ninth against Valla[15] about the reflexives "sui" and "suus." In the remaining books, I will write about other marvelous things. I will argue boldly, contradict freely. You, listeners, prepare at least some little verses for the preface, something in praise of the author and his works. The rest of you, start saving your money to buy my books. They will be offered for sale at the next fair in Frankfurt.

---

[11] Bensly: Martial 10.11.3–4: "dispeream, si tu Pyladi praestare matellam / dignus es aut porcos pascere Pirithoi." [May I die if you are worthy to hold a chamber pot for Pylades or to feed Pirithous's pigs.] Erasmus, *Ad.* 1.5.94.

[12] JS: Quintilian, 6.3.110. Erasmus, *Ad.* 1.3.86.

[13] *AM* pt. 2, sec. 2, mem. 3 (40–41): "What is the centre of the earth? is it pure element only, as Aristotle decrees, inhabited (as Paracelsus thinks) with creatures whose chaos is the earth: or with fairies, as the woods and waters (according to him) are with nymphs, or as the air with spirits?" On "as Paracelsus thinks," Burton adds this note: "Lib. de Zilphis et Pygmaeis. They penetrate the earth as we do the air."

[14] Cooper: *Condyloma*: "A swellyng of the tuell or fundament, procedyng of an inflammation." *Rhagades*: "Chappes and cleftes in the handes and other partes of the bodie."

[15] Lorenzo Valla (1406–57), *De reciprocatione Sui et Suus.*

Scena Tertia
Antonius et tibicines,   1350
Aequiuocus [*cum lucernâ.*]

ANTONIUS: Aequiuoce.
AEQUIUOCUS: Quis me vocat?
ANTONIUS: Quid hic tibi negotii?
    Hoc noctis cum lucernâ?
AEQUIUOCUS: Herum quaero.
ANTONIUS: An hac abit?
AEQUIUOCUS: Hac abit inquis. Quà non abit? Huc, illuc, vbique
    Per omnes vicos vrbis noctiuagus repit.   1355
    Ad horas omnes noctis, nunc virili habitu,
    Nunc muliebri incedens, omnes formas induens,
    Lenae, obstetricis, interdùm vero militis.
    Proteus, opinor, non est illo mutabilior,
    Nec vulpes magè versipellis aut versutior.   1360
    Sed quo te cum fidibus?
ANTONIUS: Ad amicam.
AEQUIUOCUS: Intelligo.
ANTONIUS: Sed heus, dum hi ludunt, tu canes.
AEQUIUOCUS: Quando ita vis volo.
ANTONIUS: Atque eccum propè sumus; haec ni fallor domus
    Atque hoc cubiculum vbi Camaena mea cubat.
    Haec fenestra; ludatis iam si lubet.   1365
          [*Aequiuocus canit. Tibicines ludunt.*]
      Morpheu deorum summe,
    Et insomniorum deus,
    Portas aperi corneas,
    Claude sed eburneas.
      Camaenamque seu a dextrâ,   1370
    Siue cubat a sinistrâ,
    Siue cubat haec supina,

Scene three
Antonius and lute players.
Aequivocus [*with a lantern.*]

ANTONIUS: Aequivocus.

AEQUIVOCUS: Who's calling me?

ANTONIUS: What are you doing here? And with a lantern at this time of night?

AEQUIVOCUS: I'm looking for my master.

ANTONIUS: Does he come here?

AEQUIVOCUS: Does he come here, you ask. Where does he not go? Here, there, everywhere he wanders at night, through every neighborhood of the city. And at all hours of the night, now dressed as a man, now as a woman, putting on all sorts of disguises—those of a bawd, a midwife, sometimes even a soldier.[1] I think Proteus[2] is not more mutable than he nor a fox more cunning or clever. But where are you going with lute players?

ANTONIUS: To my girl friend.

AEQUIVOCUS: I understand.

ANTONIUS: But listen, while these are playing, you should sing.

AEQUIVOCUS: If that is what you want, I will.

ANTONIUS: Look. We are close by. Unless I am mistaken, this is the house and that is the bedroom where my Camaena sleeps. That is her window. You may play now, if you please.

[*Aequivocus sings; the lute players play.*]
>
> Oh Morpheus, greatest of gods,
> Morpheus, god of dreams,
> Open your gates of horn
> Close the gates of ivory.[3]
>
> Whether she sleeps on her right,
> Whether she sleeps on her left,
> Or whether she sleeps on her back,

---

[1] *AM* pt. 3, sec. 2, mem. 2, subs. 5 (129): "Many such pranks are played by our Jesuits, sometimes in their own habits, sometimes in others, like soldiers, courtiers, citizens, scholars, gallants, and women themselves. Proteus-like, in all forms and disguises, they go abroad in the night, to inescate and beguile young women, or to have their pleasure of other men's wives; and, if we may believe some relations, they have wardrobes of several suits in their colleges for that purpose."

[2] Cooper: "Proteus: Of him came this prouerbe, 'Proteo mutabilior,' more chaungeable then Proteus, applyed to him that in his actes or woords is unstable." Erasmus, *Ad.* 2.2.74.

[3] Cooper: *Morpheus*: "The son or seruaunte of the god Somnus." The gates of horn and of ivory are the twin gates of sleep. See Vergil, *Aen.* 6.893–96, and Homer, *Od.* 19.562–63.

Tegat Morpheus a ruinâ.
    Pungens procùl esto pulex,
Cantans procùl esto culex,   1375
Funestus absit Incubus,
Magus absit et veneficus.
    Et quando aperit ocellos,
Pulchrè scintillantes illos,
Graues procùl absint curae,   1380
Seu praesentes seu futurae.
    Adsit amor et delitiae,
Dolor absit et tristitiae,
Moueaturue requiescat,
Loquaturue conticescat;   1385
    Attendat Musicus sonorus,
Atque gratiarum chorus,
Suaueolentes et odores,
Et gratissimi colores.
ANTONIUS: Salue, Camaena; salue, Tarentilla; salue, vetula.   1390
Eamus iam si placet. Illucescet enim illicò.

Scena Quarta
Polupistos. Pantomagus.

POLUPISTOS: Narraui amicis multis consilium meum
    De conditione hâc inter me et medicum.   1395
    Dehortantur, factum putant consilio malo.
    Non refert quid dicant. Prudentiores forent modò.
[*Intrat*] PANTOMAGUS: Polupiste.
POLUPISTOS: Quid uis? Quî succedit negotium?
PANTOMAGUS: Ex voto, sed interìm opus est auro nouo.
POLUPISTOS: Cui vsui?
PANTOMAGUS: Donum mittendum est praesidi Mercurio.   1400
    Ars enim sacra est.
POLUPISTOS: Cape votiuam pecuniam.
PANTOMAGUS: Benè est, sed opus etiamnum viginti minis
    Ad coemendos carbones abiegineos–

Morpheus, cover my Camaena.
    Stay far away, annoying flea;
Stay far away, stinging gnat.[4]
Deadly incubus, go away,
Enchanter and wizard, go away.
    And when she opens her eyes,
Those beautifully shining eyes,
May all her cares be far away,
Whether present or future cares.
    May love and delight be near,
Sorrow and sadness disappear
Whether she move or lie quiet
Speak or be silent.
    May sonorous music attend,
With a chorus of Graces
And sweet-smelling odors
And most pleasing colors.

ANTONIUS: Goodbye, Camaena. Goodbye, Tarentilla. Goodbye, old woman.
  We go now, please, for soon it will be light.

Scene four
Polupistos. Pantomagus.

POLUPISTOS: I have told many of my friends about my plan and about the agreement I have with the physician. They warn me against it and think it done with poor advice. But it doesn't matter what they say. They should be wiser soon.

[*Enter Pantomagus*]

PANTOMAGUS: Polupistos.

POLUPISTOS: What do you want? How are things going?

PANTOMAGUS: As promised, but meanwhile, there is need of more money.

POLUPISTOS: For what use?

PANTOMAGUS: One must give a gift to guardian Mercury. The art is sacred.[1]

POLUPISTOS: Take the votive money.

PANTOMAGUS: Good. But I also need 40 pounds to buy charcoal.

---

[4] LS: gnat is also used as a term of reproach for wanton lover.

[1] Erasmus, *Alc.* 427: "Admonebat alcumista rem felicius successuram, si Virgini matri, quae, vt scis, Paraliis colitur, mitteret aliquot aureos dono, artem enim esse sacram, nec absque fauore numinum rem prospere geri." [But the alchemist warned that the business would succeed better if he sent some gold as a gift to the Virgin Mother who, as you know, is worshipped at Paralia. For the art is sacred and does not prosper without heavenly favor.]

POLUPISTOS: Etiamne molestus?

PANTOMAGUS: Ne graueris impendere.

    Vncia quaelibet auri quam insumis hoc opere,   1405

    Meâ fide, ter centum mille rursus dabit.

POLUPISTOS: Cape quod vis.

PANTOMAGUS: Probè curabuntur omnia.

[Exit]

POLUPISTOS: Insumpsi iam quadrigentos aureolos,

    Sed ad rem, sic inquit, auri quaelibet vncia

    Ter centum mille dabit; si sic, quid quadringenta dabunt?   1410

    Subduco rationem arithmeticè, et statìm proueniunt.

[Supputat in tabulis]

    Tercentum mille, mille, millionum myriades.

    Sic est in tabulis subduxi rationem benè.

    Pergo per aequationem proportionis continuae,

    Et mille minae dabunt tres plenos modios,   1415

    Quindecem modii complebunt doliolum.

    Per tot modios quadringenta multiplicata dolia

    Implebunt ad tectum vsque totam hanc cameram.

    Aedes meae non continebunt; parabitur horreum.

Scena Quinta   1420

Theanus. Pedanus cum famulo.

THEANUS: Vnde tu tam sublimis rediisti nobis tam grauis

    Et cum famulo? Quid annon dignaris nos aspicere?

    Vnde hic pulcher habitus? Mirari satìs non queo.

PEDANUS: Annon videtur admiratione dignum?

THEANUS: Maximè equidèm.   1425

    Sed quae causa?

PEDANUS: Ipsa faelicitas.

THEANUS: Quid ais?

PEDANUS: Ter beatum, diuitem, honoratum me vides.

THEANUS: Adeo breui?

PEDANUS: Atque admodum.

THEANUS: Quaeso repete totum ab initio.

PEDANUS: Nosti qualis eram, pauper alumnus, seruus tuus.

THEANUS: Benè noui.

PEDANUS: Hinc profectus rus rectà fui.   1430

    Incidi in aedes aurati cuiusdam equitis,

    Paedagogus futurus et capellanus simul.

POLUPISTOS: Are you still bothering me?

PANTOMAGUS: You shouldn't worry about spending a little bit of money. I promise you, whatever you spend on this will be given back to you three hundred thousand times.

POLUPISTOS: Take what you will.

PANTOMAGUS: Everything will be well cared for.

[*Exit Pantomagus*]

POLUPISTOS: I've already spent 400 gold pieces, but, as he said, each little piece of gold will give back three hundred thousand. If that is so, what will 400 give? I'll add it up and find the answer right away.[2]

[*He calculates on a tablet*]

Three hundred thousand, thousand million ten thousands. Thus I have well-calculated on this tablet. If I proceed through the equation of continuous proportion, a thousand minae will give three full bushels, fifteen bushels will fill a barrel. Four hundred barrels multiplied by so many bushels will fill this whole vault right up to the roof. My house won't hold it all. I'll build a storeroom.

Scene five
Theanus. Pedanus *with a servant.*

THEANUS: Where have you come from, looking so distinguished and so serious, and with a servant? Why do you deign to look on us? Where did you get that handsome suit? I can't marvel enough.

PEDANUS: Does it seem worthy of admiration?

THEANUS: Quite. But what is the cause?

PEDANUS: Good fortune itself.

THEANUS: What are you saying?

PEDANUS: You are looking at a man three times blessed, rich and honored.

THEANUS: And in such a short time?

PEDANUS: And in full measure.

THEANUS: I beg you. Tell me all from the beginning.

PEDANUS: You know what sort of man I was, a poor scholar, your servant.

THEANUS: I know it well.

PEDANUS: After I left here, I went straight to the country. I happened upon the house of a certain wealthy gentleman. I became both his children's tutor and his chaplain.

---

[2] Erasmus, *Alc.* 426: "Interea Balbinus totus erat in supputationibus, subducebat enim, si vncia pareret quindecim, quantum esset lucri rediturum ex vnciis bis mille. Tantum enim decreuerat insumere." [Meanwhile Balbinus was absorbed in his calculations, figuring, if one ounce yielded fifteen, how much profit he would make from two thousand ounces. He had decided to spend that much.]

THEANUS: Quid inde?

PEDANUS: Nactus inde honores, opes, titulos
Et quod magìs mirêre binum sacerdotium,
Omissis iis quae mercatus sum.

THEANUS: Graecâ fide? 1435

PEDANUS: Fortasse.

THEANUS: Sed vnde honor tuus?

PEDANUS: Sequitur diuitias.
Irenarcha sum apud meos, et sacellanus Ducis.

THEANUS: Mira narras.

PEDANUS: Ita est.

THEANUS: Sed quorsum nunc venis?

PEDANUS: Ad accumulandos gradus.

THEANUS: Quos demum gradus?
Doctorne futurus, an sacrae Theologiae Baccalaureus? 1440

PEDANUS: Vterque si diis placet, et his proximis comitiis.
Sed iam festino.

THEANUS: Quo tandem?

PEDANUS: Ad ducem propero.

THEANUS: Quam ob causam?

PEDANUS: Ob bonum Reipublicae.
Timeo ne mox occidione occidant omnes populi.

THEANUS: Dii meliùs. Vnde timendum? An a pestilentiâ, 1445
Fame, bello, diluuioue?

PEDANUS: Certiora affero.
Nam vidên, nostîn apud villas in singulis domibus
Magnum esse numerum gallorum septennium;
Hos compertum est anno quouis septimo parere,
Enascique ex eorum ouis, basiliscos serpentum genus 1450
Quorum obtutu solum homines infecti pereunt,
Et si non statìm à Duce prospectum fuerit,
Actum erit a Ducatus huiusque incolis.

THEANUS: Then what?

PEDANUS: Then I found honor, wealth, titles, and what is more wonderful, two benefices, not to mention those I bought.

THEANUS: By the faith of the Greeks?[1]

PEDANUS: Perhaps.

THEANUS: But how did you gain honor?

PEDANUS: It follows wealth. I am a justice of the peace among my people, and the duke's chaplain.

THEANUS: A strange thing you tell.

PEDANUS: So it is.

THEANUS: But why have you now come here?

PEDANUS: To pile up some degrees.

THEANUS: Exactly what degrees? Will you become a Doctor or a Bachelor of Sacred Theology?

PEDANUS: Both, if it please the gods, and at the next Congregation.[2] But now I must hurry on.

THEANUS: Where are you going?

PEDANUS: To the duke.

THEANUS: Why?

PEDANUS: For the good of the state. I fear that soon the populace will be utterly destroyed.

THEANUS: Dear gods. What do you fear? Pestilence, famine, war, flood?

PEDANUS: I have more certain information. You know that in every house in the villages there is a great number of seven-year-old cocks. It has been determined that these reproduce every seven years, and from their eggs are hatched the basilisk, a kind of serpent, just the sight of which infects and kills human beings; and if the duke does not do something about this at once, it will happen to the inhabitants of this duchy.[3]

---

[1] Greek faith means perfidy. See Plautus, *As.* 199. Erasmus, *Ad.* 1.8.27.

[2] JS: "This is the term used at Oxford for the meeting at which degrees are conferred."

[3] Pontano, *Ant.* 52: A certain compater Neapolitanus [citizen of Naples], asks a peregrinus [foreigner] where he is hurrying: "PER. Ad Regem propero; ad regiam utra ducit via? COMP. Utraque; sed quaenam salutandi Regis causa? hoc enim ipsum scire cupimus, itaque vicem redde. PER. Nimis quam timeo nostrae reipublicae, ne paucis post annis occidione occidant populi. COMP. Ab gladione, an a pestilentia, an a diluvione timendum est nobis? Equidem et te siderum progressiones observasse reor, quando astrologorum est has clades praedicere. PER. Certiora affero: Maxima in singulis non modo oppidis, sed pene domibus vis est gallorum septennium; eos satis compertum est anno septimo parere enascique basiliscos serpentes, quorum obtutu homines infecti pereant. Quod nisi a rege probe prospectum fuerit, actum est de regni Neapolitani populis; opus autem esse ut singulis in oppidis singuli deligantur cauti et solertes viri, qui haec mala gallorum caede procurent videantque ne quid respublica detrimenti capiat. Ego hac de causa atque ut reipublicae prosim meae, ad Regem eo, vos valete." [FOREIGNER: I am hastening to the king. Which road leads to the palace? NEAPOLITAN CITIZEN:

THEANUS: Quid ergò suades?
PEDANUS: Vt in singulis oppidis
  Quidam deligantur qui gallorum caedem faciant,   1455
  Ne quid inde Respublica detrimenti capiat.
THEANUS: Prudentèr sane.
PEDANUS: Pleraque alia sunt etiam
  Quae maximè spectant ad Reipublicae bonum;
  De quibus singulis certiorem ducem faciam.
THEANUS: Benè fit. Praeuideo te futurum Episcopum.   1460
  Sed, Pedane, dic sodes, pro veteri amicitiâ
  Qui possim et ego tui similis euadere?
PEDANUS: Quî possis? Neque manendo in Academia
  Neque studendo; licet omnem Encyclopediam crepas,
  Ipsum superes Augustinum, aut Chrisostomum   1465
  Morum probitate ad vnguem exprimas,
  Haud curat patronus si nihil afferas.
  Si nihil attuleris, ibis, Homere, foras.
  Dum vos hic per annos aliquot famelici
  Legatis Diuum Thomam et J. Duns Scotum,   1470
  Pallentes studiis, nos indulgentes genio
  Expiscamur interìm opima quaeque sacerdotia.
THEANUS: Quod vis ergò faciam.
PEDANUS: Rus ite singuli,
  Sunt ibi patroni, proceres, reliqua omnia.
                [*Exit*]

THEANUS: What do you suggest?

PEDANUS: That in every town someone be appointed to kill the cocks, lest some harm befall the state because of them.[4]

THEANUS: Very prudent.

PEDANUS: There are many other things that especially concern the good of the state. I shall inform the duke about each of them.

THEANUS: May it turn out well. I foresee that you will be a bishop. But, Pedanus, for the sake of old friendship, tell me, my friend, how can I advance just as you have?

PEDANUS: How can you? Not by remaining at the university and not by studying. Although you may boast of encyclopedic knowledge, surpass Augustine himself, or press Chrysostomus[5] to the limit in moral virtue, patrons do not care unless you bring something. "If you bring nothing, Homer, you will be thrown out the door."[6] While you are here, suffering from hunger for so many years, while you are reading Saint Thomas and J. Duns Scotus, paling in your studies, I, indulging my genius,[7] have meanwhile been fishing for a good benefice.

THEANUS: Whatever you suggest, I'll do.

PEDANUS: Go alone to the country. That's where the patrons, noblemen, and others are.

[*Exit Pedanus*]

Both. But why do you need to speak with the King? This is what we want to know, so tell us the circumstance. FOREIGNER. I am greatly concerned that in a few years the populace of the state will be completely destroyed. CITIZEN. What should we fear: war, pestilence, a flood? I suppose you have observed the progression of the stars since it is astrologers who predict these disasters. FOREIGNER. I bring more certain information. Not only in every town but in almost every house there is a great number of seven-year-old cocks. It has been sufficiently determined that these reproduce in seven years, and give birth to basilisks. Just looking at these serpents, men may become infected and die. Unless the king does something at once, it will happen to the Neopolitan people. Moreover, in each town one careful and skillful man must be selected to carry out this unfortunate slaughter of cocks and see that no harm befalls the state. For this reason and so that I may help my state, I go to the king. Goodbye.]

[4] Bensly: This is from "the Constitutional formula by which the Senate at Rome proclaimed a state of siege, equivalent to a proclamation of Martial Law. The consuls were thereby entrusted with special powers." See Sallust, *Bellus Catilinae* 29.2.

[5] Cooper: "Chrysostomus: The name of a famous byshop of Constantinople, and also of an historian, which were so called for theyr eloquence. For 'Chrysostomus' is in englishe, a golden mouth."

[6] JS: Ovid, *Ars Amatoria* 2.279–80: "ipse licet uenias Musis comitatus, Homere, / si nihil attuleris, ibis, Homere, foras." [Although you yourself come, Homer, attended by the Muses, if you bring nothing, Homer, you will be thrown out the door.]

[7] LS: *genius* means the spirit of social enjoyment, fondness for good living, and appetite, as well as talent. To indulge the genius [indulge genio], is a term used by parasites for a patron. Erasmus, *Ad.* 2.4.74.

THEANUS: Rus ite singuli. Sequar hoc salutare consilium.   1475
Meditabor de verbis hisce noctes et dies.
Et me accingam mox ad officinam proximam.
Inde parabo vestes et reliquum viaticum,
Rus iturus illico. Quid enim semperne vixero
Solus, delirus, macer, et melancholicus,   1480
Cogitabundus de genere et spetie et de primâ materiâ,
Cacexiae, dentium dolori, et catharris obnoxius?
Scote, vale; Thomâ, vale; genus et speties,
Valete, et Musarum Mystae omnes simul.

[Canit]

    Valete, Academici,   1485
    Et combibones optimi,
    Osunensesque reliqui,
        Et nunc et in perpetuùm.
    Valete, coci et lanei,
    Sutores, crepedarii,   1490
    Propolae, proletarii,
        Et nunc et in perpetuùm.
    Sancte Petre in occidente,
    Sancte Petre in oriente,
    Cum Maria mediante,   1495
        Et nunc et in perpetuùm.
    Longùm vale, Katherina,
    Longùm vale, Thomasina,
    Et quot estis in sutrinâ
        Et nunc et in perpetuùm.   1500
    Valedicturus ego sum,
    Et discessurus pannis cum,
    Valete multum, et vsque dum,
        In saecula saeculorum.
    Si quis vestrum venit rus,   1505
    Et vos fortè sim visurus;
    Bibetur plenus cantharus,
        In gratiam amicorum.
Sic vbi fata vocant, vdis abiectus in herbis,

THEANUS: "Go alone to the country." I will follow this healthy advice. I will meditate on these very words day and night. Soon I will equip myself at a nearby shop; I'll get clothes and other provisions for the journey. I'll go at once to the country. Why should I always live alone, doting, thin and melancholy, cogitating on genus and species, primal matter, subject to cachexia, toothache and rheum?[8] Farewell, Scotus; farewell, Thomas. Genus and species, and at the same time, all initiates of the muses, farewell.

[He sings]

Farewell, Academics
And best drinking friends
And others of Osuna,
    Now and forever.
Goodbye, cooks and butchers,
Cobblers and shoemakers,
Hucksters and beggars,
    Now and forever.
St. Peter in the west,
St. Peter in the east,
With Mary in the middle,
    Now and forever.[9]
Long farewell, Katherina,
Long farewell, Tomasina,
And all at the cobbler's shop,
    Now and forever.
I'll bid you all farewell
And depart with my satchel.
Goodbye again until
    Forever and ever.
If you come to the country
Perhaps I'll see you there.
We'll drink a full cup
    To friendship.

"Thus where the fates call, cast down in damp grasses, near the shallows

---

[8] *AM* pt. 1, sec. 2, mem. 3, subs. 15 (302): "hard students are commonly troubled with gouts, catarrhs, rheums, cachexia, bradypepsia, bad eyes, stone, and colic, crudities, oppilations, vertigo, winds, consumptions, and all such diseases as come by overmuch sitting; they are most part lean, dry, ill-coloured, spend their fortunes, lose their wits, and many times their lives, and all through immoderate pains and extraordinary studies."

[9] Michael O'Connell, *Robert Burton* (Boston: Twayne, 1986), 98: These three churches "belonged to Oxford as well as Osuna: ... The university church of St. Mary's stands about halfway between St. Peter's in the East and St. Peter Bailey (the latter now a part of St. Peter's College.)"

Ad vada Maeandri concinit albus olor. 1510
Valete ad vnum omnes, et, si sapitis, sequimini.

Scena Sexta
Staphila. Tarentilla.
Camaena.

STAPHILA: O fortunatum et verè diem aureum, 1515
    Quo mihi contigit Osunam accedere.
    Quoties enìm vitae anteactae recordor meae,
    Quam vilis olìm pauper quam lacera fui,
    Inter squalorem et sordes quam miserè aetatem habui,
    Contenta pane mucido et tenui ceruisiâ— 1520
    Et quam ornatè, iam quam Iouialitèr agam,
    Quam omnigenum supellex, lautae et exoticae dapes.
    Cunctaque ferè habeam et ad animum meum.
    Tam faelix derepentè, tam fortunata videor
    Vt fortunis meis superaddi nihil queat, 1525
    Vt si quis deus optionem daret mihi,
    Non esset omnino quod optarem ampliùs.
    O me beatam ter et filiolas meas!
CAMAENA: Faelitioresque futuras si quod tuum est ageres.
STAPHILA: Quid vultis? Vesperi cubatis, mane surgitis 1530
    Quando libet, quousque placet itis, reditis etiam
    Ad libitum quo vultis, victum et vestitum omnia
    Habetis. Quid deest?
CAMAENA: Aedes angustae nimìs.
STAPHILA: Parabimus ampliores.
TARENTILLA: Sed nec victus placet.
STAPHILA: Quos vultis cibos?
TARENTILLA: Hortulanos carduos, 1535
    Pisces marinos, benè conditas cochleas,
    Vinum generosum et purissimum pollinem.
CAMAENA: Famulumque vnum et alterum.
STAPHILA: Quicquid vultis dabitur.
              [Exit Staphila]
CAMAENA: Iam solae sumus. Dic mihi bonâ fide soror,
    Quae tam diuersos experta es tam innumeros procos: 1540
    An amasium malles scholarem Academicum,
    An oppidanum, rusticum an aulicum?
TARENTILLA: Tu dic prior.
CAMAENA: Ascultat opinor hic aliquis.
TARENTILLA: Nemo, solae sumus.
CAMAENA: Cauendum tamen
    Sunt enim oculati turres, aurita moenia. 1545

of the Meander, a white swan sings."[10] Goodbye to all. If you are wise, follow me.[11]

Scene six
Staphila. Tarentilla.
Camaena.

STAPHILA: O fortunate and truly golden day when I first happened on Osuna. So often I remember my former life, how worthless I was, how poor and tattered, what a miserable life I led among the squalor and filth, content with mouldy bread and watery beer. Now how elegantly, how jovially I shall live, with all kinds of furnishings, with rich and exotic meals. I'll have almost everything and just as I want it. So suddenly blessed and fortunate I seem that nothing could be added to my fortune; even if some god should give me free choice, there would be nothing more I would desire. O three times blessed, me and my little girls.

CAMAENA: Who would be happier if you did what you should.

STAPHILA: What else do you want? You lie in bed in the evenings, get up in the mornings at whatever time you like, go wherever you wish, return as it pleases you; you have plenty of food and clothes. What's lacking?

CAMAENA: The house is too small.

STAPHILA: We'll get a larger one.

TARENTILLA: I don't like the food.

STAPHILA: What kind of food do you want?

TARENTILLA: Artichokes from the garden, fish from the sea, snails well seasoned, some fine wine and very pure flour.

CAMAENA: And a servant or two.

STAPHILA: Whatever you want will be given.

[Exit Staphila]

CAMAENA: Now we are alone. Tell me in good faith, sister. Since you are more experienced with so many and such different suitors, whom do you prefer as a lover: a scholar from the university, a townsman, a countryman or a courtier?

TARENTILLA: You tell first.

CAMAENA: I think someone may be listening.

TARENTILLA: No, we are alone.

CAMAENA: Nevertheless, we must be careful for the towers have eyes, the walls ears.

---

[10] JS: Ovid, *Heroides* 7.1-2.

[11] Bensly: Plato, *Phaedo*, 5.61B. "Joannes Serranus's Latin version printed in Henri Estienne's edition of Plato [1:61], Paris 1578, is *Haec igitur, Cebes, Eueno refer: et valere iube, et si sapiat, me sequi.*" [Therefore, Cebes, tell Evenus: I bid you well, and if you are wise, follow me.]

TARENTILLA: Scias inaequalem esse furorem hominum.
　　Alitèr vruntur adolescentes, alitèr senes,
　　Alitèr ciues, aulici, pauperes, diuites.
CAMAENA: Sed vnde discrimen?
TARENTILLA: Pauperes obsequio
　　Placere putant, at diuites muneribus,　　　　　　　　　　1550
　　Conuiuiis, pompâ, ludis, et spectaculis.
　　Ciuis amare nescit absque zelotipiâ,
　　Oppidanus amando fit omninò stultior,
　　Diues profusis rebus fit sapientior,
　　Aulicus ob amicam magna quaeuis aggreditur,　　　　　　1555
　　Nil audet ciuis.
CAMAENA: At quem interim probas?
TARENTILLA: Aulicum ego.
CAMAENA: Ego scholarem Academicum,
　　Et inter scholares vnicum Antonium.
TARENTILLA: At quam ob causam?
CAMAENA: Quam quaeris? Multiplicem;
　　Sunt ingeniosi scholares, ornati nobiles,　　　　　　　　1560
　　Iuuenes plerumque blandi, benigni, faciles;
　　Iocis et cantilenis adoriuntur amasiam;
　　Dant quicquid habent supra modum et facilè amant.
TARENTILLA: Quidni et oppidanos?
CAMAENA: Faetant de allio,
　　Hircum et canem olent, vultus habent horridos,　　　　　1565
　　Duri, deformes, agrestes, nasuti, indigi,
　　Ne curant puellam nisi cum sint ebrii,
　　Carent argento, et ferè omnes vxorem timent.
TARENTILLA: At quem locum praefers?
CAMAENA: Hunc ego singulis.
TARENTILLA: Eundem ego. Vale, Roma; valete, Venetiae,　　1570
　　Sena, Pisa, Mediolanum, ciuitatesque Italae;
　　Regiones habitare mallem Acheronticas.
　　Hic portus meus, hoc forum, quaestuarium,
　　Sint Osunenses meae delitiae.
CAMAENA: Mihi prae cunctis placent Academici.　　　　　　1575
　　Haec mea sedes, hic sunt amores mei.

Scena Septima
Pantomagus. Polupragmaticus.
Lodouicus Pantometer. Simon Acutus.
Fidicen. Promus.　　　　　　　　　　　　　　　　　　1580

PANTOMAGUS: Proh dii immortales, quis me fortunatior,
　　Qui ex obscuro bardo et impolito homine

TARENTILLA: You know that men's passion is not the same. Young men are consumed in one way, old men in another, citizens, courtiers, poor men, rich men in yet other ways.

CAMAENA: What makes the difference?

TARENTILLA: The poor think they can please by flattery, but the rich by gifts, fine meals, pomp, shows, and spectacles. A citizen does not know how to love without jealousy, the townsman becomes constantly more foolish by loving, a rich man by means of extravagant things becomes wiser, a courtier attempts great things for his girl friend, a citizen dares nothing.

CAMAENA: So which do you like best?

TARENTILLA: The courtier.

CAMAENA: I like the university scholars, and among the scholars, just one, Antonius.

TARENTILLA: Why?

CAMAENA: Do you ask why? Many reasons. Scholars are intelligent, respected, noble, very flattering young men, kind, gentle; they tell their girl friends jokes and sing little songs, they give whatever they have beyond measure, and love easily.

TARENTILLA: And why not townsmen?

CAMAENA: They reek of garlic, smell like a goat or a dog, they have bristly faces, they're harsh, ugly, boorish, have big noses, they're needy, they don't care about a girl unless they are drunk, they have no money, and almost all of them fear their wives.

TARENTILLA: But what place do you prefer?

CAMAENA: This place alone.

TARENTILLA: Me too. Goodbye Rome, goodbye Venice, Siena, Pisa, Milan and the states of Italy; I'd rather live in hell. May my port, my forum, my market be here. May the people of Osuna be my delights.

CAMAENA: The university men please me above all others. This is my home, here are my loves.

Scene seven
Pantomagus. Polupragmaticus.
Lodovicus Pantometer. Simon Acutus.
Lute player. Drawer.

PANTOMAGUS: O immortal gods! Who could be more fortunate than I? From an obscure, dull and uncultured man I have come into this honor, and so quickly.

[*The others enter*]

POLUPRAGMATICUS: Whose voice is that which sounds so near us?

SIMON ACUTUS: Pantomagus, how is it going?

PANTOMAGUS: Very, very well. I think all the gods want to bless me for in-

In hunc honorem euasi, et tam citò?
                    [*Intrant reliqui*]
POLUPRAGMATICUS: Cuia vox haec quae tam prope nos sonat?
SIMON ACUTUS: Pantomage, quid agitur?
PANTOMAGUS: Optimè, optimè.   1585
    Omnes, opinor, dii mihi benefactum volunt.
    Etenìm praeter spem in virum quendam incidi
    Qui me ditauit abundè, et supra omnem fidem.
SIMON ACUTUS: Cur tu tam tristis?
POLUPRAGMATICUS: Nostîn Aequiuocum meum?
SIMON ACUTUS: Tanquam te.
POLUPRAGMATICUS: Nosti ergo circulatorem et furem.   1590
PANTOMAGUS: Qui sic?
POLUPRAGMATICUS: Compilauit mihi scrinium
    Aufugitque; immo ne drachmam fecit reliquam.
SIMON ACUTUS: Fallere fallentem non est fraus.
PANTOMAGUS: Heus bone vir,
    Artem imponendi non surripuit tibi.
POLUPRAGMATICUS: Non nisi me vnà auferat.
PANTOMAGUS: Quid ergo dolet?   1595
    Damnum leue. Superest dum fraus, supererit pecunia.
[Intrat] LODOUICUS PANTOMETER: Amici et socii mei iamdudum vos
    sequor.
SIMON ACUTUS: Eccum Lodouicum, vnde venis, vt vales?
LODOUICUS PANTOMETER: Id ipsum volebam a vobis percontarîer.
    Rure ego.
SIMON ACUTUS: Quoniam iam rursus conuenimus   1600
    Et iam soli sumus, memorare quisque occipiat
    Quid egerit, aut quî Spartam adornarît suam.
PANTOMAGUS: En vobis hoc aurum.
POLUPRAGMATICUS: Quid illud?
PANTOMAGUS: Inditium.
SIMON ACUTUS: En vobis has literas.
POLUPRAGMATICUS: Quas, cui vsui?
SIMON ACUTUS: Ad me missas a tribus diuersis Academiis.   1605
LODOUICUS PANTOMETER: Quam ob causam?
SIMON ACUTUS: Ob professorem publicum.
POLUPRAGMATICUS: Itane Simon?
SIMON ACUTUS: Sed et vir magnus, audio;
    Si quando vel in publicum apparuero,
    Certatim ab omnibus ad me curritur,
    Velùt ad visendam noctuam reliquae auiculae,   1610
    Dicentes hic ille Simon Acutus summus philosophus.
LODOUICUS PANTOMETER: Idem vbicunque de me ferè praedicant.
SIMON ACUTUS: Molesti sunt mihi, orant, ambiunt, obsecrant

deed beyond hope I have fallen in with a certain man who has made me abundantly rich past all belief.

SIMON ACUTUS: Why are you so sad?

POLUPRAGMATICUS: Do you know my Aequivocus?

SIMON ACUTUS: As I know you.

POLUPRAGMATICUS: Then you know a jester and a thief.

PANTOMAGUS: Why is that?

POLUPRAGMATICUS: He has stolen my money chest and fled. Indeed he left not a penny.

SIMON ACUTUS: To deceive a deceiver is not deceit.

PANTOMAGUS: My good man, he has not stolen your art of imposture.

POLUPRAGMATICUS: Not unless he stole me at the same time.

PANTOMAGUS: Then why are you sad? It's a small loss. So long as trickery remains, money will remain.

[Enter Lodovicus Pantometer]

LODOVICUS PANTOMETER: My friends and comrades, I've been following you for a long time.

SIMON ACUTUS: Look, it's Lodovicus. Where have you come from? How are you?

LODOVICUS PANTOMETER: I wanted to ask the same of you. I've come from the country.

SIMON ACUTUS: Since we are together again and alone, let each one begin to recall what he has done or how he has made the most of his Sparta.[1]

PANTOMAGUS: Look at this gold.

POLUPRAGMATICUS: What is it?

PANTOMAGUS: A token.

SIMON ACUTUS: See these letters.

POLUPRAGMATICUS: What letters, what are they for?

SIMON ACUTUS: They were sent to me by three different academics.

LODOVICUS PANTOMETER: Why?

SIMON ACUTUS: Because of my public professorship.

POLUPRAGMATICUS: Is that so, Simon?

SIMON ACUTUS: I am considered a great man. Any time I appear in public, people from all over come eagerly to see me, just as other birds to see an owl. They say "There he is, Simon Acutus, the greatest philosopher."

LODOVICUS PANTOMETER: They say nearly the same thing about me everywhere I go.

SIMON ACUTUS: I find them bothersome. They beg, solicit, implore to be allowed to see me, bid me to visit them—noblemen and gentlemen—so that I might deign to teach them or their sons, or so that I might inspire them

---

[1] Erasmus, *Ad.* 2.5.1. Cooper: "A prouerbe, signifiyng, the estate or office whiche thou haste, order or applie it well."

Videre vt liceat, ad se accersi iubent
Magnates, heroes vt se et filios suos   1615
Docere digner, vt praeceptis imbuam,
Alter vt hunc vel illum locum interpreter
Respondere vt velim et in viâ derigere.
Nimia est miseria doctum esse hominem nimìs.
PANTOMAGUS: Hoc ipsum fere etiam contingit mihi;   1620
Mane surgo, pulsat statim aliquis fores.
Quis? Tuum consilium? Mox succedit alius,
Patritius, senator, aut faemina nobilis;
Vix suspiro, en anhelantem e rure aliquem.
Accersor. Eo. Absolutum me censeo—   1625
Statìm alius, receptum fratri aut patri.
Iuuo omnes. Haec ferè est vita mea,
Haec ars. Plus lucror quam medici decem.
LODOUICUS PANTOMETER: Ego per villas incedens rudemque plebeculam
Superstitiosum vulgus, et inprimis mulieres   1630
Abundè victum habeo. Nunc a Geomantiâ,
Nunc a stellis docens nubilibus viros
Promitto, mares grauibus prolemque sterilibus,
Aegris salutem, et, si quaestum non interciperent
Fratres quidam chiromantici, supra modum ditescerem.   1635
POLUPRAGMATICUS: Me censet vulgus plus quam Thaletem sapere.
Doctum, diuinum, de caelo delapsum hominem,
Dux honorat proceresque, et vos scitis probè.
Sed quorsum haec? Quasi nos inter nos non norimus.
Amici, cauendum nobis est, idque seriò.   1640
SIMON ACUTUS: Quid ita?
LODOUICUS PANTOMETER: Obsidemurne?
PANTOMAGUS: Caelumne ruet?
POLUPRAGMATICUS: Verendum ne quis prudens Academicus
Nos prodat aliquando, et fucum suboleat.
Si quis has artes in apertum proferet,
Miserè periimus, actum de nobis erit.   1645
Maturâ deliberatione opus est. Nam quod aiunt,
Fortuna nunquam perpetua est bona.

with precepts, or interpret this or that passage, or answer and set them
straight. There is misery in being too learned a man.[2]

PANTOMAGUS: Almost the same things happen to me. I rise early; at once
someone knocks on the doors. "Who is it?" "What do you advise?" Soon
someone else comes, a patrician, a senator, or a noblewoman. I hardly
breathe before there is someone, out of breath, from the country. I'm
summoned, I go. I think I have finished, when at once there's someone
else, wanting a remedy for his brother or father. I help everyone. This is
practically my life, my art. And I make more money than ten physicians.

LODOVICUS PANTOMETER: I'm quite well provided for while wandering
through the towns among the rustic poor and superstitious folk, especially the women. Instructing sometimes by geomancy, at other times by
astrology, I promise husbands to marriageable girls, males to the pregnant and children to the barren,[3] health to the sick, and if certain chiro-
mantic monks didn't snatch away part of the trade,[4] I would be rich
beyond measure.

POLUPRAGMATICUS: The common folk think that I am wiser than Thales.[5] As
well you know, the duke and governors honor me as learned, divine, a
man slipped down from heaven. But what is the purpose of these things?
As if, among ourselves, we did not know ourselves?[6] My friends, we must
be careful. Very careful.

SIMON ACUTUS: Why is that?

LODOVICUS PANTOMETER: Are we being attacked?

PANTOMAGUS: Is the sky falling?

POLUPRAGMATICUS: We should be afraid lest some prudent academic sniff
out our pretense and at some time betray us. If anyone makes known our
deceptions, we will perish miserably, it will be the end of us. We need
wise deliberation for, as they say, good fortune doesn't last forever.[7]

---

[2] JS: Plautus, *Mil.* 68. "nimiast miseria nimi' pulchrum esse hominem." [There is
misery in being too handsome a man.]

[3] Pontano, *Ant.* 92: "et profecto Caietanae mulieres cum sint superstitiosulae, satis
commode hinc victitarem, ni fratres quidam proventum interciperent, dum somnia
coniiciunt, dum iras deorum venditant, dum viros nubilibus, mares gravidis, prolem
sterilibus promittunt." [And indeed, since the women of Caieta are so superstitious, I
would make a satisfactory living here if the monks did not snatch away the crop while
interpreting dreams, selling the wrath of the gods, promising husbands to marriageable
girls, males to the pregnant, children to the barren.]

[4] Bensly: For Burton on monks and sorcery, see *AM* pt. 3, sec. 2, mem. 2, subs. 5
(129).

[5] LS: "Greek philosopher of Miletus, one of the seven wise men and founder of the
Ionic sect." Erasmus, *Ad.* 3.7.26, notes that Thales is used ironically for one who thinks he
is wise. See Plautus, *Rud.* 1003: "Stultus es. Salue Thales." [You are stupid. Goodbye,
Thales.]

[6] Terence, *Ad.* 271: "quasi nunc non norimu' nos inter nos" [As if now we did not
know ourselves among ourselves.]

[7] Terence, *Hec.* 406: "o fortuna, ut numquam perpetuo's data!" [O, fortune, you are

LODOUICUS PANTOMETER: Quid ergo vis?

SIMON ACUTUS: Quid suades?

POLUPRAGMATICUS: Eamus huic ocyùs.
    Peruagandum puto ad reliquas Academias.

PANTOMAGUS: Quasi perspicaces aequè non essent alibì.   1650

SIMON ACUTUS: Quo tandem?

POLUPRAGMATICUS: Friburgum Brisgoae, aut Hasinam Daniae,
    Pragam Bohemorum, aut Anglorum Oxoniam.

LODOUICUS PANTOMETER: Cauesis edico vt appellas Angliam ni lupum,
    Vulpem aut vrsum adiungas comitem.

POLUPRAGMATICUS: Quid ita?

LODOUICUS PANTOMETER: Ob frequentes molossos qui sunt ibi.   1655

POLUPRAGMATICUS: At cur vrsum aut lupum vis adiungam comitem?

PANTOMAGUS: Vt, te relicto, ruant molossi in eorum aliquem.

POLUPRAGMATICUS: Nugaris. Vultis visitare Academias Italas?

SIMON ACUTUS: Non.

POLUPRAGMATICUS: Quare?

SIMON ACUTUS: Sunt ibi nobis doctiores mulieres.

POLUPRAGMATICUS: Qui sic?

SIMON ACUTUS: Ob frequentem fratrum et Theologorum concubitum   1660
    Qui rorem instillant his et inspirant quendam spiritum.

LODOVICUS PANTOMETER: So what do you want?

SIMON ACUTUS: What do you suggest?

POLUPRAGMATICUS: That we leave here quickly. I think we should go to another university.

PANTOMAGUS: As if the quick-witted would not be there also?

SIMON ACUTUS: Where then?

POLUPRAGMATICUS: Freiburg in Breisgau or Copenhagen in Denmark, Prague in Bohemia, or Oxford in England.

LODOVICUS PANTOMETER: I warn you to be careful if you're considering England. Don't go there without a wolf, fox, or bear.

POLUPRAGMATICUS: Why is that?

LODOVICUS PANTOMETER: Because of the many mastiffs there.

POLUPRAGMATICUS: But why should I take along a bear or a wolf?

PANTOMAGUS: So the mastiffs can chase one of them and leave you alone.[8]

POLUPRAGMATICUS: You're being silly. Do you want to visit an Italian school?

SIMON ACUTUS: No.

POLUPRAGMATICUS: Why?

SIMON ACUTUS: Because the women there are more learned than we.

POLUPRAGMATICUS: Why is that?

SIMON ACUTUS: Because they frequently sleep with monks and theologians who sprinkle them with dew and inspire a certain spirit.[9]

---

never given forever.] The Oxford text gives "bona" as a variant for "data." [O, fortune, you are never good forever.] Burton gives the reading "Fortuna nunquam perpetuo est bona" in *AM* pt. 2, sec. 3, mem. 1, subs. 1 (129).

[8] Pontano, *Ant.* 94. Suppatius relates more of his adventures while in search of a wise man. He has been talking to a man who asked many questions, and when he noticed that the man was prepared to ask more: " 'Quando, inquam, faciendo itineri occupatus sum, quaeso, mutuum mihi redde et comitem quo Neapolim usque commodiore uti possim, edoce.' Tum ille: 'Agrum, inquit, hunc nostrum peragranti, si bene tibi consultum velis, lupum comitem adhibebis; neque enim comite alio, tot tantorumque molossorum rabiem evitaveris, atque utinam unus tibi satis sit lupus!'—'Atqui inquam, meus hic asellus uni lupo satis non est.' " [I said, "Seeing that I am about to make a journey, I ask you, tell me something in return. Tell me who would be an appropriate companion for me in Naples." Then he said, "If you want good advice, while traveling through that district, you will take a wolf as your companion, for with no other companion will you avoid the fierceness of so many and such large mastiffs, and may one wolf be enough for you!" "But," I said, "my little ass here is not enough for one wolf."] Pontano is possibly playing on the double meanings of "asellus," a little ass or a man addicted to sensuality, and "lupus femina" or "lupa," a she-wolf or a prostitute.

[9] Pontano, *Ant.* 93. When Suppatius asked about a certain woman he had met, "unde tantam mulier doctrinam hausisset" [where she had drunk in such doctrine], he was told that she did not drink from the fountain of the muses nor sleep on Parnassus, "sed vigilans in toro atque in theologi complexibus cubuit. Ex huius ipsius lingua manat eloquentia tam suavis, ex ore theologi orat tam copiose atque inundanter; spiritum huic ille inspiravit roremque instillavit unde oratio eius spirat stillatque tam suave." [but vigilant in bed she sleeps in the embrace of a theologian. Such a sweet eloquence flows from his tongue; he speaks so copiously and over-flowingly. He inspired in her a spirit and

POLUPRAGMATICUS: Vultis Salamancam?

SIMON ACUTUS: Illic nobis non est opus.

LODOUICUS PANTOMETER: Habent plures fortasse nobis non absimiles.

POLUPRAGMATICUS: Si plures, tunc nobis securis esse licet.

LODOUICUS PANTOMETER: Sed minùs lucrandum.

PANTOMAGUS: Descebtabimus aliàs.   1665
    Cessabit quisque nunc ominari malè.

SIMON ACUTUS: Congratulabimur hunc nobis faelicem diem,
    Et, si vultis, ad proximam tabernam vnà ibimus.

PANTOMAGUS: Quin euocemus cauponem huc. Heus puer.

[*Intrat*] PROMUS: Quis vocat?

LODOUICUS PANTOMETER: Insterne mensam sine morâ,   1670
    Affer huc vinum et cyathos, et qui fidibus canat.
[Accumbunt]

    Intendam vires omnes vt me strenuum potando geram.
    Laus enim nunc est. Sed congerrones accumbite.
    Simon quod faustum faelixque sit, poculum praebibo tibi.

SIMON ACUTUS: Accipio, sit salus. Heus, tibi totum hunc cyathum.   1675
[Intrat fidicen]

PROMUS: Fidicen adest.

SIMON ACUTUS: Intende neruos (bone vir)
    Et exhilera nos facetâ cantiunculâ, si quid potes.

POLUPRAGMATICUS: Vereor ne lusus hic in luctum desinat.

SIMON ACUTUS: Tace—

FIDICEN [*canit*]: Phaebus dum pererrat orbem,
    Lustrans quaque praeter spem,   1680
    Martem videt et Venerem,
    Sine thalamo cubantem.
    At nec Phaebus visa celat,
    Sed Vulcano rem reuelat.

OMNES [*canunt*]: Ex diis quidam tum facetè,   1685
    O vtinam vidisset me
    Cubantem sic cum Venere.

FIDICEN: Vulcanus fecit illicò,
    Rete quoddam de metallo,
    Inuicèm se complexantes,   1690

POLUPRAGMATICUS: How about Salamanca?

SIMON ACUTUS: There is no need for us there.

LODOVICUS PANTOMETER: They have plenty just like us.

POLUPRAGMATICUS: If there are many, then we should be safe.

LODOVICUS PANTOMETER: But we'll make less profit.

PANTOMAGUS: We'll discuss this some other time. For now each one will cease these sad prognostications.

SIMON ACUTUS: We'll celebrate our lucky day. If you wish, we'll go together to the nearest tavern.

PANTOMAGUS: Instead, let's call the taverner here. You, boy.

[*The drawer enters*]

DRAWER: Who calls?

LODOVICUS PANTOMETER: Spread a table without delay; bring us wine and cups and someone to sing to the lute.[10]

[*They recline*]

I shall direct all my strength to strenuous drinking, for this is now our glory. But, jolly companions, recline. Simon, I drink this cup to you. May it be propitious and lucky.

SIMON ACUTUS: I accept. To your health. I drink this entire cup to you.

[*Enter lute player*]

DRAWER: The lute player is here.

SIMON ACUTUS: Stretch the strings, my good man, and make us merry with a witty little song, if you are able.

POLUPRAGMATICUS: I fear this playing will end in sorrow.

SIMON ACUTUS: Be quiet.

[*The lute player sings*]

Phoebus, wandering the earth,
Saw more than he had hoped.
For he spied Venus and Mars
On their adulterous couch.
Phoebus did not conceal this,
But revealed the affair to Vulcan.[11]

ALL [*sing*]: Then one of the gods said wittily,
          "O would that he had seen me
          Lying there with Venus."

LUTE PLAYER: Immediately Vulcan made
          A certain net of metal.
          Those embracing

---

sprinkled her with dew whence her speech breathes forth and trickles so sweetly.]

[10] Bensly: "This is, presumably, an echo of Horace, *Epode* [9.33.34]. Capaciores *affer huc*, puer, *scyphos / Et* Chia *vina* aut Lesbia." [Bring here, boy, more generous bowls and wine from Chios or Lesbos.]

[11] See Ovid, *Met.* 4.167–89; Homer, *Od.* 8.266ff.

Et nil tale cogitantes
Quod ligauit tanto nodo
Vt non soluant vllo modo.
OMNES: Ex diis quidam tum facetè,
 O vtinam ligasset me   1695
 Cubantem sic cum Venere.
FIDICEN: Postquàm sic ligasset eos,
 Vocat simul omnes deos,
 Et ostendit concumbentes,
 Sese mutuò fouentes.   1700
 Haerent casse obuoluti.
 Sunt in risum dii soluti.
OMNES: Ex diis quidam tum facetè,
 O vtinam risissent me
 Cubantem sic cum Venere.   1705
PANTOMAGUS: O vtinam risissent me cubantem sic cum Venere.
SIMON ACUTUS: Profectò benè, tu iam ludes, nos canemus inuicèm.
 Incipiam si lubet, vos autem sequimini—
      [Canit]
 Exultemus et ouemus,
 Pergraecemur et potemus   1710
  Simul et amicè.
PANTOMAGUS: Sed quis vinum ministrabit,
 Sed quis potum praestò dabit,
  Multùm sitienti?
LODOUICUS PANTOMETER: Vos euocate puerum—   1715
 Cognoscentem bonum vinum,
  Idque primo visu.
PANTOMAGUS: Euge puer optime—
 Graecè bibens et latinè
  Tuum fac officium.   1720
OMNES: Haec est illa bona dies,
 Vnde nobis tanta quies,
  Facta fuit hodie.
 Nullus metus, nec labores,
 Nulla cura, nec dolores   1725
  Sint in hoc symposio.
SIMON ACUTUS: Omnes fortes sunt vinosi,
 Et potantes animosi,
  Dicit Aristotiles.
POLUPRAGMATICUS: Vbi nemo vestrum sapit,   1730
 Sed vos omnes vinum capit,
  Quid sequetur illicò?

And unsuspecting
He bound with such a knot
They could no way get free.
ALL: Then one of the gods said wittily,
      "O would that he had bound me
      Lying there with Venus."
LUTE PLAYER: After he had trapped them thus,
He called the gods together,
Displayed the two lying there,
Embracing one another and
Caught in metal covers.
The gods dissolved in laughter.
ALL: Then one of the gods said wittily,
      "O would that they had laughed at me
      Lying there with Venus."
PANTOMAGUS: O would that they had laughed at me, lying there with Venus.
SIMON ACUTUS: Well done. Now you play, we'll sing in turn. I shall begin, if
    you please, then you follow me.
                      [He sings]
      Let us rejoice and celebrate
      Let us play the Greek and drink
          Together and as friends.
PANTOMAGUS: But who will serve the wine
      And who will bring a cup
         For the very thirsty?
LODOVICUS PANTOMETER: You there, call the boy.
      He knows a good wine
         At first glance.
PANTOMAGUS: Well done, fine boy—
      Drinking in Greek and Latin
         Do your duty.
ALL: This is that good day
      Whence for us such peace
         Was made today.
      No fear, no toil,
      No care, no sorrow
         Are in this symposium.
SIMON ACUTUS: All brave men are full of wine
      And drinkers full of courage,
         As Aristotle says.
POLUPRAGMATICUS: When none of you is wise
      But all seize the wine—
         What follows then?

OMNES: Bibe, bibe, bibe, bibe,
    Tu qui sapis, bibe, bibe,
      Dum Lyeus imperat.   1735
PROMUS: Sed vos rogo, dum potatis
    Terque quater videatis—
      Ne frangatis cyathum.
PANTOMAGUS: Dulce dulci misceatis.
    Ex hoc in hoc effundatis   1740
      Vt potemus meliùs.
POLUPRAGMATICUS: Sed iam potrix turba tace
    Ne pro vestrâ tantâ pace
      Bellum fiat arduum.
OMNES: Ergò tandem desinamus,   1745
    Et potantes abeamus
      Canentes hilarè.

ALL: Drink, drink, drink, drink,
      You who are wise, drink, drink
         While Bacchus rules.
DRAWER: But I beg you, as you're drinking
      Three and four, do be careful
         Not to break the cups.
PANTOMAGUS: Mix sweet with sweet,
      Pour this into this
         That we may better drink.
POLUPRAGMATICUS: But now, fellow drinkers, be silent,
      Lest, in place of this peace,
         We find bitter war.
ALL: Therefore at last let us cease,
      And drinking, let us depart
         Singing merrily.

ACTUS QUINTUS
Scena Prima
Sordidus. Cornutus. Rubicundus.   1750

CORNUTUS: O me infaelicem et miserum! Quid agam, quid querar?
    Apud quos; vbi?
SORDIDUS: Hem Cornute, quid agis?
    Quid id est quod te tam sollicitum tenet?
    Salua domus, vxor salua, salui liberi,
    Diues es, sanus es, liber es, et quid te dolet?   1755
CORNUTUS: Dolet, et si non vidissem his ipsis oculis.
SORDIDUS: Quid vidisti, laruam, lemures, an Gorgoneum caput?
CORNUTUS: Non, sed cornigerum caput.
SORDIDUS: Doletne caput?
CORNUTUS: Dolet caput.
SORDIDUS: Apagesis cum tuo capite.
    An tu primus an tu solus in hoc oppido   1760
    Quod conuenit omni fere et sempèr? Quid te dolet?
    Annon heroes, duces, ipsi reges cornigeri?
CORNUTUS: Emat, vendat, rem familiarem coquat,
    Propinet, pitiset, vsque in diem cubat.
    Probare possem et probo, at hoc tamen.   1765
SORDIDUS: Hoc nihil.
CORNUTUS: At ipse vidi et in aedibus meis.
SORDIDUS: Certus es id tibi contigisse in indiuiduo
    Quod conuenit omnibus oppidanis in genere.
CORNUTUS: At a scholari factum.
SORDIDUS: Non refert a quo fiat modò.
CORNUTUS: Ero ludibrium.
SORDIDUS: Quibus ludibrium?
CORNUTUS: Ciuibus.   1770

ACT V
Scene one
Sordidus. Cornutus. Rubicundus.

CORNUTUS: Oh unhappy, miserable me! What am I to do? How do I make a complaint? To whom? Where?

SORDIDUS: Hey, Cornutus, what are you doing? Why are you so upset? Your house is safe, your wife is safe, your children safe, you are rich, healthy, free, so what's troubling you?

CORNUTUS: I'm troubled, even if I hadn't seen it with my own eyes.

SORDIDUS: What have you seen? A ghost, a goblin, the Gorgon's head?

CORNUTUS: No, but a horned head.

SORDIDUS: And your head hurts?

CORNUTUS: My head hurts.

SORDIDUS: Forget your head. Are you the first or the only one in this town? It happens to almost everyone and all the time. Why does it trouble you? Don't you know that noblemen, dukes, even kings themselves are cuckolded?[1]

CORNUTUS: Let her buy, sell, stir up the household, drink, sip, stay in bed all day. I would be satisfied with it, and I am. But now this.

SORDIDUS: This is nothing.

CORNUTUS: But I have seen it myself, and in my own house.

SORDIDUS: You know that what has happened to you in particular happens to everybody in this town in general.

CORNUTUS: But it was done by a student.

SORDIDUS: It doesn't matter by whom it was done.

CORNUTUS: I'll be a laughing stock.

SORDIDUS: For whom?

CORNUTUS: The townpeople.

---

[1] See *AM* pt. 3, sec. 3, mem. 4, subs. 1 (289–90).

SORDIDUS: Clodius accuset moechos. Sed Cornute, sanum consilium
    Amplectere amici et quod vides, non vides,
    Et quod scis, nescis. Tu pol si sapis atque ita
    Pacatus viues, et fortasse quaestum vberem facies.
    Ego sic soleo. Sed non omnibus dormio.   1775
[*Intrat*] RUBICUNDUS:
    Amici, populares, conciues, homines,
    Ferte opem innocenti!
SORDIDUS: Quis hic, Rubicundus furens?
CORNUTUS: Is ipse.
RUBICUNDUS: O caput, o costas, o craneum.
SORDIDUS: Quid vis, quid agis?
RUBICUNDUS: Me miserum! Scholares duo
    Omnes dentes labefecerunt mihi—   1780
    Colaphisque tuber fecerunt totum caput—
CORNUTUS: Itane? Vbi?
RUBICUNDUS: Meis ipsius aedibus—
SORDIDUS: Quâ de causâ?
RUBICUNDUS: Quod totum propinanti cyathum
    Ego tantum ebiberam demidium.
CORNUTUS: Graue facinus.
SORDIDUS: Quo telo?
RUBICUNDUS: Pugnis suis   1785
    Et crebris poculis ita saeuierunt in caput.
CORNUTUS: Ita videtur.
SORDIDUS: Sed vbi laesus interim?
RUBICUNDUS: Non sum omninò laesus, sed quod sursum pedes
    Volent aliquandò et deorsum caput.
    Ligarûnt omnes sensus magicis carminibus.   1790
CORNUTUS: Magnis credo poculis.
SORDIDUS: Tu verberatus quidem.
    Sed audi, tu te domum quamprimum conferes,
    Ibique te pronum in lectum coniicies,
    Prae te ferens verberatum, laesum grauitèr.
CORNUTUS: Quem ob finem non video.

SORDIDUS: Let Clodius condemn adulterers.[2] But Cornutus, take some good advice from a friend. If you are smart, what you see, you don't see; what you know, you don't know.[3] That way, you will live in peace and maybe even make a fat profit. That's what I do. But I don't sleep for everyone.[4]

[Enter Rubicundus]

RUBICUNDUS: Friends, countrymen, fellow citizens, men, bring help to the innocent![5]

SORDIDUS: Who is this, Rubicundus raging?

CORNUTUS: He himself.

RUBICUNDUS: O head, o ribs, o skull.

SORDIDUS: What do you want? What are you doing?

RUBICUNDUS: O wretched me! Two scholars loosened all my teeth and from blows with their fists, my whole head is one lump.[6]

CORNUTUS: Is that so? Where?

RUBICUNDUS: At my own house.

SORDIDUS: Why?

RUBICUNDUS: Because to one who toasted me with a whole cup, I drank only half.

CORNUTUS: A serious crime.

SORDIDUS: What weapon did they use?

RUBICUNDUS: With their own fists and cups they kept venting their rage on my head.

CORNUTUS: So it seems.

SORDIDUS: Where is the wound?

RUBICUNDUS: I'm not exactly wounded, but sometimes my feet would fly up and my head down. They bound all my senses with magic songs.

CORNUTUS: More likely with large cups.

SORDIDUS: You have taken a beating indeed. But listen, as soon as you get home, throw yourself prone on the couch. Let out you have been beaten, seriously wounded.

RUBICUNDUS: I don't see to what end.

---

[2] JS: "P. Clodius, enemy to Cicero, was a notorious adulterer: he was free to accuse others of the same sin, but he was caught himself, and lives in the ancient proverb which Burton quotes from Juvenal." *Sat.* 2.27: "Clodius accuset moechos" [If Clodius condemn adulterers].

[3] JS: Terence, *Heaut.* 748: "tu nescis id quod scis, Dromo, si sapies." [If you are wise, Dromo, you don't know what you know.] See also Terence, *Eun.* 722 and Erasmus, *Ad.* 3.5.99: "Quod scis, nescis" [What you know you don't know.]

[4] Cicero, *Ep. Fam.* 7.24. Erasmus, *Ad.* 1.6.4.

[5] Terence, *Ad.* 155: "Obsecro, populares, ferte misero atque innocenti auxilium." [I beg you, fellow citizens, bring help to the wretched and innocent.]

[6] Terence, *Ad.* 244-45: "omnis dentis labefecit mihi, / praeterea colaphis tuber est totum caput:" [He loosened all my teeth; moreover, my whole head is one lump from blows with the fists.]

SORDIDUS: Obsecro taceas. 1795
    Vxor primo mane querelam deferat ad ducem,
    Laesum ciuem, et coniugem semimortuum.
    Nos interim per omne dissipabimus oppidum,
    Ciuem verberatum et in ipso foro.
    Tu sis lecto aeger. Amici te visitent. 1800
CORNUTUS: Quid tum sequetur?
SORDIDUS: Audi totam fabulam.
    Scholares hoc audito soluent quod vis. Ne quid grauius
    Contingat, rem componentes vxore tuâ.
    Aut si non coram ipso Duce causam agant.
CORNUTUS: Placet hoc consilium.
RUBICUNDUS: Et fiet illicò. 1805
SORDIDUS: Tu te verberatum fortasse laetabere.

Scena Secunda
Antonius. Aequiuocus.

ANTONIUS: Quam nunquam secundus amor est vel ad exitum
    Laetum perueniat, quin hunc excipiat dolor illicò; 1810
    Malo meo demens hoc ipsum intelligo–
    Compressi virginem et ducturum me fidem dedi,
    Quae res me sic excruciat vt nihil magìs.
    Tanquam nauis iactor pelago, et ad crucem
    Statìm adigar infaelix vel ad insaniam. 1815
    Vt nubam cogit lex, pietas, aequitas, amor,
    Fides relligio; at stat e contra pater.
    Durus pater qui me praecipitem dabit.
    O vos beati qui procul ab his vinculis,
    Neptunum a terra videtis furentem procùl! 1820
    O fallaces mulieres, quae non secus ac canes feram
    Prosequuntur, apprehensum mordicùs tenent!
    O perfidum Aequiuocum pessimum omnium mortalium,
    Qui mihi malum hoc machinatus es, hanc pernitiem!
    Sed lupus in fabulâ. Subducam me attendens quid ait. 1825
[*Intrat*] AEQUIUOCUS: Sudore diffluo; ita me pondus auri premit.
    Herum compilaui, et Pantomagum medicum.
    Furtiuas claues ementiendo circumueni grauitèr.
    Sed et Antonium fraudaui hâc sicâ et clamide,
    Et iam nunc equum et baiulum seruum pcto, 1830
    Qui me leuent hoc onere, sed et artificem
    Statuarium. Statuam enim mihi fieri volo.

SORDIDUS: Be quiet, I beg you. First thing in the morning, have your wife take a complaint to the duke: a citizen has been injured, her husband half dead. We, meanwhile, will tell the whole town that a citizen has been beaten, and in the forum itself. You should be sick in bed. Friends will visit you.

CORNUTUS: Then what happens?

SORDIDUS: Hear the whole story. When these things have been heard, the scholars will pay whatever you want. Lest something more serious happen, they'll settle the matter with your wife. If not, they may have to plead the case before the duke himself.

CORNUTUS: I like this plan.

RUBICUNDUS: It will be done right away.

SORDIDUS: Perhaps you will be glad that you were beaten.

Scene two
Antonius. Aequivocus.

ANTONIUS: Love is never favorable nor has a happy outcome without sorrow coming right on its heels. Fool that I am, I know this to my misfortune: I have ravished a young maiden and promised I would marry her. This tortures me as nothing more. I am tossed about as a ship on the sea, and I, unhappy person that I am, am driven at once to destruction or to insanity. The law, piety, justice, faith, religion compel me to marry; my father is against it. He is a harsh father who will cast me down. O happy are you who are far from these chains, who see Neptune raging far from land.[1] O deceitful women who, like dogs pursuing a wild beast, hold fast their prey. O perfidious Aequivocus, worst of all mortals, who craftily devised for me this trouble, this destruction. But speak of the wolf.[2] I'll take myself away, attending to what is said.

[Enter] AEQUIVOCUS: My sweat is just flowing, this weight of gold presses me so. I have robbed my master and the physician Pantomagus. By surreptitiously copying keys, I deceived them in an impressive manner. I have also taken from Antonius this dagger and cloak and now I need a horse and a porter to relieve me of this burden. I also want a sculptor, for I wish to have a statue made of me.[3]

---

[1] Horace, *Epist.* 1.2.10.

[2] LS: Proverb: "lupus in fabula or sermone, said of the appearance of a person when he is spoken of; as we say in English, 'talk of the devil, and he appears.'" Plautus, *Stich.* 577: "lupum in sermone." Terence, *Ad.* 537; Cic. *Att.* 13.33.4: "lupus in fabula." Erasmus, *Ad.* 3.8.56; 4.5.50.

[3] Bensly: Plautus, *Bacch.* 640–41: "Hunc hominem decet auro expendi, huic decet statuam statui ex auro; / nam duplex facinus feci hodie, duplicibus spoliis sum adfectus." [Here is a man who deserves his weight in gold, who deserves a statue made of gold; for today I committed a double crime and have acquired double spoils.]

ANTONIUS: En tibi seruum et baiulum, qui te leuabit hoc onere
    Artificemque qui parabit tibi pro statuâ crucem,
    Perfidissime.
AEQUIUOCUS: Antonî suauissime per Iouem.   1835
    Ioco feci.
ANTONIUS: At seriò poenam dabis.

Scena Tertia
Polupistos. Stephanio.

POLUPISTOS: Qui vbi sunt, fuerunt, aut futuri sunt asini,
    Stulti, stolidi, buccones, blenni, fatui,   1840
    Ego longè anteo omnibus stultitiâ.
    Pudet. Perii. Me hoccine aetatis hominem
    Ludum bis factum esse; quo magis id repeto,
    Magìs vror. Excoriauit me totum medicus;
    Decoxit rem totam familiarem mihi.   1845
    Auro vsque attondit, doctis indoctum dolis.
    Hoc est quod dolet, quod paracescit modò,
    Me hoc aetatis ita ludificari hominem.
    Vix sum compos animi, ita ardeo iracundiâ.
    Sed quid sto? Quidni queror, scelestum quidni persequor?   1850
        [*Exeunti conuenit.*]
STEPHANIO: Polupiste, quo tam citus?
POLUPISTOS: Stephanio, vt vales?
    Osunam ego.
STEPHANIO: Quid succenses, quid frontem caperas?
POLUPISTOS: Quo tu demum, aut quid te tam sollicitum tenet?
STEPHANIO: A filio nuper allatae sunt mihi literae
    In quibus scribit se ciuis vitiasse filiam   1855

ANTONIUS: Here is your servant and porter who will lighten your load and the craftsman who will make you a gallows for your statue, most traitorous person.

AEQUIVOCUS: Sweetest Antonius, by Jove. I did it in jest.

ANTONIUS: But you will be punished in earnest.

Scene three
Polupistos. Stephanio.

POLUPISTOS: Of all who are, were, or ever will be asses, stupid fools, buffoons, dolts, idiots, I surpass them by far in stupidity. I'm ashamed. I'm destroyed. Me, a man of my age, to have been made a fool twice. The more I say it, the more I am tormented. The physician has completely skinned me, he has consumed my entire household. He sheared me of my gold, I who was unskilled in skillful deceit. This is what pains me, what is most unpleasant, that I at my age have been made such a fool.[1] I am scarcely composed in mind, I burn so with anger.[2] But why am I standing here? Why don't I make a complaint, why don't I prosecute the scoundrel?

[*He meets someone coming.*]

STEPHANIO: Polupistos, where are you going in such a hurry?

POLUPISTOS: Stephanio, how are you? I am going to Osuna.

STEPHANIO: What's bothering you? Why are you frowning?

POLUPISTOS: I would ask the same of you. What is troubling you so?

STEPHANIO: These letters were recently sent to me by my son. In them he writes that he has deflowered the daughter of a citizen and now is compelled by law to marry her. This tortures me. I'm going there to help, if it is possible, and to supply some remedy. But have you still heard nothing about your daughter?

---

[1] Bensly: Plautus, *Bacch.* 1087–1095; 1099–1100: "Quiquomque ubi sunt, qui fuerunt quique futuri sunt posthac / stulti, stolidi, fatui, fungi, bardi, blenni, buccones, / solus ego omnis longe antideo stultitia et moribus indoctis. / perii, pudet: hocine me aetatis ludos bis factum esse indigne? / magi' quam id reputo, tam magis uror quae meu' filiu' turbauit. / perditu' sum atque eradicatus sum, omnibus exemplis excrucior. / omnia me mala consectantur, omnibus exitiis interii. / Chrysalu' med hodie lacerauit, Chrysalu' me miserum spoliauit: / is me scelus auro usque attondit dolis doctis indoctum ut lubitumst. . . . hoc est demum quod percrucior, / me hoc aetatis ludificari, . . ." [Of all those who are, were, or will hereafter be stupid, fools, idiots, fungi, dizzards, dolts, buffoons, I alone am far ahead in stupidity and silly behavior. I am destroyed, I am ashamed: at this time of my life have I been unworthily made a fool twice? The more I say it, the more I am tormented by what stirred up my son. I am destroyed and eradicated, tortured by every means. Every evil follows me, I die by every death. Chrysalus wounded me today, Chrysalus despoiled wretched me: that villain sheared me of my gold as he pleased; I who was unskilled in skillful deceit. . . . This at length is what tortures me, to have been made a fool at this time of life.]

[2] JS: See Terence, *Ad.* 310: "vix sum compos animi, ita ardeo iracundia." [I am scarcely composed in mind, I burn so with anger.]

Et vt ducat in vxorem iam cogi a legibus.
Hoc me torquet. Illuc tendo vt subueniam
Si fieri possit, et pharmachum adhibeam.
Sed nihil etiamnum audis de tuâ filiâ?
POLUPISTOS: Nihil praeter incertos rumores quod Osunae siet.   1860
   Proficiscor illuc iam.
STEPHANIO: An ob hoc negotium?
POLUPISTOS: O Stephanio, sed inter eundum rem totam dicam tibi.

Scena Quarta
Polumathes. Philobiblos.

PHILOBIBLOS: Polumathes, quid inuenisti sapientem adhuc?   1865
POLUMATHES: Quaerendus alibi sapiens.
PHILOBIBLOS: Itane?
POLUMATHES: Ita.
PHILOBIBLOS: At inuenisti opinor doctos innumeros.
POLUMATHES: Diuites plures, paucos doctos, sapientem neminem.
PHILOBIBLOS: Non intendis fortasse.
POLUMATHES: Conueni, consului
   Summos, infimos cuiuscunque ferè ordinis.   1870
PHILOBIBLOS: Quos demus probas? De vulgo quid existimas?
POLUMATHES: Sunt benè vestiti et quoad barbam conspicui
   Incessum, vocem, vultum, humani plerumque et graues,
   Stipati famulis nonunquam et pulchro satellitio,
   Prae se ferentes gradus, titulos, insignia.   1875
   Iurares ad vnum omnes sapientes, doctissimos.
PHILOBIBLOS: Quales vero sunt?
POLUMATHES: Nostin templum Aegiptiacum?
PHILOBIBLOS: Capio quid vis; tu vero dic apertè et liberè.
POLUMATHES: Sunt ob maiorem partem Cumani asini,
   Infantes, aridi, ieiuni, steriles, straminei,   1880
   Plumbei, caudaces, bardi, fungi, stipites,
   Inertes, Idiotae, somno gulaeque dediti,
   Illiterati, arrogantes, laruati, philologi
   Armati solum barbis et impudentiâ.
PHILOBIBLOS: Tu mirus praeco mirum Encomiasten agis.   1885

POLUPISTOS: Nothing but uncertain rumors that she may be in Osuna. I'm going there now.

STEPHANIO: Because of this business?

POLUPISTOS: O Stephanio, I will tell the entire thing to you as we go.

Scene four
Polumathes. Philobiblos.

PHILOBIBLOS: Polumathes, have you found a wise man yet?

POLUMATHES: The wise must be sought elsewhere.

PHILOBIBLOS: Is that so?

POLUMATHES: Yes, it is so.

PHILOBIBLOS: But you have found many learned men, I suppose.

POLUMATHES: Many rich, few learned, none wise.

PHILOBIBLOS: Perhaps you did not look diligently.

POLUMATHES: I have met and consulted with the highest and lowest of almost every rank.

PHILOBIBLOS: Do you approve of anyone? What do you think about the common people?

POLUMATHES: They are well-dressed and are conspicuous with respect to their beards, their walk, voice, appearance; they are especially genteel and serious, always surrounded by servants and a handsome guard, pretending to hold degrees of honor, titles, and insignia. You would swear that each and every one was wise and most learned.

PHILOBIBLOS: In truth, what are they like?

POLUMATHES: Do you know Egyptian temples?[1]

PHILOBIBLOS: I understand what you mean. Tell the truth, openly and freely.

POLUMATHES: They are for the most part Cuman asses, children, greedy misers, sterile straw men, dull blockheads, soothsayers, fungi, lazy, dim-witted fools who only want sleep and food. They are illiterate, arrogant, possessed by spirits; they talk too much and are armed only with beards and impudence.

PHILOBIBLOS: You are an odd crier with an odd encomium. Perhaps because you are incensed you spew forth this anger against everyone.[2]

---

[1] JS: "The term occurs more than once in Burton's *The Anatomy of Melancholy*, and is taken to mean 'fair without but foul within.' *Cuman asses*, a few lines below, is also an expression found in *The Anatomy*; it refers to the ass in Aesop that was arrayed in the lion's skin." Erasmus, *Ad*. 1.3.66; 1.7.12. *AM* Democritus (62): "To see 'sub exuviis leonis onagrum' [an ass in a lion's skin], a filthy loathsome carcass, a Gorgon's head puffed up by parasites, assume this unto himself, glorious titles, in worth an infant, a Cuman ass, a painted sepulchre, an Egyptian temple!"

[2] Terence, *Ad*. 312: "ego iram hanc in eos evomam omnem" [I would spew forth all this anger against them.]

Incensus fortasse in omnes hanc iram euomes.
POLUMATHES: Et quidni incensus? Quis aequo animo ferat?
PHILOBIBLOS: Peregrinus quum sis tu conticescas tamen.
POLUMATHES: Egone feram tot impostores proletarios,
   Semipaganos philosophastros, nugiuendulos?   1890
   Faxo sciant et, si possum, poenas ferent.
PHILOBIBLOS: At quid in omnes inueheris?
POLUMATHES: Malè capis.
   Habet Osuna viros vndiquaque doctissimos
   Suspitiendos omni scientiarum genere
   Quos ego veneror, admiror, amplector, exosculor.   1895
   At hic plures tamen pistrinâ digni asini,
   Ex harâ producti. De Gothicis hisce loquor.
PHILOBIBLOS: Rectè sentis sed tu nimis acerbus interim.
   Non habent omnes fortasse disciplinas Encyclias
   Sed in singulis praecellunt. Quisque non est Hyppias.   1900
POLUMATHES: Nec ego quaero tam multiplicem scientiam.
   Si vel in vnâ mediocres, satis superque foret.
PHILOBIBLOS: At sunt sophistae.
POLUMATHES: Si quis altum vociferet in scholis,
   Libros vulgares et deliramenta quaedam glossamatica
   Legat et effutiat, summum habent philosophum.   1905
   Si togatus ambulet, insignem peripateticum.
PHILOBIBLOS: Insignes fortasse grammatici.
POLUMATHES: Fortasse quidem.
   Si quis emergat poetaster vel criticus,
   Qui notas fecerit aut animaduersiones aliquot:
   Deleatur d, alii legunt sic, codex meus sic habet—   1910
   Phoebus audit, literarum decus, sidus, oraculum.
PHILOBIBLOS: Profecto rem tenes et hoc malo meo didici.
   In grammatistam quendam incidi qui me conuitiis
   Onerauit, quod inter loquendum marcesco excideret.
   Satis habui incolumi pallio me inde proripere.   1915
   Et hinc opinor Rhetoricâ praesertìm praecellere.
POLUMATHES: Praecellunt sane. Si quis hinc inde flosculos
   Consarcinare possit aut quasdam sententiolas
   Ad ornandam orationem, orator audit optimus.
   Artes plerumque negligunt; hoc solum votis habent,   1920

POLUMATHES: And why should I not be incensed? Who could bear this calmly?

PHILOBIBLOS: But since you are a stranger, you should be quiet.

POLUMATHES: Should I bear such common and vulgar impostors, semi-pagan trifling philosophasters? I will let them know what I would do, and if I am able, they will pay the price.

PHILOBIBLOS: But why inveigh against all?

POLUMATHES: You don't understand. Osuna has here and there very learned men in all fields of knowledge whom I honor, venerate, admire, embrace and have affection for. But nevertheless there are here many asses worthy of the mill,[3] born in a pigsty. It is about these Goths that I speak.

PHILOBIBLOS: Your opinions are correct, but you are too harsh sometimes. Perhaps not everyone has encyclopedic knowledge, but excels in a particular area. Not everyone is Hippias.

POLUMATHES: But I'm not looking for such knowledge in many areas. If they were mediocre in just one area, it would be more than enough.

PHILOBIBLOS: But they are sophists.

POLUMATHES: If anyone speaks loudly in the schools, reads common books or mentions certain foolish, uncommon words, he is considered the greatest philosopher. If he wanders about in his toga, he is considered a distinguished peripatetic.

PHILOBIBLOS: Perhaps they are outstanding grammarians.

POLUMATHES: Perhaps indeed. If some poetaster or critic emerges who has made certain notes or some judgment—such as: "let the letter 'd' be deleted; others read thus, my manuscript reads thus,"[4]—he is considered a Phoebus, the honor of literature, a star, an oracle.

PHILOBIBLOS: You understand the situation well, and I learned this by my own misfortune. I met a certain grammarian who burdened me with reproach because, while I was talking, I let the word "marcesco" slip out. I desired nothing more than to leave there with my coat intact. From this I conclude that rhetoricians certainly excel.

POLUMATHES: Certainly they excel. If anyone from one place or another can patch together "little flowers" or certain commonplaces to adorn his speech, he is considered the greatest orator. These men especially neglect the arts. They have only one desire—a fat benefice.[5] Once they have this, they have everything.

---

[3] Cooper: *pistrinum* & *pistrina*: "A place where, before milles inuented, men vsed to bray their corne in morters. which, because of the vntollerable paynes, they vsed as a prison to punish their bondemen and slaues offending their maysters." Terence, *Heaut.* 530: "hominem pistrino dignum!" [A man worthy of the mill.]

[4] JS: See *AM* Democritus (113).

[5] JS: "The Latin 'hoc solum in votis habens, optimum sacerdotium,' occurs in [*AM* pt. 1, sec. 2, mem. 3, subs. 15 (310)], and Burton renders it 'A good Parsonage was their aim.' "

Opimum sacerdotium; hoc habito, habentur omnia.

PHILOBIBLOS: Ergò dant operam Theologiae, idque vnicum
    Elaborant, consilio non malo, sed quales erant?

POLUMATHES: Vidi Theologos per annos triginta Academicos.

PHILOBIBLOS: Tanto doctiores.

POLUMATHES: Tanto crassiores asinos,   1925
    Gulae deuotos, somno ventrique deditos
    Qui suggestum aequè ac pistrinam fugiunt.
    Sed his parco.

PHILOBIBLOS: Quales vidisti medicos?

POLUMATHES: Pudet dicere, mittoque medicinae carcinomata,
    Quibus hoc tempore nihil putidius;   1930
    Passim quod medicorum est nunc anus baiula,
    Olidus balneator, vel tonsor audaculus.
    Verbosus Paracelsita aut ignauus Empericus
    Lucellum captans imposturis agit.

PHILOBIBLOS: Soli restant Iurisperiti.

POLUMATHES: Mitto illorum vlcera;   1935
    Si videres istorum in dicendo arrogantiam,
    Iurares praeter litem nihil esse reliquum,
    Praeter os et frontem, licitumque latrocinium.

PHILOBIBLOS: Stupenda narras.

POLUMATHES: Vera ita me deus amet.
    Hi sunt quos insector, quos odio sempèr habui;   1940
    Et sanciendam legem curarem aliquem
    Quae tam enormem fraenaret licentiam,
    Et quicunque sunt cordati philosophi,
    Fauebunt sat, scio, huic instituto meo.

PHILOBIBLOS: Quod ego laudo, et reformarem libentius   1945
    Si mei iuris esset. At quid agendum mones?

POLUMATHES: Querendum est ad eos, et quorum interest,
    Academiarum praefectos, et in hoc summo duci,
    Qui mox ad Tribunal hoc aderit.

PHILOBIBLOS: Do me comitem si lubet.

Scena Quinta et vltima   1950
Interloquutores ferè omnes.

[*Intrat Dux cum supplicibus in manu libellis et multis querelas deferentibus, etc.*]

DUX: O quam deceptus fui. Quis vnquam crederet
    Sub hac togâ tantam latere nequitiam?

EUBULUS: Fronti nulla fides.

PHILOBIBLOS: Therefore they turn to theology and, not advisedly, work for that alone. But of what sort are they?

POLUMATHES: I have seen theologians spend thirty years at the university.

PHILOBIBLOS: And so they are all the more learned.

POLUMATHES: All the more dull asses, devoted to their gullets, dedicated to sleep and stomach, who flee the pulpit as they would the mill. But I pardon these.

PHILOBIBLOS: What sort of physicians have you seen?

POLUMATHES: I'm ashamed to say and I pass over this growing canker of medicine. Nothing at this time is more rotten than they. What in many places now passes for a physician is an old woman porter, a stinking keeper of baths, or a bold enough barber. A wordy Paracelsian or cowardly empiric seeking a profit, manages the deceit.

PHILOBIBLOS: Only attorneys are left.

POLUMATHES: Pass over their corruption. If you were to see their arrogance in speaking, you would swear that nothing was left in litigation except a lip, a look, and legal larceny.

PHILOBIBLOS: You speak of amazing things.

POLUMATHES: But the truth, as god loves me. I censure these men, I hold them in contempt; I would ordain some law against them which would repress such undue license. I know well enough that whatever honest philosophers there are will applaud my intention.

PHILOBIBLOS: I agree, and I would reform these men with pleasure if it were within my rights. What do you suggest ought to be done?

POLUMATHES: A complaint must be made to the prefects of the university. This matter concerns them and especially the duke who will soon hold his tribunal here.

PHILOBIBLOS: I'll accompany you if you like.

Scene five, the last
Almost all speakers

[*Enter duke with supplications in hand and others bringing many complaints.*]

DUKE: Oh, how deceived I have been. Who would ever have believed that such iniquity was hidden beneath this gown.

EUBULUS: Don't trust appearances.[1]

---

[1] JS: Juvenal, *Sat.* 2.8.

CRATINUS: Neque credendum alicui.

DUX: Sed qualis fuit qui te tantis affecit iniuriis?   1955

STEPHANIO: Quod ad professionem, Iesuitam prae se tulit;
    Ex voce, gestu, habitu, vir doctus and probus,
    Sed o in hostem me potius contingat incidere
    Quam talem! Praeter bibendi et artem mentiendi benè
    Natum meum docuit omninò nihil.   1960
    Deceptus ab eo cuius fidei commiseram,
    Inter lenam et meretrices absorpsit pecuniam.

DUX: Inter lenam et meretrices! Quas, quales, vbi?

STEPHANIO: Habitant non procul hinc in suburbanis hortulis.

DUX: Lictor accerse. Nosti hominem, si videris iterum?   1965

STEPHANIO: Plus satis damno meo.

DUX: Esto animo bono,
    Poenas dabit tanto dignas facinore.

EUBULUS: Tu bis delusus an ab eodem homine?

POLUPISTOS: Non, sed diuersis.

CRATINUS: Quibus artibus?

POLUPISTOS: Alter suauiloquus, et quoad barbam conspicuus,   1970
    In Magiâ iactabat singularem peritiam,
    At plenus erat praestigiarum, deceptionis, mendacii.

EUBULUS: Idem fortasse qui huic alteri imposuit.

POLUPISTOS: Alter Spagiricus tantam verborum Ambrosiam
    Effudit vt persuaderet se posse penitus   1975
    Aurum conficere, quibus ego factus velut ebrius
    Credebam illi fortunas meas. At ille nebulo
    Insignis pro auro carbones reliquit mihi.

CRATINUS: Mirum est hoc prae ceteris imposturae genus.

EUBULUS: A quo laesus tu?

RUBICUNDUS: Verberatus grauissimè.   1980

DUX: Per quos?

RUBICUNDUS: Duos scholares ebrios in foro.

DUX: O execrandum facinus verberare ciuem et senem,
    Et in ipso foro!

EUBULUS: Quod damnum tuum?

CORNUTUS: Damnum, sed pudet dicere.

CRATINUS: At illum non puduit facere.

CORNUTUS: Legas si placet.

EUBULUS: Quid tu quereris?   1985

SORDIDUS: Ciuis sum si placet et hic in viciniâ
    Villam habui cultam pro more rustico,
    Sed dum scholares habitarûnt hoc oppidum
    Nec aedes, nec villa, nec quid mihi reliquum.

DUX: Quid ita?

CRATINUS: Don't trust anyone.

DUKE: What sort of man was he who injured you in this way?

STEPHANIO: As to his profession, he pretended to be a Jesuit. From his voice, countenance, dress, he seemed a learned and honest man, but, oh, better that I should go against an enemy rather than such a man. He taught my son nothing at all except the art of drinking and lying well. Deceived by the one to whom I entrusted him, my son spent his money on bawds and whores.

DUKE: Bawds and whores! Who, of what sort, where?

STEPHANIO: They live not far from here in a suburban garden.

DUKE: Lictor, bring them here. Would you know this man if you were to see him again?

STEPHANIO: I'm sure of it, to my loss.

DUKE: Be assured, he will pay a penalty worthy of such a crime.

EUBULUS: You were deceived twice by the same man?

POLUPISTOS: No, by different men.

CRATINUS: By what means?

POLUPISTOS: One was well-spoken and had a respectable beard, boasted of a particular skill in magic, but was full of delusions, deceptions and lies.

EUBULUS: Perhaps he was the same one who deceived the other man.

POLUPISTOS: The other, an alchemist, poured forth such an ambrosia of words that he persuaded me he could actually make gold. I, as if drunk by this, entrusted to him my fortune. The notorious knave left me with carbon instead of gold.

CRATINUS: This sort of imposture is strange compared to the others.

EUBULUS: How were you injured?

RUBICUNDUS: I was severely beaten.

DUKE: By whom?

RUBICUNDUS: By two drunken students in the forum.

DUKE: O accursed crime! To beat a citizen and old man and in the forum itself.

EUBULUS: What is your injury?

CORNUTUS: An injury, but I am embarrassed to name it.

CRATINUS: But he was not embarrassed to do it.

CORNUTUS: You may read it, if you please.

EUBULUS: What is your complaint?

SORDIDUS: Please, I am a citizen and I have a farmhouse not far from here, a typical country farm. But since the students have inhabited this town, neither house nor farm nor anything is left for me.

DUKE: Why is that?

SORDIDUS: Suffurati sunt pene omnia,   1990
  Lignum, gallinas, fructus, anates, anseres,
  Agnos, oues, nil custodimus; equum gradarium
  Alter a me nuper conductum occidit.
STEPHANIO: Propter irruptiones etiam ferè continuas
  Nos qui habitamus ad sextum abhinc lapidem   1995
  Nec aues defensamus nec damas protegimus
  Nec leporem in aruis neque piscem in aquis.
DUX: Hine venatores?
STEPHANIO: Et piscatores etiam.
DUX: O calones, o verberones!
SORDIDUS: Audi grauissimum.
  Ignarus medicus suis virulentis pharmacis   2000
  Vxorem interemit mihi charissimam.
RUBICUNDUS: Vtinam occidisset meam!
CORNUTUS: Et si placeret diis, meam.
DUX: Proh deûm atque hominum fidem! Tot scelera—
  Tam abhorrenda quis audiuit a talibus tam breui,
  Quod tam atrox factum, quod non commiserint?   2005
  Quae fraudes imposturae, furta, caedes, adulteria,
  Luxus, ebrietas, turpe quod crimen, faedum facinus
  Quod non designarînt? Hi fructus ingenii?
  Hoc illud bonum quod persuaserunt mihi?
  Ipsa Barbaries nihil produxit immanius.   2010
  Hic si Musarum profectus, eradicabo memoriam
  Et nomen Academiae, reditus et latefundia
  Redibunt in fiscum, in milites et aulicos
  Impertientur, et in vsus bellicos.
EUBULUS: Laudo summè hanc proboque sententiam.   2015
  Hoc enim cedat in lucrum mihi.
CRATINUS: Ni fallor, et mihi.
PHILOBIBLOS: Procella grauis, quamprimùm effare, Polumathes.
POLUMATHES: Ne sic o benigne princeps. Reuoca sententiam
  Nimis seueram, iniustam, et duram nimìs.
  Parce, parce, parce, precamur te singuli.   2020
EUBULUS: Qui vos tandem?
POLUMATHES: Duo peregrinantes philosophi.
CRATINUS: Nugatores. Abite.
PHILOBIBLOS: Audi loquentem priùs
  Serenissime princeps.
DUX: Aequum petit, eloquere.
POLUMATHES: Sponte facis, quod nos ipsi petituri fuimus,
  Vt vindicares hanc corruptam Academiam.   2025
DUX: Quid ergò deprecaris vt reuocem sententiam?

SORDIDUS: They have stolen almost everything: wood, hens, fruit, ducks, geese, lambs, sheep. We have nothing left. One has recently killed an ambling horse hired from me.

STEPHANIO: Because of these almost continuous trespasses, we who live up to the sixth milestone can neither defend the birds nor protect the deer or rabbits in the fields nor the fish in the waters.

DUKE: Are they hunters?

STEPHANIO: And also fishers.

DUKE: O knaves worthy to be beaten!

SORDIDUS: Hear the most serious charge. An ignorant doctor with his poisonous drugs has killed my dearest wife.

RUBICUNDUS: Would that he had killed mine!

CORNUTUS: And, if it please the gods, mine.

DUKE: By the faith of gods and men! So many crimes—who has heard of such horrible crimes from so many people and in such a short time? What atrocities have they not committed? What frauds, impostures, thefts, murders, adulteries, riots, drunkenness, what base and filthy crimes have they not designed? Is this the fruit of talent? Is this the good which they promised me? Barbarity itself produced nothing more outrageous. If this is the return of the muses, I will erase the memory and name of the university; the revenues and estates will return to the treasury to be given to soldiers and courtiers for warlike uses.

EUBULUS: I highly praise and approve of your decision. <Aside> For this may profit me.

CRATINUS <aside>: Unless I'm mistaken, also me.

PHILOBIBLOS: A perilous crisis. Speak quickly, Polumathes.

POLUMATHES: Let it not be so, O kind prince. Recall your sentence; it is too severe, unjust, too harsh. Please, please, please, one by one we beseech you.

EUBULUS: Who are you?

POLUMATHES: We are two wandering philosophers.

CRATINUS: Triflers. Go away.

PHILOBIBLOS: First, hear what we have to say, most serene prince.

DUKE: A fair request. Speak.

POLUMATHES: What you are doing of your own accord is what we were about to ask—that you reform this corrupt university.

DUKE: Then why do you ask that I revoke my sentence?

POLUMATHES: Ne simul cum malis exularent etiam boni,
Aut ars malè audiret ob abusum artificis.
Habet Osuna viros doctos, illustres, graues,
Qui verè et sincerè colunt philosophiam,   2030
Atque horum causâ, princeps serenissime,
Obnixè oraui vt reuocares sententiam.
DUX: At qui demùm sunt in quos inueheris?
POLUMATHES: Quos tu rebaris dignos Academicos
Et admittebas priùs in hanc scholam tuam,   2035
Fungi plerumque erant Idiotae, asini,
De faece plebis, balatrones, circumforanei;
Iam si vis benè mereri de republicâ literariâ,
Coerce errores istos, faecem hanc amoue,
Atque horum vice viros substitue bonos,   2040
Statuta noua sancties, leges nouas.
Sic eris Musarum decus, pater patriae,
Et nomen tuum Musae in aeternum canent.
DUX: Cordatè loqueris, et iam reuoco sententiam.
Sed quî destinguam probos hosce ab improbis,   2045
Philosophastros a veris?
POLUMATHES: Dicam breuitèr.
Promulgari statìm curabis per omnem Academiam,
Vt qui iactarit se philosophum, poteritque
Latine saltem loqui aut sillogismum conficere,
Ad distributionem mox in arcem veniat.   2050
Singulis enim minae dabuntur duae.
DUX: Laudo hoc commentum. Lictor promulge statìm.
PHILOBIBLOS: Hoc promulgato, mox turmatìm ruent,
Inhiantes famae et lucro; at boni interim
Cordatique contemnent, Musis addicti suis.   2055
Sic eos agnoscas, et turba supplicantium
Coram videns impostorem designet suum.
POLUMATHES: Videbis statìm velut ad praedam lupos
Iamdiù deuorantes hoc aurum animis,
Huc concurrentem turbam praecipitem.   2060
EUBULUS: Sed eccum Philomusas?
                    [Intrat lena cum filiabus]
DUX: Quales hae faeminae?
STAPHILA: Honesta materfamilias, atque hae sunt filiae meae.
Sumusque si placet sutrices Academicae.
CRATINUS: Vel quod veriùs dicas meretrices Academicae.
STEPHANIO: Haec est illa lena et meretrix vetula   2065
Composta ex vulpe, leone, et simiâ
Quae inescauit et corrupit filium meum.

POLUMATHES: Lest the good be exiled with the bad, or lest art be held in poor esteem because of the abuse of artifice. In Osuna are learned, illustrious, and serious men who are truly and sincerely devoted to philosophy; for their sake, most serene prince, I have begged in earnest that you revoke this sentence.

DUKE: But who are those against whom you inveigh?

POLUMATHES: Those whom you judged worthy academics and first admitted to your school. They were dolts, fools, idiots, asses, the dregs of society, rascals, hustlers. If you wish a place for learning worthy of this state, halt those errors, remove these dregs and replace them with good men, sanction new statutes, new laws. Thus you will be worthy of the muses, father of the fatherland, and the muses will sing your name forever.

DUKE: You speak wisely, and I now revoke my sentence. But how do I distinguish the good from the wicked, the philosophasters from the true scholars?

POLUMATHES: I'll speak briefly. At once you will make known throughout the university that anyone who boasts himself a philosopher—and is able at the very least to speak in Latin and compose a syllogism—should come soon to the castle for a disbursement, for four pounds will be given to each one.

DUKE: I praise your suggestion. Lictor, make this known at once.

PHILOBIBLOS: At this announcement they will rush forth in a throng, gasping for fame and money. But the good men, meanwhile, will discreetly scorn it, intent on their own muses. In this manner you will distinguish them, and this crowd of suppliants, seeing them openly, will point out their deceivers.

POLUMATHES: You will see them at once, rushing here in a precipitous throng, and like wolves near their prey, already devouring the gold in their minds.

EUBULUS: But look. Are these Philomuses?[2]

[Enter the bawd with her daughters.]

DUKE: Who are these women?

STAPHILA: I'm an honest housewife, and these are my daughters. And we are, if you please, seamstresses for the university.

CRATINUS: Or to speak more truly, the whores of the university.

STEPHANIO: This is that bawd, the old whore, part fox, lion and ape, who deceived and corrupted my son. And these are the Eumenides,[3] and this is

---

[2] Cooper: *Philomusus*: "That loueth or fauoureth good letters."

[3] Cooper: *Eumenides*: "Furies of hell."

Et hae sunt Eumenides, hoc illud Barathrum
In quod obliguriuit et profudit opes meas.
POLUPISTOS: Hem, quid video meamne filiam an alteram?   2070
Quam ego iamdiù credideram demortuam,
Nata mea vt vales?
CAMAENA: Pater ignosce, veniam peto.
Seducta ab hac anu hunc in modum delitui
Per annos aliquot.
POLUPISTOS: At quis te fecit grauidam?
CAMAENA: Antonius Stephanionis huiusce filius vnicus.   2075
Atque eccum opportunè adest.
               [*Intrat Antonius cum Aequiuoco et auro.*]
ANTONIUS: Saluete iudices.
Praesento vobis furem.
POLUPISTOS: Et impostorem eximium.
Hic ille magi seruus et medico a consiliis
Qui me supplantauit.
STEPHANIO: Et qui corrupit filium meum.
DUX: Cuius hoc aurum?
POLUPISTOS: Meum quod a me medicus   2080
Surripuit ille forsan a medico.
AEQUIUOCUS: Ita est, iudices.
DUX: Aurum tuum tibi restituo.
POLUPISTOS: Deus benefaxit tibi.
DUX: De hoc videbitur alias. Rectâ nunc ad carcerem eat.
EUBULUS: Sed heus adolescens; tune hanc fecisti grauidam?
STEPHANIO: O scelus, vt stas? Vbi pudor, vbi verecundia?   2085
Quid ad haec ais?
ANTONIUS: Vis dicam verbo. Reus sum.
Pater, da veniam quaeso, obsecro, ignoscas, pater.
STEPHANIO: Et fateris te vitiasse hanc virginem?
ANTONIUS: Fateor.
POLUPISTOS: Et in vxorem duces hanc?
ANTONIUS: Ducam lubens.
STEPHANIO: Vt ducas meretricem? Egone vt ad haec annuam?   2090
CAMAENA: Non sum meretrix. Pudicè et probè me habui
Ad reliquos omnes, hunc vnum si excipias.
ANTONIUS: Sine, te exorem pater.
EUBULUS: Lex hoc ipsum petit.
DUX: Stephanio, iniquus nimis es, aequum vterque postulat.
Vt ducat, lex iubet.
STEPHANIO: Quando ita leges volunt,   2095
Age ducat habeatque, quum tibi sic visum fuerit.
ANTONIO: O lenissimum patrem!

that pit where he devoured and poured forth my wealth.

POLUPISTOS: Hem, do I see my own daughter or someone else? My daughter, whom for so long I believed dead, are you well?

CAEMAENA: Father, forgive me. I pray for lenience. I was stolen away by this old woman; I have hidden away in this manner for many years.

POLUPISTOS: But who has made you pregnant?

CAEMENA: Antonius, the only son of Stephanio here. And look, he is conveniently here at hand.

[*Enter Antonius with Aequivocus and his gold.*]

ANTONIUS: I salute you, judges, and present to you a thief.

POLUPISTOS: And notable impostor. This is that servant of the magician and counselor to the physician who defrauded me.

STEPHANIO: And who corrupted my son.

DUKE: Whose gold is this?

POLUPISTOS: Mine, which the physician stole from me, and he perhaps from the physician.

AEQUIVOCUS: It is true, judges.

DUKE: I return your gold to you.

POLUPISTOS: May god bless you.

DUKE: We will see to this man later. For now, let him be taken directly to jail.

EUBULUS: But you, young man. Did you make this girl pregnant?

STEPHANIO: O crime, how can you stand there? Where is your shame, your modesty? What do you say to this?

ANTONIUS: If you wish, I will say it in a word. I am guilty. Father, pardon me, I beg, I pray you, forgive me, Father.

STEPHANIO: And you confess that you have violated this maiden?

ANTONIUS: I confess.

POLUPISTOS: And you will marry her?

ANTONIUS: I will marry her willingly.

STEPHANIO: You will marry a whore? Am I to agree to this?

CAMAENA: I am not a whore. I have kept myself modest and pure to all the others. He's the exception.

ANTONIUS: Allow it, I beg you, Father.

EUBULUS: The law demands it.

DUKE: Stephanio, you are too unjust. Both ask the same thing: the law ordains that he marry.

STEPHANIO: Since it is the law, and since it seems best to you, go. Let him marry her, let him have her.

ANTONIUS: O most gentle father!

POLUPISTOS: Et dotis loco
  Totum hunc Thesaurum do.
EUBULUS: Laudo factum tuum.
DUX: En gregem.
                    [*Intrant philosophastri*]
CRATINUS: Pape vt erumpunt instar apum.
  Impletur arx multitudine impellentium.   2100
  Vestrumne quisquam norît horum aliquem?
STEPHANIO: Hunc accuso; hic est ille impostor celebris,
  Iesuitam prae se ferens, qui natum corrupit meum.
POLUPISTOS: Eundem ego pro mago. Sed hic ille medicus
  Qui me emunxit argento.
RUBICUNDUS: Hic ille iuuenis   2105
  Qui me verberauit.
SORDIDUS: Hic conduxit equum meum.
CORNUTUS: Hic nepos vxori meae tam gratus, hic nebulo.
POLUMATHES: Hi sunt impostores et execrandi Hyppocritae
  Qui nos omnes affecerûnt hâc iniuriâ,
  Quorum causâ Musae et artes malè audiunt.   2110
  Sed iam capti aliquandò paenas dabunt.
PHILOBIBLOS: Exuite hos habitus vt planè cognoscamini—
                    [*Detegit scruntatur*]
  En frontes nouas.
DUX: O imposturam egregiam!
PHILOBIBLOS: Quid hic?
AEQUIUOCUS: Pera.
PHILOBIBLOS: At quid in eâ latet?
AEQUIUOCUS: Libri.
PHILOBIBLOS: Quid hic? Pecten, vnguentum, speculum.   2115
POLUMATHES: Quid hic? Pictae chartae, cultelli, tali, tesserae.
  Quid tu cirucmfers cantilenas, pocula?
  Hae musae tuae?
PHILOBIBLOS: Haec vestri exercitii viatica?
EUBULUS: O prophanum gregem!
DUX: Quod dignum supplicii genus
  Excogitabimus?
POLUMATHES: Illud incumbat mihi.   2120
DUX: Quod vis fac, committo rem totam arbitrio tuo.
POLUMATHES: Sic statuo. Quatuor hisce sycophantis egregiis
  In exemplum et terrorem reliquorum omnium,
  Vtramque genam stigmate inuri volo.
  Sit vero deustionis figura vulpes aut simia,   2125
  Deturbari deîn gradu, et expelli Academiâ.
LICTOR: Statìm fiet.

POLUPISTOS: And in place of a dowry, I give this entire treasure.

EUBULUS: I applaud your deed.

DUKE: Look, the flock.

[*Enter philosophasters*]

CRATINUS: A wonderful thing! They burst forth like bees. The castle is filled with a multitude of them pushing forward. Do any of you recognize any of them?

STEPHANIO: I accuse this one. He is that noted impostor, pretending to be a Jesuit, who corrupted my son.

POLUPISTOS: I accuse the same man as a magician. And this is the physician who stripped me of my gold.

RUBICUNDUS: This is the young man who beat me.

SORDIDUS: This one hired my horse.

CORNUTUS: This is the prodigal so pleasing to my wife, the knave.

POLUMATHES: These are the impostors and accursed hypocrites who brought injury to us all, and because of whom the muses and arts are held in poor esteem. But now that they have been caught, they will pay the price.

PHILOBIBLOS: Take off those habits that you may be clearly known.

[*He takes off their hoods and examines their faces.*]

Ah, new fronts.

DUKE: O, outstanding imposture!

PHILOBIBLOS: What is this?

AEQUIVOCUS: A satchel.

PHILOBIBLOS: What is hidden in it?

AEQUIVOCUS: Books.

PHILOBIBLOS: What is this? A comb, ointment, a mirror.

POLUMATHES: What is this? Cards, little knives, dice, score cards. Why are you carrying around songs and wine cups? Are these your muses?

PHILOBIBLOS: Are these the traveling provisions for your study?

EUBULUS: A flock of knaves!

DUKE: What worthy punishment will we exact?

POLUMATHES: Let me decide.

DUKE: Do what you will. I commit the whole matter to your judgment.

POLUMATHES: Thus I decree. For these four outstanding imposters, as an example and warning to all the rest, I decree that both cheeks be branded. Let the brand be in the shape of a wolf or an ape. Then let them be stripped of their degree and be expelled from the university.

LICTOR: It will be done at once.

[Philosophastri exeunt inurendi et mox intrant.]

EUBULUS: Diuinator, cur non hoc ante praedixeras?

POLUMATHES: Hi vero reliqui quod sit delictum minus,
    Et quod prae se ferant quaendam indolem,
    Abrasis primum barbis tragicâ nouaculâ,   2130
    Religantur per annum vnum ad Antyceras
    Vbi postquam nugis, soelicismis et ineptiis
    Purgati fuerint restituantur ad locum suum.

EUBULUS: De lenâ quid fiet?

CRATINUS: Ducatur ad carcerem
    Vbi per dies aliquot macerata cum fuerit,   2135
    Aquam caenosam et panem depascens plebeium;
    Circumducatur curru per omnes plateas,
    Atque inde flagelletur ex Academiâ.

EUBULUS: Vna superest muliercula.

CRATINUS: In medium profer.

DUX: Commiseratione digna videtur ob formam suam.   2140

CRATINUS: Paenitetne vitae anteactae tuae?

TARENTILLA: Seriò paenitet.

DUX: Age vero quis horum tecum rem habuit?

TARENTILLA: Omnes.

DUX: Itane? Ex omnibus vnum elige
    Quem virum malles, atque erit vir tuus.

TARENTIALLA: Hunc volo.

DUX: Tibine placet conditio?   2145

PANTOMAGUS: Placet.

DUX: Benè sit nuptis et faelicitèr.
    Qui inuruntur reliqui, exulent illicò.
    Vtque in posterum occurratur hisce nequitiis,
    Volumus, ordinamus, et per praesentes statuimus,
    Vt omnes popinae minus necessariae   2150
    Tollantur illico, malorum omnium initia;
    Praeesse volumus in posterum viros duos,
    Virtute et morum probitate conspicuos,
    Annatìm eligendos publicis suffragiis,
    Qui vicatim inambulantes noctù et interdiù   2155
    Plectant authoritate sua et curent haec fieri.
    Vos autem duo primam hanc vicem gerite,
    Et honoris ergò hunc habete habitum.

EUBULUS: Probo hoc inuentum.

CRATINUS: Placetque edictum mihi.

DUX: Vos ergo quibus hoc mandatum est officium,   2160
    Et quos ego elegi fideles ministros meos,
    Curate munus vestrum et exercete sedulò.

[The philosophers leave to be branded and soon return.]

EUBULUS: Prophet, why have you not foretold this?

POLUMATHES: These others, since their offense is somewhat less and since they show a certain disposition toward good, let their beards be publicly shaven[4] and let them be exiled for one year to Anticyras; after they have been purged of their silliness, let them be restored to their own places.

EUBULUS: What should be done about the bawd?

CRATINUS: Take her to jail where she can fast for some days on foul water and cheap bread. Then let her be carried around through the streets in a cart, then thrashed from the university.

EUBULUS: One little whore remains.

CRATINUS: Bring her forward.

DUKE: She seems worthy of pity because of her beauty.

CRATINUS: Do you repent of your previous life?

TARENTILLA: Earnestly I repent.

DUKE: Tell us, in truth, which of these men has had you.

TARENTILLA: All of them.

DUKE: Is that so? Pick one of them, whichever man you prefer. He will be your husband.

TARENTILLA: I want this one.

DUKE: Is this condition pleasing to you?

PANTOMAGUS: Yes, it is pleasing.

DUKE: May the marriage be good and happy.[5] Those who remain are branded; let them be exiled from here. So that such negligence may be prevented hereafter, we wish, we ordain and we decree for now that all unnecessary taverns, the root of all evil, be demolished. Hereafter, I want placed in authority two men, noted for their virtue and moral probity, elected annually by public vote. Walking along the streets by night or day, they may of their own authority punish and oversee that these things be done. Moreover, you two shall take the first turn in this office and have this apparel as a mark of dignity.

EUBULUS: I approve of this decision.

CRATINUS: The edict pleases me.

DUKE: Therefore, you to whom this duty has been mandated and whom I have chosen as my faithful ministers, take care of your tasks and exercise them with diligence.

---

[4] Literally: "with a tragic razor," i.e., in grand style or as a spectacle.

[5] Cf. the final scene of Shakespeare's *Measure for Measure* where the Duke returns to mete out punishment and arrange marriages.

POLUMATHES: Serene princeps, mandatis tuis obsequentissimi
   Hoc munus nostrum exequemur illicò.
   Operamque dabimus vt quod in nobis fiet   2165
   Longum efflorescat Osuna Academia.
DUX: Laudo paratum animum, et si quid deest,
   Secus corrigendum vestrae committo fidei.
                    [*Exit Dux et consiliarii*]
POLUMATHES: Sic restauratâ in longùm Academiâ,
   Tamque auspicato rebus compositis,   2170
   Hymnum canamus in laudem philosophiae.
   Vos autem ciues quondam malè habiti,
   Ab execrandis hisce pseudoacademicis,
   Laeti et iucundi celebrate hunc diem,
   Canentes nobiscum vnà, et vnanimi laetitiâ.   2175
            [*Vnus canit solus to the tune of Bonny Nell*]:
   Magistri, Bacchelaurei,
   Tyrones, Abcedarii,
   Doctores, Academici
   Et iuuenes Dypondii
OMNES: Cantate serenissimae   2180
   Triumphum Philosophiae.
VNUS: Philosophantes, Medici,
   Studentes, et Philologi,
   Rhetores, Causidici,
   Magi et Mathematici,   2185
OMNES: Cantate serenissimae
   Triumphum Philosophiae.
VNUS: Vos Scotistae, vos Thomistae,
   Vos Poetae, Grammatistae,
   Oratores et Sophistae,   2190
   Et qui sunt Musarum mystae,
OMNES: Cantate serenissimae
   Triumphum Philosophiae.
VNUS: Europaei, Asiani,
   Afri et Americani,   2195
   Continentes, insulani,
   Lauti ciues, oppidani,
OMNES: Cantate serenissimae
   Triumphum Philosophiae.
VNUS: Vos Germani, vos Hispani,   2200
   Vos Insubres, et Britanni
   Cimbri, Sardi et Siculi
   Poloni, Mosci, et Itali,
OMNES: Cantate serenissimae

POLUMATHES: Serene prince, we, most obedient to your commands, accept this task. We will work to the best of our ability to see that the University of Osuna flourishes for a long time.

DUKE: I praise your ready mind, and if anything is left to be put right, I entrust it to your faith.

[*Exit duke and councilors*]

POLUMATHES: Thus at length the university has been reformed and thus auspiciously matters composed. Let us sing a hymn in praise of philosophy. Moreover, you citizens, once abused by these accursed pseudoacademics, happily and joyfully celebrate this day, singing with us in happy unanimity.

[*One sings alone to the tune of Bonny Nell*]:

Masters, Bachelors,
Freshmen, teachers,
Doctors, academics,
And young halfpennies

ALL: Sing the triumph of most serene philosophy.

ONE: Philosophants, physicians,
Students, philologues,
Rhetoricians, attorneys,
Magicians, mathematicians

ALL: Sing the triumph of most serene philosophy.

ONE: You Scotists, Thomists,
Poets, grammarians,
Orators, sophists,
Priests of the muses,

ALL: Sing the triumph of most serene philosophy.

ONE: Europeans, Asians,
Africans, Americans,
Continentals, Islanders,
Rich and wealthy citizens,

ALL: Sing the triumph of most serene philosophy.

ONE: You Germans and Hispanics,
Lombards and Britons,
Cimbri, Sardinians, Sicilians,
Poles, Muscovians, and Italians,

Triumphum Philosophiae.   2205

Finis.
Plauserunt.
Feb. 16to
1617

Epilogus   2210

Sortita finem est longa tandem fabula,
Nullis referta iocisue, aspersa salibus,
Quae in aliorum fabulis haberi solent.
Fatemur, et capax subiectum non fuit.
Si quid aberratum aut absoletum quid nimìs   2215
Offendat aures, praemonimus ab initio
Vndecem abhinc annis hanc scriptam fabulam.
Molestiores aequo si forsan fuimus,
Non nostra culpa est; iis hanc culpam imputent
Quorum malignitas hoc in scena petiit.   2220
Asperius in quem si quis hic putet inuehi,
Is demum impudentes, non bonos carpi sciat.
Si quid molestum stilo aut subiecto fuerit,
Emeritus poeta veniam petit.
At nos de grege si quid forsan aberrauimus   2225
(Aliis vtcunque vobis, opinor, non imposuimus)
Voce aut manu, si quid erratum fuerit,
Date veniam; nec histriones sumus.
Sed non veremur vestrem fauorem, Iudices,
Benignitatem et gratiam. Fremat, frendat licet.   2230
Vnus et alter laesus. Bonus quisque dabit
Iam renouatae plausum Academiae.
Longùm efflorescat Osuna Academia
Et quo quisque vestrum Musis amicitior
Erit, is tanto plausum alacriorem dabit.   2235

Plauserunt.
Feb. 16to
Aede Cristi
1617

ALL: Sing the triumph of most serene philosophy.

The end.

They applauded.
February 16, 1617.

Epilogue

At last our long story has reached its alloted end,
Neither stuffed with jokes nor salted with the wit
As often is found in the comedies of others.
We confess: we had no room for them.
If anything amiss or too well-worn
Offends your ears, we warned you from the beginning
That this story was written eleven years ago.
Equally, if perhaps we have been rather bothersome
The fault is not ours; it belongs to those
Whose ill will invited this play to the stage.
If any here thinks himself too harshly inveighed
Let him know that the wicked, not the good, are attacked.
If anything was unpleasant in writing or subject,
The poet emeritus begs forgiveness.
But if we in the cast have perhaps gone astray,
(I think we have not imposed on you, but on others)
If anything was wrong in voice or gesture,
Be lenient: we are not stage players.
But we do not doubt your favor,
Goodwill and indulgence, judges. Let one or the other
Who has been wounded, rage and grind his teeth.
Each good man will now give
Applause to the renovated university.
May the University of Osuna long flourish.
And each of you, by as much as you would be more friendly to the muses,
Give to us the same amount of cheerful applause.

They applauded.
February 16, 1617,
at Christ Church.

Actorum Nomina

Desiderius Dux — Sr. Kinge, the Bishop of Londons sonne.
Eubulus — Mr. Gorges, Sr. Arther Gorges sonne.
Cratinus — Mr. Bartlit, a gentleman commoner.
Polumathes — Sr. Bennet, Sr. John Bennettes sonne.
Philobiblos — Sr. Haywood, student, bac. 2245
Polupragmaticus — Mr. Goffe, Mr. of Artes, student.
Aequiuocus — Mr. Jonson, Mr. of Artes, student.
Simon Acutus — Sr. Fortye, student, bac.
Lodouicus Pantometer — Sr. Westlye, student, bac. arte.
Pantomagus — Sr. Osboston, student bac. of artes. 2250
Amphimacer — Limiter, scholler of the house, stud.
Theanus — Sr. Vauhan, student bac.
Pedanus — Morly, scholler. stud.
Stephanio — Sr. Arundall, stud. bac.
Polupistos — Sr. Price, bac. art. student 2255
Dromo — Hilsinge, scholler of the house.
Sr. Ingolsby, Harris, Parsons — 3 Townsmen.
Staphila — Benefeilde, scholler of the house.
Camaena — Price, scholler of the house.
Tarentilla — Stroude, scholler of the house. 2260
Lictor, Promus — Cotton, scholler of the house.
Portry, Blunt, Serle — Patientes.
Hersen — Fidicen. A Quirister.

Acted on Shrouemunday night 1617. Feb. 16. die lunae.
It begane about .5. at nyght and ended at eight. 2265

Auctore Roberto Burton
Linliaco Lecestrense.

Textual Notes

F = Folger MS. V.a. 315
F¹= Folger MS. V.a. 315, Hand b
G = Harvard MS. Thr. 10.1
H = Harvard MS. Thr. 10
om. = word omitted
add. = word added at end of line
* = emendations to copy text

(4)	agunt *om.*
(7)	magis] *F¹*
(8)	quam] *F¹*
(12)	feci] *F¹*
(12)	Comoedia] *F¹*
(15)	Scripta] *above canceled* Inchoata
(16)	reuisa] *above canceled* renouata *H,*
(22)	die *before* decimo *canceled H; add.* die *before* decimo *F*
(35)	et] *F¹*
(47)	tandem ab ipso] ab ipso tandem *F*
(68)	technis] *above cancellation F¹*
(79)	sicut] *above cancellation F¹*
(81)	rithmos] *interlinear F¹*
*(84)	fit] sit *H*
(85)	alumni] *F¹*
(89)	ruri] rure *F*
(100)	se deuouet] se deuouit *F¹*
(101)	emungat] *F¹*
(105)	e] a *F*
(105)	et] *F¹*
(114)	queritur] *above cancellation F*
(119)	incensus] *interlinear*

*(136)	sancitis] F^1
*(136)	Philobiblo] Philoblo *H, F*
(141)	redeunt] reddunt F
(141)	et *om.* F
(157)	Pantometer] *over erasure* F
2	nunc *following* nunc *canceled* F
3	ludis] *above canceled* vsus F^1
6	peruulgatum] permulgatum F
8	nuperâ] *above canceled* vulgari H
8	aut] *above canceled* ne H
10	delituit] F^1
11	damnata] F^1
17	terra] *interlinear* F^1
24	plura] *above canceled* cuncta H
28	est] *interlinear* F^1
31	nostrae] nostro F
31	re] *over canceled* gregi H
34–36	Lodouicus ... apparatu *om.* G
37	loquuntur] loquentur F
37	se parant] se separant F
46	Stipes] Vnde? stipes G
47	*add. canceled* Polupragmaticus H; *add.* Polupragmaticus F
47	Edisce] Et edisce G
48	hâc] haec F
49	Sic *om.* G
49	in colloquio] ad colloquium G
52	dic] secus G
53	ac] et G
59	dato] data G
60	aut exaedron] octohedron G
65	vocali *after* Musica *canceled* G
69	aptè] apti F
70	et] *interlinear* G
75	demonstrari] demonstrare G
76	Tum] Tunc G
76	a et c et ab a ad d et l] A ad C et ab A D et C G
77	rectam per n] rectum per L G
77	ipsum *om.* G
78	altero] alterum G
79	possit] potest F
87	Vnica] vna G
88	feres] feras G
95	te] se F
96	sermo] seruo F

97	aut *om.* G
97	de *before* Marte *canceled*
98	platico] *above cancellation* G
102	linguas, artes, scientias] artes, linguas, et scientias G
104	Sed] Vultis G
104	Sed ... feram *om.* F
105	Cur] Quid G
110	sedulitate] *above cancellation of* celeritate G
118	*add.* Actus primus G
120	Lictor ... Etc.] pseudophilosophi G
126	amet] amat F
140	mauis ... semèl.] vel si verbo dictum vultis,sum Iesuita. G
142	Medicinâ ... Sceneographiâ] Scenographia, statica G
146	siem] sim F
158	hoc *om.* F
163	doceo] doces F
164	cogo] rogo F
168	exerceo] exercere F
173	omnes] omne F
181	vt] et F
200	vos] *interlinear* F
*202	suum] suam H,F
204	cedat] sedet F
208	τοὺς ἄλλους Θεούς] F^1
*208	Μἀ] Με H,F
209	Concertatur ... Pedano *om.* F
211	vitae] vita F
214	Eubulus: ... percitus] *interlinear* G
215	*add.* exeunt G
223	Immo *om.* F
227	hanc] hac F
*228	cessuram] cessurum H,F
228	nostram] nostrum F
228	in incommodum] incommodum F
*233	cessuram] cessurum H,F
236	sequentur] sequuntur F
237	nunc] *interlinear* H
*251	soluant] soluat H,F
255	vxorum pudititia] vxorem de puditia F
261	adirent] audirent F
263	Contemnent] Contemnant F
266	dum] *interlinear* F
270	de rebus hisce] *interlinear* H
280	suspecta] suspectus F

281	quam *following* olim, *canceled F*
281	a multis] *interlinear H; om. F*
285	halitum] habitum *F*
289	Sed] Se *F*
293	sum] cum *F*
*296	huc] hac *H,F*
*302	vili] vila *H*
308	et] aut *F*
323	sunt] sint *F*
331	rimetur] *F¹*
340	terrarum] terram *F*
347	saeuiret] seruiret *F*
349	causa] causae *F*
355	fiunt] fuit *F*
371	Vidistîn] vidisti *F*
372	instructam ... tum] instructa eorum bibliotheca quam *F*
*380	mensem] mensum *H*
381	at] *interlinear H*
382	communices] com *F*
*383	Polumathes:] Philobiblos: *H,F*
383	Cautum] *written over* tantum *F¹*
385	cum seruo *om. G*
392	Quod] Quid *G*
395	sicut ego] quales sum ego *G*
395	opus existimo] opus esse existimo *G*
398	sex metaphisicae] tot metaphisicae *G*
399	At] et *G*
404	multum pollicetur] multum mihi pollicetur *G*
405	hoc adolescente] huius adolescentuli vulta *G*
*406	elatam] elatum *H,F,G*
407	habet] summe *G*
*407	conspicuam] conspicuum *H,F*
407	*add.* tum *G*
408	et, et] vnus et *G*
408	ipse] ipsi *G*
408	oculus] *F¹*; oculi *G*
409	bonamque] bonam *F*
413	meam] meum *F*
413	Factum puta] Ita *G*
416	maiori] maiore *F*
419	ad] a *F*
427	fidei committes] committes fidei *G*
*430	Stephanio *om. H,F*
430	valere] saluere *G*

431	*add.* exit *G*
438	excidit *om. F*
440	furum *om. F*
443	legens . . . eos *om. F*
445	necessaria] necessarium *F*
447	Id est *om. F*
454	erat] fuit *F*
454–5	pauperibus munificus] munificus pauperibus *F*
461	num] *interlinear F*
473	scio] *interlinear F¹*
476	tu *before* non, *canceled F*
477	quid *before* Quid, *canceled F*
482	et] *interlinear F*
488	possem] possum *F*
491	Ilicèt] *F¹*
500	Testor . . . Olympum] *written over erasure F*
504	hominem] hominum *F*
*506	exemplum] exemplo *H*
507	Regia . . . erat] Regio Solus erit *F*
508	pyropo *om. F*
510	radiabant] radiabunt *F*
512	vacat, non vacat] non vacat *written over erasure F*
514	Intrat Aequiuocus *om. F*
516	at] aut *F*
528	vbi *before* quam, *canceled H*
541	ἢ ἄπιθι] *F¹*
*545	Theanus *om. H*
558	ignoretis] ignoret *F*
560	hominem] hominum *F*
566	quaerat] quaeret *F*
567	libris] *interlinear H;* horis *F*
571	emunctoralitèr *om. F*
577	peruulgati] permugat *F*
588	Purgo] *F¹*
601	Natura] Naturae *F*
614	compotationes] compotates *F*
618	apponere] opponere *F*
622–3	Qui . . . cogitaueris *om. F*
626	cantu] *below canceled* sanctu *F*
629	hospes] hospis *F*
654	Supersedebimus] supersedimus *F*
655	in] *above canceled* cum *F*
665	nouam Patriticus *om. F*
666	Nouam . . . Hagesius *om. F*

667	haec *om. F*
677	cubandique] interlinear *H*
680	mihi *om. F*
690	concionari] concionare *F*
715	reluctaris] reluctarit *F*
719	Adonidi *om. F*
721	sis] sic *F*
729	amantis] amantes *F*
745	*add. canceled* Ta. quaenam illa *H*
753	at] *interlinear H*; aut *F*
770	Aequiuocus. Dromo] Dromo, Aequiuocus *G*
773	inumerabiles] immemorabiles *F*
778	catenis *om. F*
780	gallicareum *om. F*
783	ligulas] ligula *F*
785	operculum] opusculum *G*
786	petis] cupis *G*
786	possis] posses *G*
788	e] de *G*
790	boum] *written over* locum *F¹*
793	vnius ope] ope vnius *G*
796	Batauos] Gallos *G*
799	medium] medio *F*
802	Nil] Nihil *F*
802	quid] quod *G*
803	accolas *om. F*
810	quod fuit] Dicam quod fuit *G*
810	ad] sit ad *G*
811	quidem *om. F*
812	in loco] in hoc loco *G*
814	enim] ego *F*
822	furem] *above canceled* thenar *G*
823	posthâc] posthaec *F*
824	per] interlinear *G*
826	homini] hominem *F*
830	Polupragmaticus] *below canceled* Polupistos *F*
830	in *om. G*
831	Campo] *above canceled* pante *F*
832	Toleti ... veteri] *interlinear G*
832	signum] figure *G*
832	foro] in foro *G*
834	e] a *F*
834	Erebi *om. F*
837	ais *om. G*

844	sternes] sternas *G*
847	at] et *F*; sed *G*
852	ludetisque] ludetis *G*
852	*add.* exeunt *G*
858	flammam] flammas *F*
859	Enceladus] *F¹*
873	curaturâ] creatura *F*
881	Quid faciam] *interlinear H*
885–89	Aequiuocus: Mitte . . . geram *om. F*
892	ducturum] *above canceled* nupturum *H*
902	pecunias] pecunia *F*
912	miserit] miserat *F*
926	suam *om. F*
940	malae] male *F*
941	adigit] adiget *F*
*951	*add.* Pantomagus *H,F*
966	aliquis] reliquis *F*
*968	expertae] experti *H,F*
976	vestram] vestra *F*
988	cito] *above canceled* facilè *H*
992	halitum] habitum *F*
1023	admirandam] admirandum *F*
1023	peritiam] *following canceled* stultitiam *F*
1025	Exit Dromo *om. F*
1029	aut *om. F*
1033	miserum] miseram *F*
*1051	Pedanus:] Philobiblos: *H,F*
1055	vrbanam] vrbana *F*
1060	in] *interlinear H*
1061	Honestè . . . incongruè] *beneath canceled line F*
1068	Vbi] *interlinear H*
1069	ob] ad *F*
1076	meum] meam *F*
*1077	ipse] ipsus *H,F*
1079	quispiam] *interlinear H*
1086	iam *om. F*
1088	Et . . . oppidulo] *beneath canceled line F*
1098	tibi *om. F*
1101	cados] vados *F*
1109	tu *following* amorem, *canceled F*
1114	vt] *interlinear F*
*1129	commissuram] commissurum *H,F*
1135	opes *above canceled* pretium *H*
*1154	quae] qui *H,F*

*1155 edoctae] edocti *H,F*
1161   vt] et *F*
1210   parturit] parturat *F*
1219   Azon] zon *F*
1228   vitra] vita *F*
*1230 Pantometer] Polupistos *H,F*
*1230 *add.* exit *H*
1234   et *om. F*
1243   Desertum] Deserta *F*
1245   meo] *interlinear H*
1256   veniunt] venit *F*
*1270 *add.* Polupragmaticus *H,F*
1272   sesquialtera] sesquiatem *G*
1276   Ne roges] Ne quid vltra de hoc roges. *G*
1279   et] est *G*
1289   quis sis] qui sis ipse *G*
1290   cuius ... vtaris *om. G*
1290   proferes] proferas *G*
1291   Bene vestitus *om. G*
1294   pralectiones ... quicquid] praelectiones, praefationes, aut quic-
      quid *G*
1298–1309 Polupragmaticus: Hoc ... exibila *om. G*
1300   librumque *before* Vel, *canceled F*
1301   vel] et *F*
1302   Librumque] Librum *F*
*1305 Simon Acutus] Polupragmaticus *H,F*
1312   Nostîn ... aliquod] Aut nostin paradoxon absurdum aliquid *G*
1314   Moueri ... huiusmodi] Terram mouere, incoli lunam, et stellas et
      huiusmodi *G*
1316–22 Qui ... eruditio *om. G*
1320   matellam] metallum *F*
1322   omnis] omnes *F*
1326   leno ... simia *om. G*
1327   superbus, iactator] superbus procar iactator *G*
1328   irrisor ... homo *om. G*
1328   sublimiloquus] sublimiloquitur *F*
1329   ita] sic *G*
1329   Exit] Exeunt *G*
1337   aget] agit *F*
1352   tibi] *above canceled* agis *H*
1357   omnes] omne *F*
*1363 Antonius] ET *H,F*
1383   tristitiae] tristiae *F*
1400   est *om. F*

1400	praesidi] praedi *F*
1402	est *following* opus, *canceled F*
1402	etiamnum *om. F*
1425–26	Theanus: Maxime ... ais *om. F*
1428	Pedanus: Atque ... initio *om. F*
1454–56	Vt ... capiat] *above canceled lines F*
1481	primâ] imâ *F*
1523	Cunctaque] Cuncta *F*
1537	pollinem] pollinenem *F*
1539	Exit] *written over* exeunt *H*
1542	an] *interlinear F*
1551	pompâ] *interlinear F*
1556	At] Aut *F*
1559	At] *interlinear F*
1563	habent] *above canceled* amant *H*
1566	deformes] deformis *F*
1570	Valete] Vale *F*
1577	septima] octava *G*
1580	Fidicen. Promus *om. G*
1584	Polupragmaticus] Pantomagus *G*
1585	Simon Acutus] Polypragmaticus *G*
1590	circulatorem ... furem] sycophantem, circulatorem, furem *G*
1596	supererit] superit *F*
1607	et *om. F*
1608	publicum apparuero] politicum aparuare *F*
1615	magnates] magnatos *F*
1618	et] *interlinear F*
1619	nimia] ninimia *F*
1637	diuinum de] diuinum et de *G*
1639	nos inter ... norimus] non novimus nos inter nos *G*
1640	Amici] *F[1]*
1641	Caelumne] An caelum *G*
1644	proferet] proferat *G*
1648–49	Simon ... Academias *om. G*
1652	Oxoniam] Oxonium *G*
1656	At cur ... comitem?] At quid vrsum, et lupum? *G*
1658	Nugaris ... visitare] Nugas. Omnino vultis visitare *G*
1659	Non] Nihil minus *G*
1659	doctiores] doctissimes *G*
*1665	Lodouicus Pantometer] Polupragmaticus *H,F*
1670	Intrat] Intrat Promus *F*
1670	Lodouicus Pantometer *om. F*
*1676	Intrat] Intrant *H*
1677	potes] poteris *G*

1681	et] *interlinear* F^1
1685	Omnes *om. F*
1691	nil] nihil *F*
1731	capit] cepit *G*
1737	quater] quaterque *F*
1741–44	Vt potemus ... arduum] *interlinear G*
1744	Bellum ... arduum] ab arduum bellum *G*
1747	*add.* Tarentilla: Haec condo. Polypragmaticus: Quando ita vis, placet. Finis. *G*
1753	id *om. F*
1756	ipsis] istis *F*
1763	vendat] *above canceled* heroes *F*
1767	es *om. F*
1768	omnibus] *interlinear F*
*1778	ipse] ipsus *H,F*
1782	ipsius] *interlinear F*
1801	tum] tu *F*
1802	quid *om. F*
1806	Tu te] Tune *F*
1841	stultitiâ] stultia *F*
1842	hoccine aetatis] haccine aetate *F*
*1848	aetatis] aetates *H,F*
1851	conuenit *om. F*
1857	vt] et *F*
1860	siet] fiet *F*
1861	ob] ab *F*
1862	sed *om. F*
1862	dicam tibi] tibi dicam *F*
1866	sapiens] sapientens, *F*; adhuc *following* sapientens, *canceled F*
1878	vero] vere *F*
1886	euomes *om. F*
1887	quidni] quid *F*
1890	nugiuendulos *om. F*
1895	amplector] *interlinear H*
1895	amplector exosculor] ex amplector osculor *F*
1903	Si quis] Si sis quis *F*
1908	vel] *interlinear H*
1910	deleatur] debeatur *F*
1913	conuitiis] comiis *F*
1934	imposturis] imposturos *F*
1935	illorum] eorum *F*
*1940	*add.* Polumathes *before* Hi sunt *H,F*
1947	eos] deos *F*
1949	me] mihi *F*

1952	Intrat ... etc. *om. F*
1985	tu quereris] *above canceled* quaeso damnum tuum *H*
1988	oppidum] oppido *F*
1989	villa] villam *F*
1995	qui] quidam *F*
2003	hominum] hominem *F*
2005	quod ... commiserint *interlinear F*
2016	in *following* enim, *canceled F*
2029	Osuna] Osunam *F*
2033	hos *following* sunt, *canceled F*
*2046	Philosophastros] Philosophastris *H,F*
2051	minae *om. F*
2069	obliguriuit] obligarint *F*
2092	ad *om. F*
2099	vt] et *F*
2101	quisquam] horum *F*
2105	emunxit] *F¹*
*2113	nouas] nouos *H*
2127	philosophastri ... intrant *om. F*
2127	ante] aut *F*
2141	tuae *om. F*
2142	vero *om. F*
2148	nequitiis] nequiis *F*
2176	To ... Nell *om. F*
2199	Philosophiae] Philosophi *F*
2212	salibus] fidibus *F*
2215	aut absoletum quid] aut si quid absoletum *G*
2216	praemonimus] praemonibus *F*
2221	Asperius] Asperit *G*
2221	si] sic *G*
2226	opinor *om. G*
2227–33	voce ... Academia *om. G*
2227	*add.* Hoc stigma nostrum, vestres manus deleant *G*
2236–39	Plauserunt ... 1617 *om. G*
2238	add. Oxon. *F*
2246	Mr. Goffe *om. F*
2249	arte *om. F*
2250	of *om. F*
2254	Sr. *om. F*
2261	Lictor ... house *om. F*
2264	add. Oxon. *F¹*

Appendix I

ADDITIONS AND CORRECTIONS TO
FOLGER MS. V.A. 315

Folger MS. V.a. 315 contains 106 additions or corrections made by a hand other than that of the principal scribe. The additions and corrections are scattered throughout the manuscript. Forty-two occur in the first part of the manuscript: the notes on prosody, the title page, argument and prologue. Thirty-seven occur in the main text of the play itself, one in the epilogue, and twenty-four, including twenty virgules following character names, in the Actorum Nomina.

The additions or corrections are of various types. Four are serifs, eight are accent marks, five are palaeographic *notae*, and twenty-two are punctuation marks. Thirty-five additions or corrections are graphs or series of graphs. Thirty-two additions are words or series of words. Twenty-two of these added words or series of words are written in spaces left in the manuscript by the principal scribe.

Line*	Folger MS reading	Additions / Corrections
(3)	Iambus	serifs on initial "I"
(7)	magis	word, in space left blank
(8)	quam	word, in space left blank
(12)	feci	word, in space left blank
(12)	Comoedia	word, in space left blank
(32)	latefundiis	"fundiis," in space left blank
(32)	et	word, in space left blank
(34)	causâ	accent mark

---

* *Line numbers are those of this text.*

Line	Folger MS reading	Additions / Corrections
(35)	caeterisq$_3$	"isq$_3$," in space left blank
(36–7)	vndiquaq$_3$	accent mark on "q$_3$"
(44)	conuiuiū	*nota* over final "u"
(49)	nobilē	"e" and *nota* over "e"
(53)	circumueniens	"ueniens," in space left blank
(56)	technis	word, above cancellation
(61)	Simon serifs on "S"	
(61)	Acutus	"A" in space left blank
(62)	sicut	word, above cancellation
(64)	liberiùs	accent mark
(65)	rithmos	word, inserted above line
(69)	alumni	word, in space left blank
(71)	pauper	initial "p," in space left
(79)	circumueniente	"ueniente," in space left
(80)	se deuouit	words, in space left blank
(80)	emugat	word, in space left blank
(82)	adiutus	"iutus," in space left blank
(83)	egregiâ	accent mark
(83)	formâ	accent mark
(89)	et	word, in space left blank
(90)	commendârat	accent mark
(106)	santitis	word, in space left blank
(106)	Duce	"D" over another graph
(106)	pacatus	"c" over graph "r"
3	lusis	word, above canceled "vsus"
4	benignâ	accent mark
5	solenni	"i" over "e"
8	nuperâ	accent mark
10	delituit	"ui" before first "t" canceled; "uit" in space
11	damnata	word, in space left blank
11	tenebras	"t," in space left blank
17	terra	word, inserted above line
28	est	word, inserted above line
31	nostro	final "o," over another graph
208	ἄλλους Θεούς	words, in space left blank
331	rimetur	word, in space left blank
332	(comma)	punctuation mark after "aliquando"
383	cautum	word, over "tantum"
394	omniscum	"sc," in space left blank
396	dabā	final "a" over "o"; *nota* over final "a"

Line	Folger MS reading	Additions / Corrections
408	oculus	word, in space left blank
471	scio	word, inserted above line
491	Ilicèt	word, in space left blank
541	πìθι ἤ ἄπιθι	θι ἤ ἄπιθι in space left blank
588	purgo	word, in space left blank
790	boum	word, over "locum"
796	Italia	serif on "I"
859	Encedadus	word, in space left blank
1065	caecutus	"ae" over "a"
1087	Sabbato	second "a" inserted above line
1098	erras	"er," in space left blank
1366	summe	"e" over "a"
1369	claude	"u," inserted above line
1386	Attendat	second "a," above line, over canceled "u"
1059	vocant	"c," inserted above line
1581	quid	"d," inserted above line
1640	Amici	word, in space left blank
1680	praeter	first "e," in space left blank
1681	et	word, inserted above line
1683	visa	"a," in space left blank
1839	Polupistos	first "o," in space left blank
1870	sum̄os	*nota* over "m"
1871	quos	"s," in space left blank
1872	vestitim	second "i" over "a"
1901	quaero	"ae" over "e"; a final "r" canceled
1902	mediocres	"i," in space left blank
1905	sum̄um	*nota* over first "m"
1962	absorpsit	"psit," in space left blank
1970	quoad	"o," inserted above line
2105	emunxit	word, in space left blank
2176	Bacchelaurii	"e," over another graph, "lau" in space left blank
2236	Plauserunt	"Pl," over other graphs
2241–60	(virgules)	punctuation, after character name
2264	Oxon	word, in space left blank
2265	It	serif on "I"
2265	.5.	number, in space left blank
2265	(comma)	punctuation mark, after "nyght"

Fourteen gaps remain in the text of Folger MS V.a. 315, where the principal
scribe left blank spaces for words that were not filled in. Most of these gaps
occur at the end of a line of verse (marked "eol" in table below) and many
are marked by an "x" in the margin ("x" in table below).

210	Harvard reads "a multis"
382	Folger has "com"
	Harvard reads "communices"
438	(eol), (x) Harvard reads "excidit"
440	(eol), (x) Harvard reads "furum"
508	(eol), (x) Harvard reads "pyropo"
571	(eol), (x) Harvard reads "emunctoraliter"
719	(eol) Harvard reads "Adodndi"
780	(eol) Harvard reads "gallicareum"
803	(eol), (x) Harvard reads "accolas"
834	(eol), (x) Harvard reads "Erebi"
1219	Folger has "zon"
	Harvard reads "Azon"
1886	(eol), (x) Harvard reads "euomes"
1890	(eol), (x) Harvard reads "nugiuendulos"
2051	Harvard reads "minae"

Appendix II

Following are variations in orthography in the three manuscript copies of *Philosophaster*.

> F = Folger MS. V.a. 315
> G = Harvard MS. Thr. 10.1
> H = Harvard MS. Thr. 10
> * = emendations to copy text

(19)	Cristi] Christi *F*
(20)	Cristi] Christi *F*
(37)	peregrinantes] perigrinantes *F*
(39)	pseudophilosophorum] pseudephilosophorum *F*
(42)	Academicâ] Accademiâ *F*
(77)	Tyro] Tiro *F*
(78)	mendatiorum] mendaciorum *F*
(95)	opportunè] oportune *F*
(97)	sistit] sisstit *F*
*(106)	sancitis] sanctitis *H*
(112)	Peregrinantes] perigrinantes *F*
(118)	Mathematicus] Mathematecus *F*
14	Comoediae] Commoediae *F*
20	vndequaque] vndiquaque *F*
21	admittendi] addmittendi *F*
33	scena] scaena *G*
34	Polupragmaticus] Polypragmaticus *G*
42	admittendi] addmittendi *F*
51	Paralologrammum] paralelogrammum *G*
52	Romboidem] Rhomboidem *F,G*
53	Poligonum] Polyganon *G*
53	Trapesium] Trapezium *G*

54   Icosaeadron] Icoseodron *G*
55   cylindrum] colindrum *F*
55   paralapippidum] par lappidum *F*; paralelapippedum *G*
59   octeadro] octoedro *G*
60   docaedron] decahedron *G*
63   sursolidis] subsolidis *G*
64   zinzizanzizeqique] zinzizanzizenique *F*;
              zinzizanzezenique *G*
66   Rithmicâ] Rythmica *G*
68   b fa b] be fa be *G*
70   diateseron] diatesaron *G*
71   proslambomenos] proslambanomenos *G*
73   lichanos] Lychanos *G*
82   Exietate] haeccietate *G*
89   Parimiro] Paramiro *G*
90   Elixir] Elixer *G*
92   Saturnus] Saternus *F*
93   Iuppiter] Iupiter *F,G*
*97   retrogrado] retrogado *H,F*
106   gynesia] gonesia *F*
135   Hippias] Hyppias *G*
138   alyptes] aliptes *G*
143   Vraniscophiâ] Vranoscophia *G*
144   Chyrosophiâ] Chirosophia *F*; Cheirosophia *G*
144   Bial] Biel *G*
147   Polupragmaticus] Polypragmaticus *G*
158   Admittatur] addmitatur *F*
161   perepateticus] peripateticus *F*
169   Concionator] Conscionator *F*
173   tricolos] Tritolas *F*
174   dicolos] Dicolas *F*
174   coriambos] coryambos *F*
191   Hipodidasculus] Hypodidasculus *F*
*223   praetorem] pratorem *H*
223   praetor] prator *F*
225   loquutus] locutus *F*
242   Immo] Imo *F*
257   vberimus] vberrimus *F*
284   nauseant] naseant *F*
288   exhalet] exhaulet *F*
*289   Alia] alea *H,F*
306   gipsum] gypsum *F*
*312   simulac] simulat *H,F*
313   Briseîn] Brisseia *F*

323	hyacinthini] hyacinthyni *F*
326	emplaustris] emplastris *F*
*333	obscenum] obsenum *H,F*
345	Pulchra] Pulcra *F*
385	Polupragmaticus] Polypragmaticus *G*
405	phisiognomos] physiognomos *G*
411	hebdabodis] hebdomadis *G*
422	baronum] baronium *G*
426	Philippo] Phillippo *F*
438	Sesquipedale] Sesquipedalia *F*
444	Crysiari] Chrysiari *F*
448	Cecarrasoraomi] Cecarasiorami *F*
454	Aristotiles] Aristotelis *F*
460	duplicitèr] duplicitur *F*
489	Aristotiles] Aristoteles *F*
500	Olympum] Olimpum *F*
515	diluculò] diliculò *F*
518	Tarentillam] Tarrentillam *F*
534	Calapinum] Calopinum *F*
547	melancholichus] malancholicus *F*
*554	Scena] Scaena *H*
562	Idiotas] Ideotas *F*
*568	omnino] omino *H*
572	sulphere] sulphur *F*
592	dilicculò] diliculò *F*
625	sollicitus] solicitus *F*
636	peregrinantes] perigrinantes *F*
652	Hydrangirii] Hyrargirii *F*
664	Brahe] Brache *F*
665	Roeslin] Ruslin *F*
*675	omnino] omino *H*
682	Papionani] Paphioni *F*
687	iuditium] iudicium *F*
695	Tarentilla] Tarrentilla *F*
700	quum] cum *F*
704	melancholicam] malancholicam *F*
706	nympha] nimpha *F*
735	rutilante] rutillante *F*
739	capessere] capescere *F*
750	horshewe] horseshewe *F*
757	Stockfishe] Stokefishe *F*
761	Cynthia] Cinthia *F*
764	faciam] fatiam *F*
768	Scena] Sena *F*; scaena *G*

769	Polupragmaticus] Polypragmaticus *G*
769	Polupistos] Polypistos *G*
771	gallicinium] gallicineum *G*
773	inumerabiles] innumerabiles *G*
777	nonagesimi] nonagessimi *F*
780	comederûnt] commederunt *F*
781	artocreas] atrocreas *F*
789	mus] mous *G*
789	dimoueat] demoueat *F*
790	quadringenta] quadraginta *F*
803	Colocynthropiratos] Colocynthopyratos *G*
803	accolas] acolas *G*
819	biothonandum] biothinandum *F*
820	Saturnina] Saturnia *F*; Staternina *G*
831	Calatraue] Colotraui *G*
831	Pante] Panton *G*
835	seorsìm] seorsum *G*
838	viginti] vigenti *G*
840	furcifur] farcifur *F*; furcifer *G*
890	pathicas] pathecas *F*
897	imitere] imittere *F*
*897	simulacque] simulatque *H,F*
926	committo] commito *F*
968	monachosque] monochosque *F*
969	tentandum] tontandum *F*
1009	annulum] anulum *F*
1013	istaec] isthaec *F*
1031	querar] quarar *F*
1058	exertitatio] exercitatio *F*
1086	paedagogus] pedagogus *F*
1090	opportunè] oportunè *F*
1091	sollicitum] solicitum *F*
1111	Medeam] Mediam *F*
1111	Mynois] Minois *F*
1120	Hymenis] Himenis *F*
1132	pulcherima] pulcherrima *F*
*1150	Camaena] Camena *H*
1167	Rithimicum] Rithmicum *F*
1168	Rithimica] Rithmica *F*
1195	Pantomagus] Pantomagos *F*
1219	Borregor] Borrigor *F*
1222	Auri] Asuri *F*
1222	exhilerat] exhilarat *F*
1240	Hyrciniam] Hyrcinium *F*

1241	Moeotidem] Maetidem *F*
1242	Hyberboreos] Hyperboreos *F*
1243	vberima] vberrima *F*
1251	Europae] Aeuropae *F*
1252	Dorobornium] Dorrobornium *F*
1254	exercitum] exertitium *F*
1255	mediterraneo] mediterranio *F*
*1262	delicatè] deliatè *H,F*
1263	Scena] Scaena *G*
1264	Polupragmaticus] Polypragmaticus *G*
1269	Ascultat] Auscultat *G*
1282	compendiosissimam] compendiosassimam *G*
1285	comitiis] commitiis *F*
1291	illustrissimis] illustiossimis *G*
1294	pralectiones] praelectiones *G*
1301	adiectiunculus] adiiciunculis *F*
1320	matellam] metallum *F*
1337	Thaumaturgicis] Thomaturgicis *F*
1344	desputabo] disputabo *F*
1358	lenae] laenae *F*
1379	scintillantes] scintellantes *F*
1390	Tarentilla] Tarrentilla *F*
1403	abieginieos] abiegineos *F*
1412	myriades] myrriades *F*
1419	parabitur] parrabitur *F*
1441	comitiis] commitiis *F*
1460	Episcopus] Aepiscopus *F*
1480	melancholicus] malancholicus *F*
1484	Mystae] Mistae *F*
1540	innumeros] inumeros *F*
1545	moenia] menia *F*
1566	deformes] deformis *F*
1577	Scena] Scaena *G*
1578	Polupragmaticus] Polypragmaticus *G*
1592	immo] imo *G*
1651	Hasinam] Hascinam *G*
1653	appellas] appelas *F*
1659	mulières] Muliebres *F*
1681	Martem] Myrtem *F*
1699	concumbentes] concumbantes *F*
1729	Aristotiles] Aristoteles *F*
1732	sequetur] sequitur *F*; sequaetur *G*
1732	illicò] ilico *G*
1751	querar] quaerar *F*

1753	sollicitum] solicitum *F*
1757	Gorgoneum] Gorgonium *F*
1762	heroes] haeroes *F*
*1788	omninò] ominò *H*
1817	relligio] religio *F*
*1820	Neptunum] Nuptunum *H,F*
1840	stolidi] stollidi *F*
1853	sollicitum] solicitum *F*
1867	innumeros] inumeros *F*
1874	nonunquam] nonnumquam *F*
1904	glossamatica] glossomatica *F*
1979	ceteris] caeteris *F*
1986	viciniâ] vaciniâ *F*
1992	gradarium] gradiarum *F*
2021	peregrinantes] perigrinantes *F*
2023	Aequum] equum *F*
2036	Idiotae] Ideotae *F*
2049	sillogismum] syllogismum *F*
2096	quum] cum *F*
2108	Hyppocritae] hypocritae *F*
2129	quaendam] quandam *F*
2131	Antyceras] Anticeras *F*
2141	anteactae] antiactae *F*
2232	plausum] plasum *F*
2234	amicitior] amititior *F*
2235	plausum] plasum *F*
2243	Bartlit] Barlet *F*
2244	Bennet] Benet *F*
2244	Bennettes] Bennets *F*
2247	Jonson] Johnson *F*
2249	Westlye] Westly *F*
2251	Limiter] Lymiter *F*
2256	Hilsinge] Hiling *F*
2258	Staphila] Staphilla *F*
2263	Quirister] querrister *F*
2265	nyght] night *F*
2267	Linliaco] Lindliaco *F*

Siena secunda·

Theanus Pedanus /

Th Quid cis pedane? p· et chartæ huic nomen apponas si placet

Th quid sibi vult? ped· Testimoniales literæ /

Th fiet· sed quam nunc illa rationem inis?

p· Rus eo docturus nobilis cuiusdam filios·

Th Teste caput· p· bene est· Th· ita velo tege caput·

pedane, et tibi primum rus adituris cave

Et sit gestus gravis, et quam cito poteris

A sint testes intida· cavendum id timeri

sit vultus comis plerumque, et blandus, nisi sit in schola·

Tum vero nasū corruga et frontem caperra·

pe· fiet· Th· sed si cis insignis haberi grammaticus

comparabiles sunt libri plures in folio

pe· Habeo Calepinum et cum commento Virgilium·

Th· sic oportet· sed si fueris ad mensā adhibitus,

sit sermo plerumque de rebus philosophicis·

quam diu amant culex et apis, vel de Meteoris

sed in quibusvis sis supra modum Criticus

pe· Attendo· Th· inter confabulandum debes historiolā

Inserere aliquando, vel e græcis sententiam·

Ὡς ναι ἰγὶς και το κακον· ἡ τοιβι και ἀφρδι·

pe· Imitare· sed in scholā quid agendum mones?

tu grammu· suades an ferulā? Th· non refert· quam velis·

uni hanc nunc illā· pe· sed quot plagas oportebit dare·

[add· [Th·]] Erras, non est dicendu oportebat sed oportuit·

plebeio sex, tres tantum generosi filio

nisi sit bene potus, melancholicus·

pe· quot ingenuis dare debueram· Th· illas iterum

Fig. 1. Folger MS V.a.315, fol. 9r, by permission of the Folger Shakespeare Library.

Quod est poetis nunc, nunc quod antiquis fuit
Solenne, et usu semper in suetis erit,
Orare adesse ut mente benigna velitis,
pro more solenni nos petituri sumus.
Siquid peruulgatò hac fabula fuerit
Absolutu si quid, qd minus arriserit
Emendicatò à nuperâ forma aut quis putet,
Sciat quod undecim abhinc annis scripta fuit,
Inter blattas et tineas in hunc diem delituit.
Ab authore in aeternas damnata tenebras,
Aliorum importunitate nunc in scenam venit.
Et hoc in praesentiarum scire vos aequum fuit.
Comoedia sumam eloqui non est opus,
Nomen ut ipsum quae sit abunde docet.
Scenae prima. ne quis ignoret tamen,
Hec totius quá vos tenet est Andalusia
Hoc oppidum Osuna, a duce huiusce loci
Iam de nupero erecta Academia —
Viros undiquaq accersiuit doctissimos —
Mox aderunt, una omnes admittendi illico.
Hic non agitur de bonis, pseudophilosophi.
Quid perpetrauerint, fabulae finis docet.
Nec plura dicam, cuncta si sponte explicent
vos unus hoc obiter admonitos volo.
philosophastros, siqui tales saltem sunt
Quam primum ut fiant, plene, primarie sumus.
Qua salua res, nullus exurgit loco.
Nemo sedet, digni omnes Academici,
opere magno rogatos vos omnes volo.
Attentioni nostrae ut praestatis ingenui.
Saltem Theatro quanta vulgari datur.

Fig. 2. Harvard MS Thr. 10, fol. 27r, Harvard Theatre Collection.

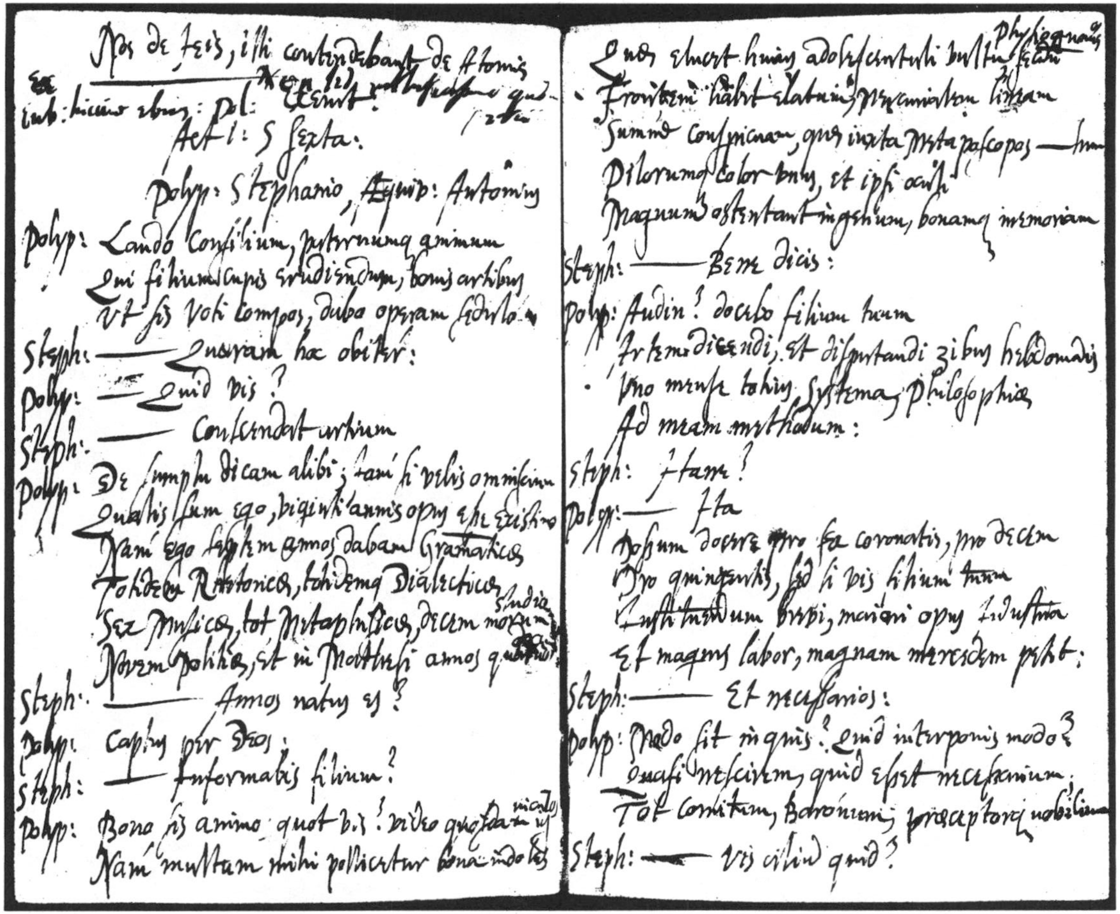

Fig. 3. Harvard MS Thr. 10.1, fol. 51, Harvard Theatre Collection.

Philosophaster, Burton's Latin play written in 1605 and presented at Christ Church, Oxford in 1617/18, is an excellent example of academic satire and classical comedy. The play is also a self-parody—it is an attack on pedants by one of the most self-consciously pedantic English writers. Burton's "philosophasters" are pseudophilosophers, frauds, and quacks who ensconce themselves in a university to use (and confuse) their fellow academics, young scholars, and local townspeople.

Three manuscript copies of the play are extant, including one holograph. Professor McQuillen has based her edition on Burton's holograph. She provides detailed annotation of Burton's patchwork of allusions, borrowings, quotations and misquotations. Text and translation, with notes, are on facing pages.

Philosophaster—an academic play written, produced, and performed by seventeenth-century university students—should prove interesting to university students of the twentieth century. In addition, it will be valuable to Neo-Latinists as an example of unstylized Neo-Latin as written by a seventeenth-century scholar. And it will be especially interesting to all those interested in seventeenth-century English literature and culture.

Connie McQuillen, who teaches at the University of Idaho, has published articles about Burton in *Selecta* and *Manuscripta*. She was the recipient of a Blackburn Fellowship at Washington State University in 1987–88.

mRts

medieval & Renaissance texts & studies
is the publishing program of the
Center for Medieval and Early Renaissance Studies
at the State University of New York at Binghamton.

mRts emphasizes books that are needed —
texts, translations, and major research tools.

mRts aims to publish the highest quality scholarship
in attractive and durable format at modest cost.